Lynda Weinman's | Hands-On Training

ActionScript 3.0

for Adobe® Flash® CS3 Professional

Includes Exercise Files and Demo Movies

lynda.com

By Todd Perkins

ActionScript 3.0 for Adobe® Flash® CS3 Professional Hands-On Training

By Todd Perkins

lynda.com/books | Peachpit Press
1249 Eighth Street • Berkeley, CA • 94710
510.524.2178 • 510.524.2221(fax)
www.lynda.com/books
www.peachpit.com

lynda.com/books is published
in association with Peachpit Press,
a division of Pearson Education
Copyright ©2008 by lynda.com

ISBN-13: 978-0-321-29390-9
ISBN-10:   0-321-29390-8

0 9 8 7 6 5 4 3

Printed and bound in the
United States of America

H•O•T Credits

Director of Product Development and Video Production: Tanya Staples

Senior Editor: Karyn Johnson

Production Editor: Tracey Croom

Compositors: Myrna Vladic and David Van Ness

Technical Writer: Lauren Harmon

Copyeditor: Kim Wimpsett

Proofreader: Liz Welch

Interior Design: Hot Studio, San Francisco

Cover Design: Don Barnett

Cover Illustration: Bruce Heavin (bruce@stink.com)

Indexer: Jack Lewis

H•O•T Colophon

The text in *ActionScript 3.0 for Adobe Flash CS3 Professional H·O·T* was set in Avenir from Adobe Systems Incorporated. The cover illustration was painted in Adobe Photoshop and Adobe Illustrator.

This book was created on an Apple Macintosh using Mac OS X. It was printed on 60 lb. Influence Matte at Courier.

Table of Contents

Table of Contents

Introduction

A Note from Lynda Weinman

Most people buy computer books to learn, yet it's amazing how few books are written by teachers. Todd Perkins and I take pride that this book was written by experienced teachers who are familiar with training students in this subject matter. In this book, you'll find carefully developed lessons and exercises to help you learn ActionScript 3.0 in Adobe Flash CS3 Professional—one of the most powerful and popular animation and authoring tools for the Web.

This book is targeted to beginning-level and intermediate-level Web designers and Web developers who need a tool for creating powerful, compelling, and highly interactive digital content for the Web. The premise of the hands-on approach is to get you up-to-speed quickly with ActionScript while actively working through the lessons in this book. It's one thing to read about a program, and it's another experience entirely to try the product and achieve measurable results. Our motto is, "Read the book, follow the exercises, and you'll learn the program." I have received countless testimonials, and it is our goal to make sure it remains true for all our hands-on training books.

This book doesn't set out to cover every single aspect of ActionScript, and it doesn't try to teach you everything this extremely powerful programming language can do. What we saw missing from the bookshelves was a process-oriented tutorial that teaches readers core principles, techniques, and tips in a hands-on training format.

I welcome your comments at **books-errata@lynda.com**. If you run into any trouble while you're working through this book, check out the technical support link at **www.lynda.com/info/books/as3**.

Todd Perkins and I hope this book will improve your skills in ActionScript. If it does, we have accomplished the job we set out to do!

—Lynda Weinman

About lynda.com

lynda.com was founded in 1995 by Lynda Weinman and Bruce Heavin in conjunction with the first publication of Lynda's revolutionary book, *Designing Web Graphics*. Since then, lynda.com has become a leader in software training for graphics and Web professionals and is recognized worldwide as a trusted educational resource.

lynda.com offers a wide range of Hands-On Training books, which guide users through a progressive learning process using real-world projects. lynda.com also offers a wide range of video-based tutorials, which are available on CD-ROM and DVD-ROM and through the lynda.com Online Training Library. lynda.com also owns the Flashforward Conference and Film Festival.

For more information about lynda.com, check out **www.lynda.com**. For more information about the Flashforward conference and film festival, check out **www.flashforwardconference.com**.

Register for a Free 24-hour Pass

Register your copy of *ActionScript 3.0 in Adobe Flash CS3 Professional HOT* today, and receive the following benefits:

- Free 24-hour pass to the lynda.com Online Training Library with more than 20,000 professionally produced video tutorials covering more than 300 topics by leading industry experts and teachers

- News, events, and special offers from lynda.com

- The lynda.com monthly newsletter

To register, visit **www.lynda.com/register/HOT/as3**.

Additional Resources from Peachpit and lynda.com

To help you master and further develop your skills with Flash CS3, Web design, and Web development, check out the following resources:

Advanced ActionScript 3 with Design Patterns, Joey Lott and Danny Patterson (peachpit.com)

Flash CS3 Professional Advanced for Windows and Macintosh, Visual QuickPro Guide, Russell Chun (peachpit.com)

Flash CS3 Professional Essential Training, with Rich Schupe (lynda.com)

Illustrator CS3 and Flash CS3 Professional Integration, with Mordy Golding (lynda.com)

About the Author

Todd Perkins is an Adobe Certified Instructor and spends much of his time teaching people how to use Adobe Web development software. Todd has several years of experience teaching people of all ages and backgrounds, and he is an expert at teaching complex concepts in a way everyone can understand. Todd is half of the dynamic duo behind All Things Adobe: The Chad and Todd Podcast and has authored a vast array of video training titles. Todd also loves to teach in classrooms, consult with businesses, and train people online, but what he loves most is playing video games with his amazing wife, Jessica.

Acknowledgments from Todd Perkins

I want to give thanks to all the people who helped make this book possible. My brother, Chad, thanks for introducing me to the amazing folks at lynda.com and inspiring me to learn Flash. Tanya and Lauren, thank you for all your hard work. You guys are awesome! Jessica, thanks for all the support you've given me in writing this book and for motivating me to work hard. Thanks to everyone at lynda.com; I love working with all of you! Last, I want to thank *you* for reading this book.

How to Use This Book

The following sections outline important information to help you make the most of this book.

The Formatting in This Book

This book has several components, including step-by-step exercises, commentary, notes, tips, warnings, and video tutorials. Step-by-step exercises are numbered. File names, folder names, commands, keyboard shortcuts, and Web addresses are in bold so they pop out easily: **filename.htm**, the **images** folder, **File > New**, **Ctrl-click**, **www.lynda.com**.

Commentary is in dark gray text:

This is commentary text.

Interface Screen Captures

Most of the screen shots in the book were taken on a Macintosh computer using Mac OS 10.4. I also own, use, and love my PCs, and I note important differences between the two platforms when they occur.

What's on the ActionScript HOT CD-ROM?

You'll find a number of useful resources on the **ActionScript 3.0 HOT CD-ROM**, including the following: exercise files, video tutorials, and information about product registration. Before you begin the hands-on exercises, read the following sections so you know how to set up the exercise files and video tutorials.

Exercise Files

The files required to complete the exercises are on the **ActionScript 3.0 HOT CD-ROM** in a folder called **exercise_files**. These files are divided into chapter folders, and you should copy each chapter folder onto your desktop before you begin the exercises for that chapter. For example, if you're about to start Chapter 5, copy the **chap_05** folder from the **exercise_files** folder on the **ActionScript 3.0 HOT CD-ROM** onto your desktop.

On Windows, when files originate from a CD-ROM, they automatically become write-protected, which means you cannot alter them. Fortunately, you can easily change this attribute. For complete instructions, read the "Making Exercise Files Editable on Windows Computers" section later in this introduction.

Video Tutorials

Throughout the book, you'll find references to video tutorials. In some cases, these video tutorials reinforce concepts explained in the book. In other cases, they show bonus material you'll find interesting and useful. To view the video tutorials, you must have Apple QuickTime Player installed on your computer. If you do not have QuickTime Player, you can download it for free from Apple's Web site: **www.apple.com/quicktime**.

To view the video tutorials, copy the videos from the **ActionScript 3.0 HOT CD-ROM** to your hard drive. Double-click the video you want to watch, and it will automatically open in QuickTime Player. Make sure the volume on your computer is turned up so you can hear the audio content.

Making Exercise Files Editable on Windows Computers

By default, when you copy files from a CD-ROM to a Windows computer, the files are set to read-only (write-protected), which will cause a problem with the exercise files because you will need to edit and save many of them. You can remove the read-only property by following these steps:

1 Open the **exercise_files** folder on the **ActionScript 3.0 HOT CD-ROM**, and copy one of the subfolders, such as **chap_02**, to your **Desktop**.

2 Open the **chap_02** folder you copied to your **Desktop**, and choose **Edit > Select All**.

3 Right-click one of the selected files, and choose **Properties** in the contextual menu.

4 In the **Properties** dialog box, select the **General** tab. Deselect the **Read-Only** option to disable the read-only properties for the selected files in the **chap_02** folder.

Making File Extensions Visible on Windows Computers

By default, you cannot see file extensions, such as **.htm**, **.fla**, **.swf**, **.jpg**, **.gif**, or **.psd**, on Windows computers. Fortunately, you can change this setting easily. Here's how:

1 On your **Desktop**, double-click the **My Computer** icon.

Note: If you (or someone else) changed the name, it will not say My Computer.

2 Choose **Tools > Folder Options** to open the **Folder Options** dialog box. Select the **View** tab.

3 Deselect the **Hide extensions for known file types** option to makes all file extensions visible.

Adobe Flash CS3 Professional System Requirements

Windows

- Intel Pentium 4, Intel Centrino, Intel Xeon or Intel Core Duo processor (or equivalent) and newer

- Windows Vista, Windows XP

- 512 MB RAM (1 GB recommended)

- 1024 x 768, 16-bit display (32-bit recommended)

- 2.5 GB available disk space

Mac

- 1 GHz PowerPC G4 or G5 or multicore Intel processor

- Mac OS X 10.4.8

- 512 MB RAM (1 GB recommended)

- 1024 x 768, thousands of colors display (millions of colors recommended)

- 2.5 GB available disk space

Getting Demo Versions of the Software

If you want to try demo versions of the software used in this book, you can download demo versions from the following Web page:

www.adobe.com/downloads

1

Getting Started

You may already be an accomplished Adobe Flash user, but creating fully interactive presentations requires using ActionScript 3.0, the internal programming language in Flash CS3 Professional. It's similar, but not identical, to Java. However, you do not have to know Java or JavaScript or be a programmer to include ActionScript in your movies. Though it is a little more difficult to learn than ActionScript 2.0, ActionScript 3.0 runs faster (in many cases), is more consistent, and overall is more powerful than ActionScript 2.0.

ActionScript is important because you can't accomplish many basic Flash activities—such as stopping a movie, restarting a movie, or controlling audio volume—without it. ActionScript also extends the power and flexibility of your project by letting you navigate the main **Timeline**, link to other URLs (**U**niform **R**esource **L**ocators) on the Internet, load other movies into a Flash CS3 movie, and do much more. By the time you are finished with this chapter, you will have a solid understanding of how to add ActionScript to your Flash movies. You will also learn most of the "must-know" ActionScript required for your own Flash projects.

Working with ActionScript code is one of the most technically challenging aspects of Flash CS3. This book will not teach you everything there is to know about ActionScript, but it will cover the basics and give you a solid foundation on which to build.

Introducing ActionScript 3.0

ActionScript 3.0 is an object-oriented programming language used to power the Flash Player. It's an ECMAScript language, similar to JavaScript, so if you want to learn other ECMAScript languages, ActionScript 3.0 is a great place to start. The latest version of ActionScript brings it into full compliance with ECMA standards.

ActionScript 3.0 can be embedded in a Flash project (**.fla**) file in Flash CS3, written as a stand-alone ActionScript (**.as**) file, or created in Flex Builder, a new tool built on Adobe's Flex framework that offers developers an environment for creating RIAs (**R**ich **I**nternet **A**pplications). This book will focus on using ActionScript 3.0 to enhance your Flash CS3 projects.

Why You Should Learn ActionScript 3.0

If you're a Flash designer, chances are you've gotten only so far using Script Assist. Learning ActionScript 3.0 will help you to leap that hurdle and create fully interactive applications, including dynamic Web applications and interactive video games. If you have learned ActionScript 1.0 or 2.0 and are intimidated by the language differences in ActionScript 3.0, consider that ActionScript 3.0 has several key benefits over the previous version, including fast downloading speed, precise visual control, advanced interactivity, the capability to combine bitmap and vector graphics and include video or animation, and scalable and streaming content.

NOTE: | **Download Speed**
ActionScript is executed by the AVM (**A**ctionScript **V**irtual **M**achine) in the Flash Player. ActionScript 3.0 introduces AVM2, which results in download speeds up to 30 times (30 times!) faster than legacy versions.

What's New in ActionScript 3.0?

ActionScript 3.0 offers a vast array of new features. The following chart outlines some of the new features:

ActionScript 3.0 New Features	
Feature	**Description**
Packages	ActionScript 3.0 classes are organized into **packages**, folders that hold similar ActionScript class files. Packages existed in ActionScript 2.0 but are used much more in ActionScript 3.0.
Document class	Flash CS3 has introduced something called a **document class**. In previous versions of Flash and ActionScript, the main **Timeline** was always a movie clip symbol. Now, you can create your own custom class for the main **Timeline**.
ActionScript tools	Flash CS3 has many new ActionScript tools in the **Actions** panel that help you learn how to write and organize code more effectively than ever. There are now many buttons to create comments and collapse blocks of code.
Scripting improvements	Flash CS3 now includes a new ActionScript debugger that offers improved flexibility and feedback and is consistent with Adobe's Flex 2 debugger. You can also convert animations directly to ActionScript and copy and paste ActionScript animation properties from one object to another.
Language consistency	If you are familiar with ActionScript 2.0, you may have noticed some inconsistencies in the language. ActionScript 3.0 is far more consistent in syntax, so the language is much more intuitive once you know the core concepts.

Differences Between ActionScript 1.0/2.0 and 3.0

ActionScript 3.0 includes many key differences, as you can see in the previous chart. Here's a practical example that will illustrate these differences more clearly.

Let's say you want to add a text field to your Flash document. Using ActionScript 2.0, the code would look like this:

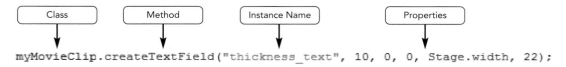

```
myMovieClip.createTextField("thickness_text", 10, 0, 0, Stage.width, 22);
```

In the first line of code, you call the movie clip class. In legacy versions of ActionScript, all components had to be embedded in movie clips. Next, you use the **createTextField** method to add the text field. An instance name, in parentheses, is required for all components when you use ActionScript. The text field properties, the width and height and positioning on the **Stage**, follow the instance name.

In ActionScript 3.0, the same code would look like this:

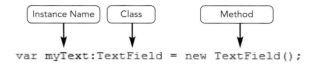

```
var myText:TextField = new TextField();
```

In ActionScript 3.0, you simply create a new instance of the text field class. You can supply the text field properties later.

Here's another example. The following line of ActionScript 2.0 code imports a movie clip symbol from your **Library** panel into the SWF file at run time:

```
myMoveClip.attachMovie("MySymbol", "moviename_mc", this.getNextHighestDepth());
```

Again, you must call the movie clip class, the **attachMovie** method, the symbol's name, the new instance name, and a depth value.

In ActionScript 3.0, you simply create a new instance of the movie clip class. You can add the properties, such as the instance name, symbol name, and **Stage** depth, later. The syntax is basically the same to create a text field or a movie clip.

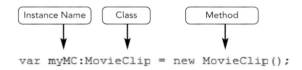

```
var myMC:MovieClip = new MovieClip();
```

Note this is just an isolated example. Not every function in ActionScript 3.0 requires less code than in previous versions. ActionScript 3.0 isn't necessarily a simpler language but, more important, is standardized. It doesn't matter whether you're creating a text field, a movie clip, a shape, or any other object. This standardization makes it easier to learn and easier to use.

ActionScript 3.0 Elements

In this chapter, you will learn about several core ActionScript 3.0 elements, including the following:

Variables

Instances

Properties

Functions and methods

Events, event handlers, and event listeners

Classes

Conditional statements

These are not *all* the elements of ActionScript 3.0, but knowing how to use these elements will allow you to do most of the common ActionScript tasks. The following sections can act a reference for you to understand each of the ActionScript 3.0 elements used in this book. If you get to a section in a later chapter that seems difficult or confusing, return to this chapter and review these terms.

Variables

Variables are containers that hold data. To understand variables, think of a game where the player has a score. The information (or **data**) about how many points the player has is contained in a variable. When the player gets more points, the number in the **score** variable increases. Thus, the **score** variable acts as a container (or variable) for a number (or data).

The data in a variable is not limited to numbers only. Variables can hold many types of data. Variables can hold text values, such as a user name, password, or text in a text field. They can also hold **true** or **false** values, such as whether or a user logged into a Web site has administrator status. The type of data a variable holds is called its **data type**.

In ActionScript 3.0, you create variables using the keyword **var**. The code to create a variable called **score** is **var score**.

Whenever you create a variable in ActionScript 3.0, you must give the variable a data type. To tell Flash CS3 the type of data a variable will hold,

type a colon and then the data type. Most data types begin with a capital letter. The code to tell Flash CS3 that the **score** variable will hold a **Number** data type is **var score:Number**.

The name of the data type that holds text is **String**, and the name of the data type that holds **true** or **false** values is **Boolean**.

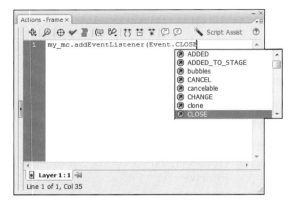

Note: If you typed code such as that shown in the illustration here in the **Script** pane in the **Actions** panel, you may have noticed that after you typed the colon, a small menu appeared. This menu is called the **Code Hint** menu and is a useful tool in writing ActionScript 3.0.

You give a value to a variable using an equals sign. You can do this on the same line as you create your variable. The code used to assign a value of **0** to a variable called **score** is **var score:Number = 0;**. The code to create a variable called **text** with a value of **"This is my text"** is **var text:String = "This is my text";**.

Note: Notice the quotation marks around the text variable's value. Anytime you use the String data type, the value must be in quotation marks, or Flash CS3 will think you are referencing a variable. All other data types do not use quotation marks.

Also notice the semicolon after the Number value in **var score:Number = 0;**. A semicolon in ActionScript 3.0 is similar to a period in a sentence. Both denote the end of a statement.

Many variables do not contain the same value forever. Consider a player's score again—it may start at 0, but as the player gets more points, the value can change to 100; 500; or 1,948,762. To assign a new value to a variable that has already been created, do not use the **var** keyword. Instead, on a different line of code, type the variable name, an equals sign, and then the new value (followed by a semicolon, of course). The code to assign a value of **100** to a variable called **score** that was initially created on a previous line of code with a value of **0** is **score = 100;**.

Instances and Instance Names

You are already familiar with instances. When you drag a symbol from the **Library** panel in Flash CS3, you are creating an **instance** of that symbol. One symbol can have many instances, but each instance is linked to only one symbol.

In Flash CS3, you must name instances if you want to communicate with them via ActionScript. For example, if you want your Flash movie to stop playing when you click a button, you must give that button an instance name. You can give instance names to movie clips, buttons, and text fields but not to graphic symbols. To give an instance name to an instance, select the instance, and type an instance name in the **Instance Name** field in the **Property inspector**:

In ActionScript, you refer to individual instances by their instance names, not by their symbol names in the **Library** panel. The name you give your instances is important and is similar to how you must name your symbols. Always start with a lowercase letter, and do not use spaces or special characters other than underscores. It is a best practice to pick a naming convention and use it consistently. Instance names should also be descriptive but brief (so you don't have to type more than necessary). Some examples of good instance names are **contact_btn** , **nav_mc**, and **body_txt**.

Note: If you end your instance names with **_mc** for movie clips, **_btn** for buttons, and **_txt** for text fields, Flash CS3 will give you access to code hinting in the **Actions** panel. This makes writing code much easier and faster.

Properties

Believe it or not, you are already familiar with properties by this point. Properties are simply variables that are attached to an instance of a symbol. If that sounds a little cryptic, think of properties as attributes you can modify in the **Property inspector**. Specifically, the *x* and *y* positioning and the width and height of an instance are some of its properties. Working with movie clips or buttons, some other properties include alpha, blend mode, and even filters. You can modify properties in ActionScript using **dot syntax**, which means you type the instance name, a dot, the property you want to modify, and then the value you want to give that property using an equals sign (just like setting the value of a variable). The code to modify the X position of a movie clip with an instance name of **my_mc** and set it to **100** is **my_mc.x = 100;**.

Functions and Methods

When using ActionScript 3.0, you will often write large blocks of code that you reuse many times. Copying the same code several times can be frustrating and tedious. Fortunately, you can write a block of code one time and recycle it using functions and methods. Functions and methods are essentially the same—both are reusable blocks of code.

Many functions already exist in Flash CS3. If you want to stop a movie from looping continuously, you can use the prebuilt **stop()** function. To use a function, type the name of the function, and then type a pair of parentheses. The code to run the **stop()** function is **stop();**. Another common prebuilt function in Flash CS3 is **gotoAndPlay()**. The **gotoAndPlay()** function plays the Flash movie starting at a particular frame. When you run the **gotoAndPlay()** function, you tell Flash CS3 the frame you want to play in the parentheses. For example, the code to play a movie from the fifth frame is **gotoAndPlay(5);**.

Note: The parentheses are what make the function run, and they differentiate a function from a variable. If you just typed **stop** with no parentheses, Flash CS3 would think you were referring to a variable called **stop**.

Some functions do not already exist in Flash CS3, so you will have to create them. Writing custom functions requires a few steps. First, you must tell Flash CS3 you are creating a function by using the **function** keyword. Next, you tell Flash CS3 the name of your function. If you wanted to create a function called **myFirstFunction**, you would type **function myFirstFunction**. The next step is to type a pair of parentheses. You will learn more about what the parentheses are for when you learn about events. After the parentheses, you need to tell Flash CS3 the return data type using a colon (similar to how you set a data type for a variable). The return data type for all functions used in this book will be **void**. Last, you put all the code block that you will reuse inside curly braces. For example, the code to create a complete function called **myFirstFunction** is as follows:

```
function myFirstFunction():void
{
    (Block of code goes here)
}
```

Running a custom function is similar to running a prebuilt function. Simply type the name of the function and then the pair of parentheses. The code to run a function called **myFirstFunction** is **myFirstFunction();**.

Events, Event Handlers, and Event Listeners

Events are things that happen while a Flash movie is playing. Many types of events exist, such as when a visitor to your Web site clicks a button, presses a key on the keyboard, or starts downloading a file. You can utilize events by running functions when events happen. The special functions that run when events happen are called **event handlers**.

To write an event handler, simply create a basic function. The only difference with an event handler

function is that it receives information about the event that made the function run. The code to create an event handler function called **playMovie** that reacts to a button click is as follows:

```
function playMovie(event:MouseEvent):void
{
}
```

Note: The **event:MouseEvent** code in the parentheses is significant. This is how you capture information about what caused the function to run. The **event** part represents the event that happened, and the colon specifies the data type of this event, which is **MouseEvent**. Before this function will run when you click a button, you need to attach the event handler function to the event (the button click).

To attach an event to an event handler, you need to use something called an **event listener**. Event listeners wait for events to happen, and when the events happen, the appropriate event handler function runs. To understand event listeners, think of a radio station broadcasting music as an event. It broadcasts whether or not you listen to it. Tuning your radio to a station is like listening for an event. When you hear the music, you choose how to react to it (that is, sing along, change the station, or turn the volume up). In the same way that your selection of a radio station connects you to the signal being broadcast, event listeners connect event handlers to events.

To have a button or any object in Flash CS3 listen for an event, use the **addEventListener** method (**method** is synonymous with **function**) of any object. You do this by typing the instance name, typing a dot, and then typing **addEventListener**. Then in parentheses, tell Flash CS3 the event the instance is listening for, type a comma, and then type the name of the function that will run when the event happens. For example, if you had a button with an instance name of **play_btn** and you wanted to run a function called **playMovie** when you clicked it, you would type the following:

```
play_btn.addEventListener(MouseEvent.CLICK,
playMovie);
```

Note: In Flash CS3, events start with the data type of the event (in this case `MouseEvent`), then have a dot, and then have a specific event name in all caps. Also note that anytime you send multiple values to a function, you separate the values with commas.

Classes

Classes might be somewhat familiar to you already. A **class** is a blueprint, or concept, of something. Think of movie clip symbols and button symbols. What are some differences between the two? Movie clips have nearly an unlimited number of frames, and they play when your Flash movie is running unless you use ActionScript to tell them otherwise. Buttons have a **Timeline** with only four frames and do not play unless you roll over or click them. The `MovieClip` class is the blueprint for all movie clips. Though each movie clip symbol may look different, all movie clips have certain similarities. Classes all begin with a capital letter, and all classes are also data types. `Number`, `String`, and `Boolean` are all classes.

When you drag instances of movie clip or button symbols out of your **Library** panel and put them on the **Stage**, you are creating instances of the `MovieClip` or `Button` class. Many classes are not visual, so you must create instances of those classes with ActionScript using the **new** keyword. After the **new** keyword, type the class name and a pair of parentheses. One nonvisual class is called **Loader** and is used to load external content. To create a new instance of the **Loader** class called `myLoader`, you would type the following:

```
var myLoader:Loader = new Loader();
```

Note: This code creates a new instance of the **Loader** class and is similar to creating instances of many other nonvisual classes. After the **new** keyword, notice the name of the class and the pair of parentheses. This looks similar to the syntax used to run a function—because it *is* a function. It's a special function called a **constructor function** that creates a new instance of that particular class.

Conditional Statements

Conditional statements allow you to run a block of code based on a condition being true or false. Picture yourself getting dressed in the morning (or whatever time of the day you prefer to get dressed). Assuming you are planning to wear both shoes and socks that day, you put your shoes on only if you are already wearing socks. If you don't have socks on, then you put socks on and then shoes.

In ActionScript 3.0, conditions are computed in a similar way. Consider a variable called `socksOn` with a **true** or **false** data type (Boolean). To write a conditional statement, you first use the keyword `if`, then you place the expression that is evaluated as **true** or **false** in parentheses, and finally you place the code that executes in curly braces. In code, a conditional statement that would put shoes on if socks were already on would look like this:

```
if(socksOn)
{
    (Put shoes on)
}
```

Note: If the `socksOn` variable had a value of **true**, the code that says **(Put shoes on)** would run. Everything in the parentheses after the keyword `if` is evaluated as **true** or **false**.

You can also run a block of code if a condition is not true. To do that, use the keyword **else**, and place the code you want to run in curly braces. Using the previous code, if you wanted to put shoes on if `socksOn` were true and put socks on if `socksOn` were false, you would type the following:

```
if(socksOn)
{
    (Put shoes on)
}
else
{
    (Put socks on)
}
```

Note: You don't need any parentheses after the **else** keyword.

Moving Beyond Script Assist

If you've done a lot of Flash design, chances are you have used Script Assist, which is a feature in Flash that helps you write ActionScript. It can be helpful when you know the functions or methods you need to call but can't remember the correct syntax. To turn on Script Assist, open the **Actions** panel by choosing **Window > Actions** or by hitting **F12** (Windows) or **Opt+F12** (Mac) on your keyboard and clicking the **Script Assist** button in the upper-right corner of the screen:

Double-click any method, and you'll be prompted to type the required properties:

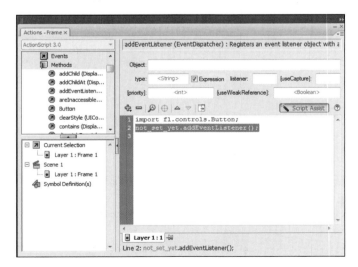

Script Assist is a great tool for writing simple ActionScript. However, if you don't have a solid understanding of ActionScript to begin with, Script Assist is not going to work very well for you. This book will lay the foundation that you need to write solid, concise ActionScript, and you may very well find that as your skills improve, you may move beyond Script Assist. When you create the code yourself, you can add advanced interactivity and add more power to your applications.

Caution: Player Required!

Flash CS3 content is not visible in a browser unless either the Flash Player or the Shockwave Player has been installed in that browser. In the past, this was seen as a serious limitation of the format, although over the past few years the number of Internet users who have the player has increased exponentially because current browsers now come with the Flash Player preinstalled. Shockwave was designed to view content created with Adobe Director and has not reached quite the same level of popularity as Flash.

Adobe has hired an independent consulting firm to maintain an estimate of the number of Flash Players in use. At the time of this writing, the Flash Player is installed on 98 percent of Internet-enabled desktops globally, and more are 200 million Flash-enabled mobile devices are in existence. Flash Player 9 comes preinstalled on all new browsers shipped by AOL, CompuServe, Microsoft, and Netscape. Additionally, all versions of Microsoft Windows 98 and newer and Apple OS 8 and newer include the plug-in.

The following chart describes the two players:

Adobe Players	
Description	**Player**
Flash Player	The Flash Player is used for viewing Flash content on the Web. You can download the latest version of the Flash Player at **www.adobe.com/downloads/**. This player installs in the player folder for your browser of choice.
Shockwave Player	The Shockwave Player is used for viewing Director content on the Web. You can download the latest version of the Shockwave Player at **www.adobe.com/downloads/**.

Beyond ActionScript 3.0

Flash CS3 is an incredibly powerful tool by itself. However, it can't perform a few functions. The following sections present some of the Web technologies you should know about if you want to extend Flash CS3 beyond its basic capabilities. Using these technologies is beyond the scope of this book. However, it is good to understand what these technologies are, especially if you plan to further your ActionScript skills when you are finished with this book.

What's AIR?

Adobe Air (Adobe Integrated Runtime), formerly code-named Apollo, is a cross–operating system runtime, or a framework that works along with the operating system to support applications written specifically for the framework. C++ is an example of an existing popular runtime. For years, Web developers have been developing RIAs for the Web. With AIR these developers can use the programming knowledge they already have (such as HTML, Flash, Ajax, and so on) to build and publish desktop applications. Unlike Web applications, AIR applications will not have to run within a browser environment and can support traditional desktop application features, such as drag-and-drop interactivity, desktop shortcuts, Clipboard access, and integration with other desktop applications. It's an exciting prospect and one that Flash users are eagerly anticipating.

For further information about AIR, please check out the following URLs:

http://labs.adobe.com/technologies/air/

www.codeapollo.com/

What's CGI?

A CGI (**C**ommon **G**ateway **I**nterface) script is a program that defines a standard way of exchanging information between a browser and a server. You can write CGI scripts in any number of languages (Perl, C, ASP, and others). If you plan to create a complex Web application that requires using something like CGI, it is recommended that you work with a Web engineer who has experience creating these kinds of scripts. Flash CS3 can communicate with CGI scripts, although that topic is beyond the scope of this book.

For further information about using CGI, please check out the following URLs:

www.cgidir.com/

www.cgi101.com/

www.icthus.net/CGI-City/

What's XML?

XML (e**X**tensible **M**arkup **L**anguage) is a standard that handles the description and exchange of data. With XML, developers can create markup languages that define the structure and meaning of information. Therefore, an XML document is much like a database presented in a text file. You can transform XML content into a variety of formats, including HTML, WML (**W**ireless **M**arkup **L**anguage), and VoiceXML.

XML differs from HTML in that it is not predefined—you create the tags and attributes. You can also use XML to create your own data structure and modify it for the data you want it to carry. In Flash CS3, you can use the XML object to create, manipulate, and pass that data. Using ActionScript, a Flash CS3

movie can load and process XML data. As a result, an XML-savvy Flash CS3 developer can develop a movie that dynamically retrieves data from the external XML document instead of creating static text fields within a project file.

Just as HTML provides an open, platform-independent format for distributing Web documents, XML has become the open, platform-independent format for exchanging any type of electronic information. Like CGI, XML is also a topic beyond the scope of this book.

For further information about XML, take a look at the following URLs:

www.ait-usa.com/xmlintro/xmlproject/article.htm

www.xml.com/

www.xmlfiles.com/

JavaScript and Flash CS3

ActionScript is based on JavaScript, another scripting language. Although ActionScript and JavaScript share a similar syntax and structure, they are two different languages. One way to tell them apart is that ActionScript uses scripts processed entirely within the Flash Player, independently of the browser used to view the file. JavaScript, on the other hand, uses external interpreters that vary according to the browser used.

You can use ActionScript and JavaScript together because Flash CS3 lets you call JavaScript commands to perform tasks or to send and receive data. A basic knowledge of JavaScript can make learning ActionScript easier, because the basic syntax of the scripts and how objects are handled are the same in both languages. However, JavaScript is not a requirement for learning ActionScript.

For further information and tutorials about JavaScript and how to use it in conjunction with Flash CS3, check out the following URLs:

www.javascript.com/

http://javascript.internet.com/

www.flashkit.com/links/Javascripts/

That's a wrap for this chapter. You've familiarized yourself with the basic concepts of ActionScript 3.0, the differences between 3.0 and legacy versions, and how to extend Flash content even further using various technologies. Now it's time to dive into the details of ActionScript 3.0 and start writing some actual code. On to the next chapter!

2

Communicating with ActionScript

In this chapter, you'll learn how to communicate with different objects in your Adobe Flash CS3 Professional project and even with other people who may be working on the project using ActionScript 3.0. The lines of communication flow both ways; you can use ActionScript to send messages to objects, such as when you transform a symbol instance's properties, or to provide feedback, such as when you run a trace statement. Alternatively, you can embed comments directly in the code so other people who are working on the same Flash project can read them. Before you start adding interactivity to your Flash movies using ActionScript, you need to learn how to communicate with the objects in them. So, let's get started!

1 | Communicating to Movie Clips

The first step in communicating with objects is to transform the object into a **symbol**, a type of predefined class, so ActionScript can interact with it. In this exercise, you'll convert a shape to a movie clip symbol and add named instances to the **Stage** so that later you can call them with ActionScript.

1 Start Flash CS3. The **Welcome** screen should appear automatically by default. If you have modified your preferences to hide it, choose **Edit > Preferences** (Windows) or **Flash > Edit Preferences** (Mac), and choose **Welcome Screen** in the **On launch** pop-up menu in the **General** category of the dialog box.

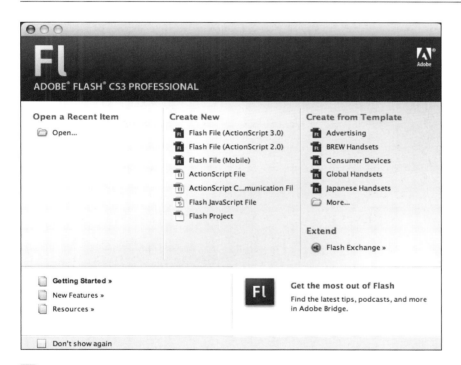

2 Choose **Flash File (ActionScript 3.0)** under the **Create New** heading on the **Welcome** screen.

A new document opens with a blank Stage. Next, you'll draw a simple object on the Stage and convert it to a movie clip.

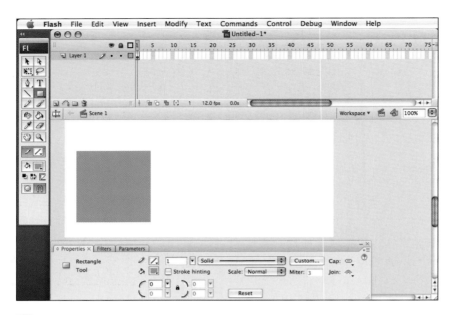

3 Select the **Rectangle** tool in the **Tools** panel. Select a green color in the **Fill Color** box, and make sure you have the **Object Drawing Model** button at the bottom of the **Tools** panel deselected. Click and drag to draw a rectangle on the **Stage**. The rectangle can be as large or as small as you want.

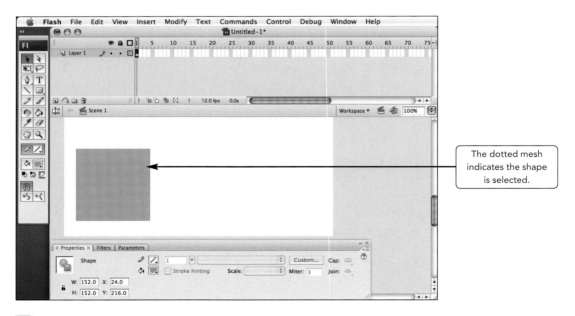

The dotted mesh indicates the shape is selected.

4 Select the **Selection** tool in the **Tools** panel, or press **V** on your keyboard. Click and drag a selection area around the rectangle to select the entire object.

You will know the rectangle is selected by the mesh that appears over the object when it is selected.

Selecting Shapes

Ordinarily, you click to select objects on the **Stage** with the **Selection** tool, but when you are working with merged shapes, you can move and transform the stroke and fill independently of one another. To make sure you select the entire shape, select the **Selection** tool, and click and drag a bounding box around the shape or double-click the shape's fill to select both the stroke and the fill.

5 Choose **Modify > Convert to Symbol** or press **F8** on your keyboard to open the **Convert to Symbol** dialog box.

6 Type **mcRectangle** for the symbol name, and choose **Movie clip** for **Type**. Leave the **Registration** setting in the upper-left corner, and click **OK**.

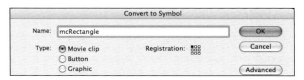

Now the shape on the Stage has been converted to an instance of the new symbol, and the symbol itself appears in the Library panel. If the Library panel is not open, choose Window > Library or press Ctrl+L (Windows) or Cmd+L (Mac) to open it.

Symbol Naming Conventions

As you start creating symbols and instances, you'll need to name them. In more complex Flash projects that include ActionScript, instance names become important, especially for movie clip symbols. For this reason, you need to adhere to some guidelines when naming symbols, instances, and document files in Flash CS3. Following these rules will keep you out of a lot of trouble.

Do use the following:

Lowercase letters (a–z) for the first character: Symbol names starting with numbers or uppercase letters can confuse ActionScript. For this reason, start symbol names with a lowercase letter. You can use numbers (1–9) for symbol names but not as the first character. Restricting your names to only lowercase letters makes them easier to remember.

Descriptive names: Try to use descriptive, easy-to-remember names. For example, use **mcRectangle** rather than **symbol6**. When using multiword names, capitalize the first letter of each word (except the first word) so you can read it easier. However, you must remember that when you refer to an object in ActionScript, you reference the symbol with the same capitalization you used in its name.

Don't use the following:

Special characters: Special characters (such as !, @, #, &, $, and many others) are forbidden. Many of these special characters have a specific meaning to Flash CS3 and can cause problems with ActionScript. To avoid accidentally using a special character, avoid everything but numbers and letters.

continues on next page

NOTE:

Symbol Naming Conventions *continued*

Spaces: Never use spaces in your names. Instead, string your words together, or use underscores. For example, instead of **my first symbol**, use **myFirstSymbol** or, even better, **my_first_symbol** (no uppercase letters to remember!).

Periods: Never put periods in your file or symbol names (other than the three-letter extension). For example, **snow.boarder.fla** will cause problems. Instead, use **snow_boarder.fla**.

Forward slashes: Forward slashes are misinterpreted as path locations on a hard drive. Never use them. For example, **my/new/symbol** would be interpreted as the **object** symbol located in the **new** folder located in the **my** folder.

7 Deselect the symbol instance by clicking the gray artboard around the **Stage**. Choose **Window > Properties > Properties** to open the **Property inspector**, if it is not already open. Click to the reselect the rectangle on the **Stage**, and then look in the **Property inspector** to examine the rectangle's properties.

The Instance Behavior pop-up menu in the upper-left corner should say Movie Clip, and the Instance Name field should have the <Instance Name> placeholder text, as in the illustration shown here. To communicate with the movie clip in ActionScript, you must assign every symbol instance an instance name. That's the next step!

---

8 Type **rectangle_mc** in the **Instance Name** field.

Instance names should follow the same naming conventions as symbol names. To avoid confusion, don't use the same name for a symbol and one of its instances. In this case, you're just inverting the two parts of the name, separated by an underscore. The _mc part actually has a special significance, as you'll discover in Exercise 2.

---

9 Select the **Free Transform** tool in the **Tools** panel, or press **Q** on your keyboard.

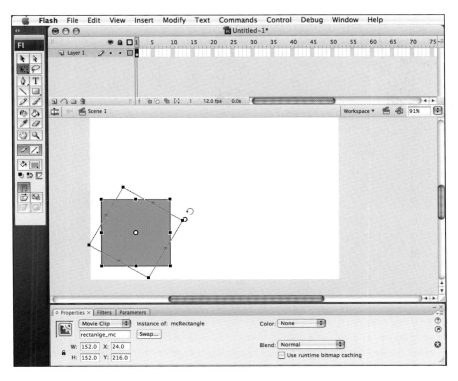

10 Eight handles will appear around the edges of the shape. Position your cursor over one of the outside corners, and then click and drag to rotate the shape. Click and drag any of the handles on the sides of the shape to make the shape larger or smaller.

11 In the **Library** panel, click and drag the **mcRectangle** symbol to the **Stage** to add another instance to the document. Click and drag to add a third instance to the **Stage**.

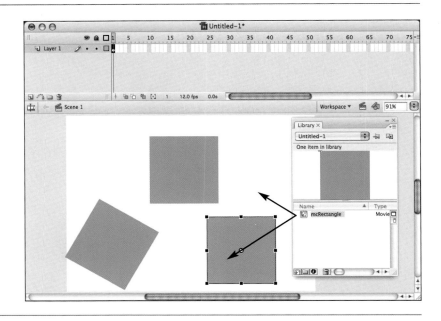

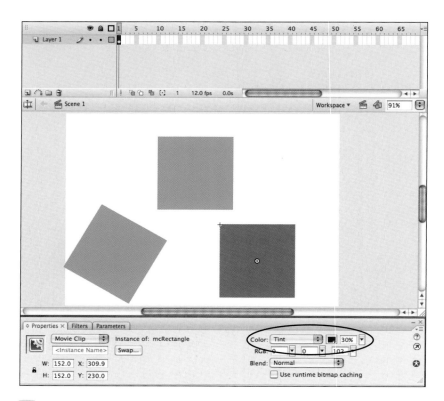

12 Select the **Selection** tool, and select one of the **mcRectangle** instances on the **Stage**. Go to the **Property inspector**, and choose **Tint** in the **Color** pop-up menu. Click the **Fill Color** box, and choose a blue color to tint the rectangle. Type **30%** in the **Tint Amount** field.

Now you have three instances of the original symbol on the Stage. As most Flash users know, no matter how you modify the instances, the original symbol will remain the same until you choose to modify it.

You'll learn how to change instance properties, including size, rotation, and tint, using ActionScript in the next exercise. The critical part to remember from this exercise is that you won't be able to do so, or communicate with the instances at all, unless you assign them each a valid instance name. The instance name is what differentiates the objects from one another.

Now you have one named instance of **mcRectangle** on the **Stage**. In the next exercise, you'll dive into ActionScript and learn how to modify some of its basic properties.

2 | Modifying Movie Clip Properties

In this exercise, you'll learn how to modify a movie clip's properties with ActionScript. Properties are attributes of an object, such as color or size, that you can also modify in the **Property inspector** in Flash.

---

1 Copy the **chap_02** folder from the **ActionScript HOT CD-ROM** to your desktop. Open **MovieClip_Properties.fla** from the **chap_02** folder.

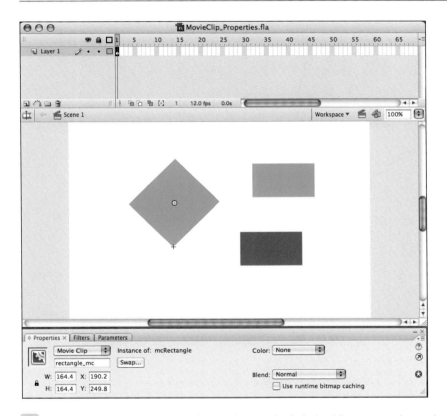

2 Select the **Selection** tool in the **Tools** panel. Click the blue rectangle on the **Stage**, and go to the **Property inspector**.

Notice that for this particular object you can modify the following properties: the width, the height, the object's position on the Stage (via the X and Y values), the color, and the blending mode for the object. The properties in the Property inspector will change depending on the type or **class** of object selected.

---

3 Change **Height** to **125**, and watch the rectangle on the **Stage** get taller.

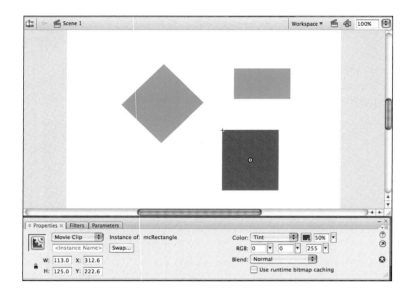

4 Change the **X** position to **145**, and watch the rectangle move to the left.

You can also change properties of objects on the Stage using the tools in the Tools panel.

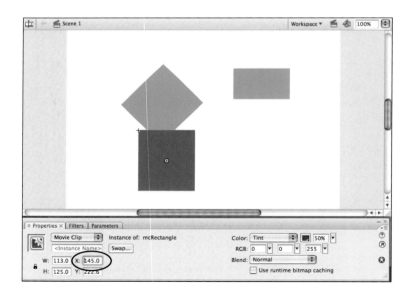

5 Select the **Free Transform** tool in the **Tools** panel. Select the same rectangle, and rotate it counterclockwise to watch the position properties in the **Property inspector** change.

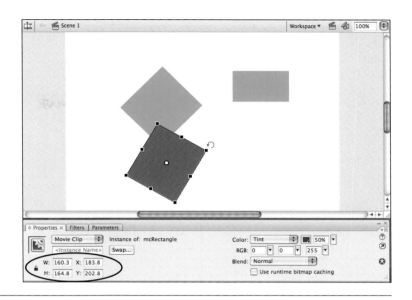

6 Press **Ctrl+Z** (Windows) or **Cmd+Z** (Mac) to undo the shape rotation.

Now that you understand how you can change properties by modifying the shape on the Stage, you will modify the properties through ActionScript. However, first each of these objects needs an instance name.

7 Press **V** to switch to the **Selection** tool. Select the blue rectangle. Choose the **Property inspector**, and change the instance name to **rectangle1_mc**.

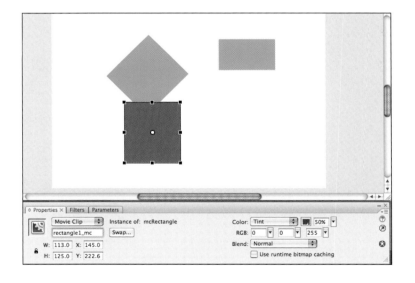

8 Select the rectangle in the upper-right corner of the **Stage**. Go to the **Property inspector**, and type **rectangle2_mc** in the **Instance Name** field. Choose the last rectangle, which has already been named **rectangle_mc**, and change the instance name to **rectangle3_mc**.

9 Click the **Insert Layer** button at the bottom the **Timeline** to create a new layer. Double-click the name of the new layer, and type **actions** to rename the layer.

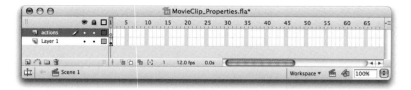

Click and drag the **actions** layer to the top of the layer order if it is not already there.

You're not required to rename this layer. You don't even need a separate layer for your actions, but it is considered best practice. By default, when a SWF files loads, the layers are loaded from the bottom up in the order they appear in the Timeline. Keeping the actions in a separate layer at the top of the Timeline ensures all the objects are fully loaded before the ActionScript tries to run.

---

10 Click the dot under the **lock** icon on the **actions** layer to lock the layer.

Locking the layer prevents you from accidentally adding contents to the actions layer but still allows you to add ActionScript.

---

11 Select **Frame 1** on the **actions** layer, and choose **Window > Actions** to open the **Actions** panel. The keyboard shortcut for this is **F9** (Windows) or **Opt+F9** (Mac).

The Actions panel has three basic areas: a Script pane, where you type the ActionScript code; the Actions toolbox, which contains a listing of all the classes, their methods, their events, and their parameters; and a Script navigator, which allows you to navigate to the different frames containing ActionScript.

The Actions toolbox

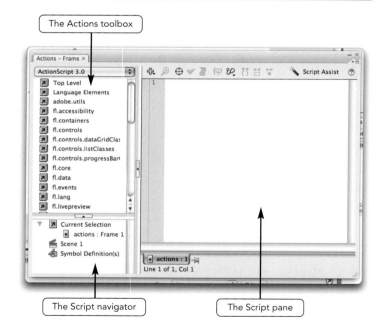

The Script navigator

The Script pane

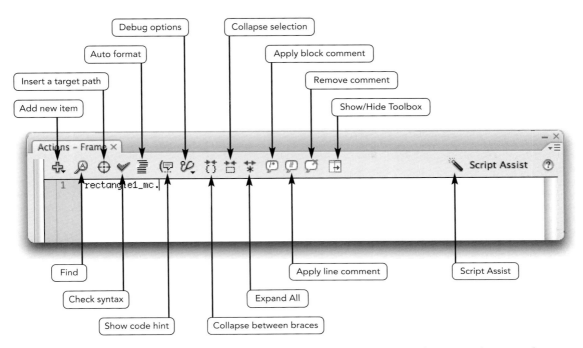

You'll also see 15 buttons above the Script pane, as shown in the illustration here. You don't need to know them all to start coding, but rest assured, you will be using these buttons throughout this book. For now, to start typing code, you need to make sure Script Assist is off. Script Assist is a feature that prompts you to type code through a form field.

12 If the **Script Assist** button above the **Script** pane is pressed, click it again to turn it off.

In this exercise, you won't be using the Actions toolbox. Instead, you'll be typing the code by hand. To make more room to type, you will close this pane, along with the Script navigator.

13 Click the **triangle** button in the middle of the split bar separating the **Script navigator** and **Actions toolbox** from the **Script** pane to hide them.

Now you're ready to code. The first step is to call the object you want to transform, using the instance name.

14 Insert your cursor on Line 1, type **rectangle1 _mc**, and then add a period.

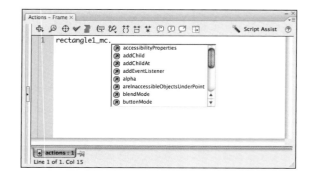

A pop-up menu will appear containing methods you can use with this movie clip object. This is Flash's code hinting feature. Flash happens to recognize that the object is a movie clip because of the _mc extension you added to the instance name and suggests a number of properties and methods that you can pick from. As I mentioned in Exercise 1, the _mc is optional, but it is handy when it comes time to type your code.

TIP:

Turning Code Hinting On and Off

Code hinting is just one of the features of Flash CS3's code editor; other features include syntax checking, code coloring, and autoformatting. You can turn these features on and off by choosing **Edit > Preferences** (Windows) or **Flash > Preferences** (Mac) and selecting the **ActionScript** category.

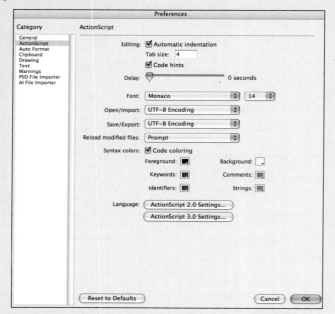

When code hinting is turned on, the hints disappear as soon as you finish typing or choose a selection in the pop-up menu. If you need to access the **Code Hint** pop-up menu again, position your cursor in the correct location, and click **Show Code Hint** in the **Script** pane toolbar, the sixth button from the left.

15 Type **al**. The **Code Hint** menu will filter through the results for anything that starts with **al**. (**alpha** should be the only highlighted entry.) Press **Enter** (Windows) or **Return** (Mac), and Flash will complete the rest of the word.

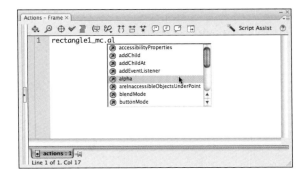

---

16 After `alpha`, press the **spacebar**, and type the following:

`= .5;`

Now you are telling Flash that the object's alpha property, or transparency, should be equal to .5, or 50 percent. The semicolon ends the statement. It's kind of like a period in a sentence.

If you're familiar with ActionScript 2.0, you'll notice two things about this property that are different. One is that the property has been changed from `_alpha` to just `alpha`. Second, the range for the alpha is no longer from 0 to 100; it's from 0 to 1.

---

17 Minimize the **Actions** panel by double-clicking the panel's tab. On the **Stage**, select **rectangle1_mc**.

Notice that the rectangle is still fully opaque. Why? The ActionScript does not come into play until the movie is published, which you'll see next.

---

18 Press **Ctrl+Enter** (Windows) or **Cmd+Return** (Mac) to test the movie.

There you have it. The rectangle is now semitransparent. To be precise, it's exactly 50% transparent.

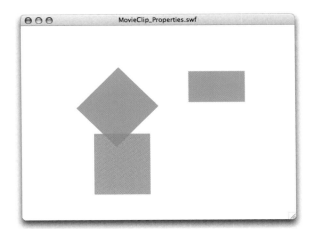

---

19 Close the movie preview window, and double-click the **Actions** panel tab to maximize the panel.

NOTE: | **Selection Cannot Have Actions Applied**

If you get the message "Current selection cannot have actions applied to it" when you open the Actions panel, don't panic. This simply means you have selected the wrong frame in your Timeline. You must type actions in a blank keyframe. Return to the Timeline, and select the blank keyframe in your actions layer; the Actions panel will allow you to type the code again.

---

20 Change the first line of code to read as follows:

```
rectangle1_mc.alpha = .15;
```

This will make the rectangle even more transparent. On the scale from 0 to 1, 0 is completely transparent and 1 is completely opaque.

---

21 Press **Ctrl+Enter** (Windows) or **Cmd+Return** (Mac) to test the movie again.

The rectangle in the movie is even more transparent, but once you close the preview window, you'll notice that the object on the Stage is still completely opaque.

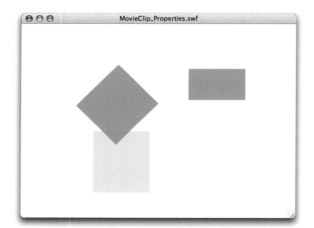

---

22 Close the preview window, and return to the **Actions** panel.

So now you know how to modify a movie clip's properties, but you still might be thinking, how am I going to remember all the possible values for each property? How will I remember that **alpha** accepts a value between 0 and 1? Well, Flash has another helpful feature you can use.

---

23 Highlight the `alpha` property in the code to select it. Press **F1** on your keyboard.

Pressing F1 opens the Help menu, which in Flash CS3 is context-sensitive, so it opens right to the `alpha` property. The Help menu contains very detailed information on all the ActionScript properties, including their accepted values. Once Help is open, you can use the Search field to look for properties, but I find the other method a little faster.

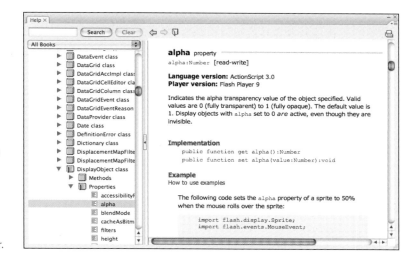

---

24 When you are finished, close **MovieClip_Properties.fla**. You don't need to save your changes.

Understanding Variables

A **variable** is basically a container that holds information. In the illustration shown here, the box on the left represents the variable that holds the data. The data is the user names on the right. The container (the variable) is the same for every user, but every time a different user logs in, that container is going to hold different data.

Understanding this concept is going to be important in the next exercise, where you will be creating variables with ActionScript.

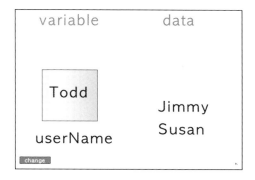

VIDEO: | **understandingvariables.mov**

For more explanation of the concept of variables, check out **understandingvariables. mov** in the **videos** folder on the **ActionScript HOT CD-ROM**.

3 Setting Variable Data Types

In this exercise, you'll learn how to create variables and how to assign different data types in ActionScript 3.0.

1 Choose **File > New**, and select **Flash File (ActionScript 3.0)** in the **New Document** dialog box. Click **OK**.

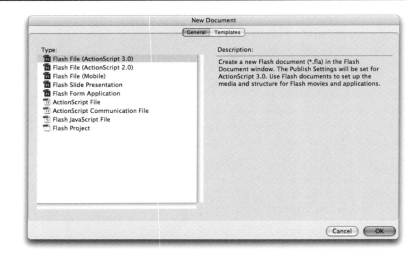

2 Double-click **Layer 1**, and rename the layer **actions**.

New Flash documents always open with one layer by default.

3 Select **Frame 1** on the **actions** layer. Press **F9** (Windows) or **Opt+F9** (Mac) to open the **Actions** panel.

To create a variable, the first task you need to perform is to type the word *var*.

---

4 Position your cursor on the first blank line, and type **var** followed by a space. After the space, type **userName**.

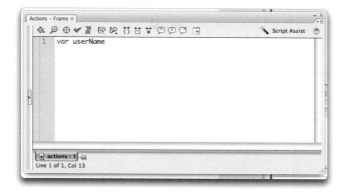

var is a keyword in Flash. Notice that the word turns blue. After the space, you type the variable name, in this case **userName**. You always have to start with **var**, but the variable name can be anything you want. However, note variable names are subject to the same rules as symbol and symbol instance names—no spaces, no special characters, and so on.

Now you will type a value for the variable. In this case, it will be text data, the user's actual name. Text data is called a **string**. Strings in general can be any combination of numbers, letters, spaces, and special characters. Whatever the characters it contains, when you're defining a string in Flash, you always put the string between quotation marks.

---

5 After **userName**, type a space, and then enter the following:

= "Todd";

You can type your own name if you want here. Now comes the important part: setting the variable data type. The variable data type does exactly what it sounds like. It defines the type of data that is going to be held inside the variable. Sometimes it will be numbers, and sometimes it will be text, as you see here. You'll specify the data type for this variable in the next step.

---

6 Position your cursor after **userName**, and type a colon (:). The **Code Hint** pop-up menu appears again. This time Flash recognizes that the statement is creating a variable and supplies variable data types.

---

7 Type the letters **Str**. Press **Enter** (Windows) or **Return** (Mac) as soon as the word **String** is highlighted in the **Code Hint** pop-up menu.

Make sure to type a capital *S* in this step, or the code hint won't work.

Once you hit Enter (Windows) or Return (Mac), your ActionScript statement is complete. You can change the variable name and the text string to anything you want, but *var* is required. The variable data type isn't required to make this

statement work, but as you'll see later, typing it prevents Flash from accepting garbage data. If you were to accidentally type a special character for a Number type variable, you'd want Flash to let you know.

---

8 Close the **Actions** panel, and close the Flash file. You don't need to save your changes.

In the next exercise, you'll use something called a trace statement to check a value inside a variable.

---

4 | Using Trace Statements

One way to make sure your code is syntaxed and running properly is to use trace statements. A **trace statement** pops up in the **Output** panel when you test or publish the movie. It's kind of like a message to whomever is working on the file, and it stays internal to Flash. The message won't display, for example, if you publish the SWF file on the Web. In this exercise, you'll learn how to set up a trace statement.

---

1 Choose **File > Open**, and open **Trace_Statements.fla** from the **chap_02** folder you copied to your desktop.

---

2 Select **Frame 1** on the **actions** layer, and press **F9** (Windows) or **Opt+F9** (Mac) to open the **Actions** panel.

This file contains a similar variable statement to the one you created in Exercise 3. I'm going to use *Sammy* for the text string this time.

---

3 Position your cursor after the first line of code, and hit **Enter** (Windows) or **Return** (Mac) three times until your cursor is at the beginning of Line 4. Type the following:

trace

trace is another keyword, so it will turn blue like **var**.

Note spaces between lines of code are not required for the ActionScript to run properly; they just provide a visual separation between statements.

---

4 Press the spacebar after **trace**, and type the following:

(userName);

It's important to pay attention to the casing of the variable name on Line 1 in this statement. Otherwise, your trace statement won't return an accurate value.

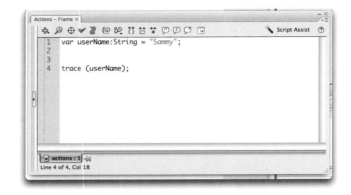

5 Press **Ctrl+Enter** (Windows) or **Cmd+Return** (Mac) to test the movie.

Notice that the Output panel opens when the movie is exported. (It may open in a different area of your screen.) The Output panel contains the variable value, **Sammy**. Now this might not seem valuable information, but consider you have a project containing hundreds or even thousands of lines of code and that code contains an error. The Output panel gives you no information or a coded error message that you can't understand. That's when trace statements become really valuable. They can help you check the code and isolate any problems.

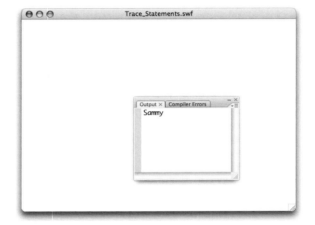

6 Close the **Output** panel and the preview window.

7 In the **Actions** panel, delete `userName` from the **trace** statement, and type **"This code is running properly."** (Make sure to include the quotation marks.)

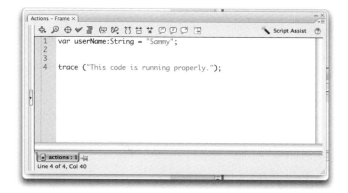

The trace statement checks against whatever portion of the code in which it's inserted. `userName` was just the message it returned after checking the code, not the actual code it was checking. You can change the string, as you just did, to tailor the output message to the particular needs of your project. If you had multiple trace statements, you could tailor the message to the blocks of code in which they were located.

8 Press **Ctrl+Enter** (Windows) or **Cmd+Return** (Mac) to test the new message. When you are finished, close the preview window and the **Actions** and **Output** panels, and then close **Trace_Statements.fla**. You don't need to save your changes.

It might still not be entirely clear why or where or when you use trace statements, but when you start to work with more complicated files in the next few chapters, they will be easier to understand. In the next exercise, you'll learn how to make comments in your code.

Using Comments

In this exercise, you'll learn how to insert comments in your code. Comments are notes, usually to your-self or to other coders looking at the file. Comments can explain coding decisions, such as the file organization, or can simply annotate the code. You can also temporarily turn off a block of code using a comment.

---

1 Choose **Flash File (ActionScript 3.0)** in the **Create New** section of the **Welcome** screen.

---

2 Double-click the name of the first layer, and rename it **actions**.

---

3 Select **Frame 1** on the **actions** layer, and press **F9** (Windows) or **Opt+F9** (Mac) to open the **Actions** panel.

First you'll practice temporarily turning off a line of code.

---

4 Position your cursor on the first blank line, and type the following:

`trace("something");`

You may have noticed that whenever you place a word or phrase in quotation marks, it turns green in the Actions panel. (If you have modified your ActionScript preferences, it may turn a different color.) This is another Flash code assistance fea-ture, called **code coloring**. Keywords are colored blue by default, as you saw in a previous exercise. Strings, such as this text string, are colored green. Comments, which you'll add in a moment, are gray. You can turn off code coloring or change the default colors by going to the ActionScript category of the Preferences menu.

---

5 Press **Ctrl+Enter** (Windows) or **Cmd+Return** (Mac) to test the movie.

The preview window should be empty when the SWF loads, because you didn't add any content to the movie. Because of the trace statement you added, the Output panel should open and contain the word *something*.

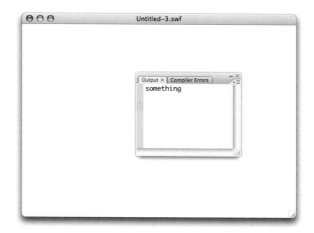

6 Close the preview window and the **Output** panel.

7 In the **Actions** panel, position your cursor before the trace statement, and type **//** (two slashes).

Notice that the entire line of code turns gray. Two slashes signal to Flash that the line of code is a comment and shouldn't be used in the final movie.

8 Press **Ctrl+Enter** (Windows) or **Cmd+Return** (Mac) to test the movie.

Even though the trace statement is still in the code, the Output panel should not open when the movie is exported because you disabled the code.

You can also use comments to leave messages for other coders. Messages can use any combination of characters.

9 Close the preview window, and return to the **Actions** panel. After the trace statement, press **Enter** (Windows) or **Return** (Mac) twice. Type **//** to start a new comment.

10 Type a message of your choice, such as Hey fellow coder, line 1 has been disabled until we have more code to trace.

Both the comment code and the text will turn gray.

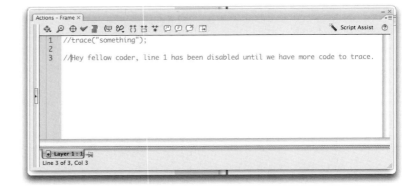

11 Position your cursor before Line 1, and delete the two slashes. Click and drag to select the entire trace statement. Press **Ctrl+C** (Windows) or **Cmd+C** (Mac) to copy it.

12 Press **Enter** (Windows) or **Return** (Mac) to go to the next line. Press **Ctrl+V** (Windows) or **Cmd+V** (Mac) to paste the trace statement.

To disable, or **comment out**, multiple lines of code such as you have here, you'll use a multiline comment.

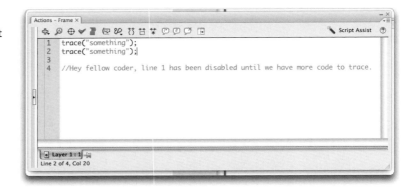

13 Position your cursor before the first trace statement, and press **Enter** (Windows) or **Return** (Mac). Press the **up arrow** key to go to the new first line. Type **/***.

Notice that both lines of code are now gray.

14 Position your cursor on the next blank line after the second trace statement, and type ***/** to close the multiline comment. Press **Enter** (Windows) or **Return** (Mac), and on the new line, press **Ctrl+V** (Windows) or **Cmd+V** (Mac) to paste the trace statement again.

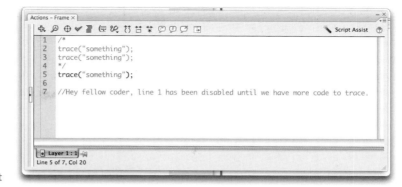

Notice that the trace statement outside the commented block of code stays active.

There's one more feature to comments I want to show you: the comment tools. The comment tools are located above the Script pane and can be used to insert or delete both single-line and multiline comments, without having to type the // or */.

---

15 Select the third trace statement, and click the **Apply line comment** button.

Flash adds the comment marker before the line, and the code turns gray. Notice that Flash inserts the markers on the same line as the code. I prefer to separate them, as you've done in this exercise, to keep the markers and original code visually separated, but it's not absolutely necessary. To remove the comment, you simply reselect the code and click the Remove comment button.

---

16 Close the **Actions** panel, and then close the Flash file. You don't need to save your changes.

Congratulations! You've completed the first set of exercises. Now that you know the basics of ActionScript—how to use correct syntax, how to modify properties, how to create variables, and so on—you can move on to building functions. In the next chapter, you'll learn how to use ActionScript's built-in functions, called **methods**, and how to write custom functions of your own.

3

Using and Writing Functions

In this chapter, I'll explain what functions are and how to use them. Functions, to put it simply, do things. They are sometimes referred to as the "brains" of ActionScript. Functions contain a statement or group of statements that perform certain tasks, and they're a powerful and important part of any ActionScript code. You can reuse functions multiple times; you write code once, and then you can use it over and over again. Functions can be run on different objects and even accept different values depending on the targeted object. Functions can even return values that can be used in other statements. In this chapter, you'll review all the features of functions in depth.

Understanding Functions

A **function** is a reusable block of code. In the illustration shown here, the block in the middle represents a block of code. The blue blocks represent the instance name (**boarder**) and the properties (**move** and **rotate**) of the snowboarder object at the bottom right of the illustration. This illustration is actually from a workable file, **Functions.swf**, provided on the **ActionScript HOT CD-ROM** for you to follow along.

To run the function, you need to add both an object and a property to the function. In this case, you can add **boarder** and **move** to the function, and the boarder will jump the hill. You can add **boarder** and **rotate** to make the boarder just spin. Or you can add **boarder**, **move**, and **rotate**. The idea here is not only that you can use any combination of properties in the function but that you can use the function over and over again with different objects. Theoretically, you could run this same function on the snow if you wanted rotating snow. In the following exercises, you'll see how this works in detail.

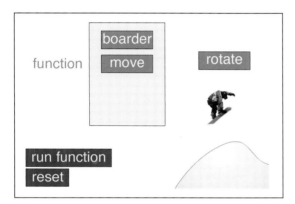

VIDEO: | **functions.mov**

For more information on the basic properties of functions, check out **functions.mov** in the **videos** folder on the **ActionScript HOT CD-ROM**.

1 | Using Methods

In this exercise, you'll learn how to use functions that are built into Flash, called **methods**. A method is a type of function that runs on a particular class of objects in ActionScript.

1 Copy the **chap_03** folder from the **ActionScript HOT CD-ROM** to your desktop. Open **Using_Functions.fla** from the **chap_03** folder.

The visibility is turned off on the guide layer.

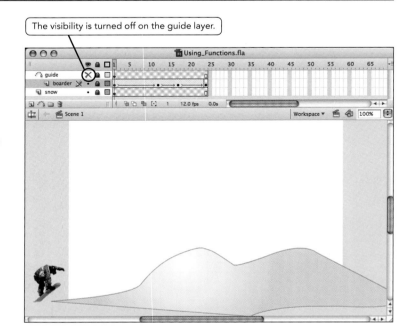

This file contains a simple tween animation with a motion guide layer. The visibility on the guide layer is turned off so that it doesn't distract you.

2 Press **Ctrl+Enter** (Windows) or **Cmd+Return** (Mac) to preview the movie.

3 Close the preview window. Click the **Insert Layer** button below the **Timeline**, and rename the new layer **actions**. Move the layer to the top of the layer stack.

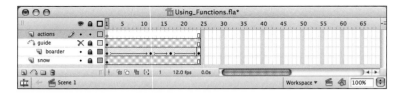

On this layer, you'll be adding functions that will stop the movie from playing automatically.

Now, if you've used Script Assist or any form of ActionScript, you should be familiar with methods. You have probably used the **stop()** method to stop your movies from playing automatically. Stop is actually a method.

4 Select **Frame 24**, the last frame, on the **actions** layer. Press **F7** to insert a new blank keyframe, or choose **Insert > Timeline > Blank Keyframe**.

An empty circle appears in Frame 24 indicating it is a blank keyframe. Remember that actions need to be added to keyframes. Even though a keyframe can contain both art and code, it's good practice to place ActionScript in blank keyframes.

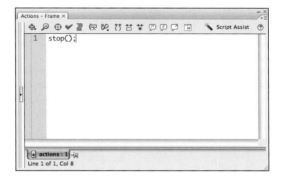

The empty circle in the frame represents the new blank keyframe.

5 Select the new blank keyframe, and press **F9** (Windows) or **Opt+F9** (Mac) to open the **Actions** panel.

6 Position your cursor on the first line, and type the following:

```
stop();
```

Make sure you're on Frame 24 of the actions layer! Otherwise, the animation won't play at all.

TIP:

Finding Methods in the Actions Toolbox

This book focuses on programming ActionScript without using Script Assist or other tools so you have a firm understanding about how code is constructed and why it is constructed that way. However, sometimes you may be starting to code on your own and forget what a certain function does or what built-in functions are available when you are working with certain objects. Enter the **Actions toolbox**. The **Actions toolbox** is really no more than an index of classes and their functions and properties, but it can be very helpful when you need to jog your memory.

For example, let's say you were trying to draw a circle on the **Stage** at a certain point in the movie and you knew there was a method for the **Graphics** class. You could go to the **Actions toolbox** and expand the **flash.display** package, the **Graphics** class, and then the **Methods** category and review all the available methods, including the one you want, **drawCircle**. Simply double-click **drawCircle** to add it to the **Script** pane.

continues on next page

TIP:

Finding Methods in the Actions Toolbox *continued*

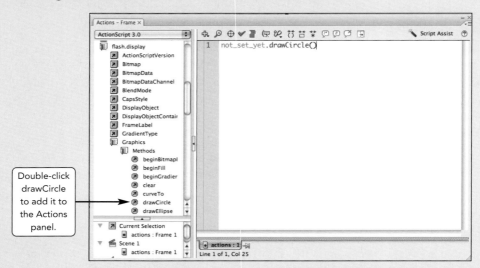

Double-click drawCircle to add it to the Actions panel.

If you're not sure of the package or class of the method, use the **Index** category at the end of the list. Simply expand the category, and type the first letter of your search term.

The Index category lists events, methods, and properties in alphabetical order.

Position your cursor over an item in the Actions panel to reveal the tool tip for that item.

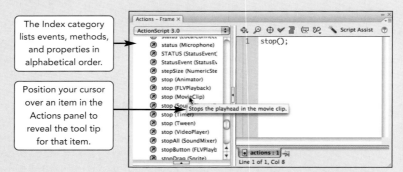

Another helpful feature of the **Actions** panel is that a tool tip will appear when you position your cursor over a method. The tool tips provide brief explanations of what the method does. If you need more, press **F1** or choose **Help > Flash Help** to open the context-sensitive **Help** menu, which will take you right to the definition and usage of the selected method.

7 Press **Ctrl+Enter** (Windows) or **Cmd+Return** (Mac) to test the movie again.

The animation will play once and then stop. Let's run one other function that you may already be familiar with.

---

8 Close the preview window, and return to the **Actions** panel. Make sure **Frame 24** is still selected on the **Timeline**. Select the **Stop** function, and press **Delete**.

---

9 Type the following:

`gotoAndStop(2);`

This function instructs the movie to play until the frame included in the parentheses, Frame 2. Frame 2 is where the snowboarder first appears on Stage.

---

10 Press **Ctrl+Enter** (Windows) or **Cmd+Return** (Mac) to test the movie again.

The movie will play once and then start over and end on Frame 2.

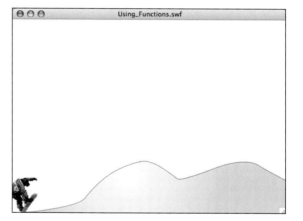

---

11 When you are finished, close the preview window, and then close **Using_Functions.fla**. You don't need to save your changes.

This exercise has been an overview of methods, which are functions that, most likely, you already know. In the next exercise, you'll dive into creating your own custom functions, which can be far more complex.

---

2 | Writing Custom Functions

In this exercise, you'll write a custom function that modifies several properties of the same object.

1 Choose **File > Open**, and open **WritingFunctions.fla** from the **chap_03** folder.

This composition should look pretty familiar by now. The file contains a movie clip, mcBoarder, which can be located in the Library panel. The movie clip was created by converting the boarder_logo.png file, also stored in the Library panel, to a movie clip symbol. You'll be writing a custom function that will both move the snowboarder and rotate him slightly.

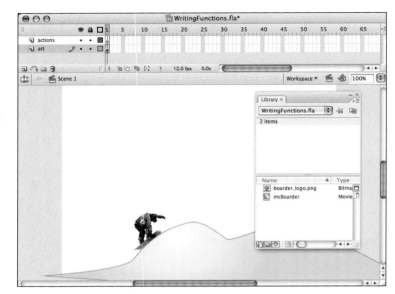

2 Click the **mcBoarder** instance on the **Stage**. Check the **Property inspector** to make sure the snowboarder has the instance name **boarder_mc**.

If you recall from Chapter 2, adding the _mc extension to movie clip instance names helps Flash recognize the symbol type and provide the correct code hints.

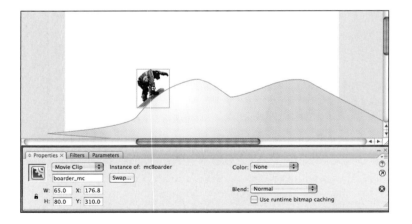

3 Select **Frame 1** on the **actions** layer, and press **F9** (Windows) or **Opt+F9** (Mac) to open the **Actions** panel.

4 Position your cursor on the first line, and type the following:

```
function moveBoarder
```

Defining a function is similar to defining a variable. You just type *function*, followed by a space, followed by a name of your choosing.

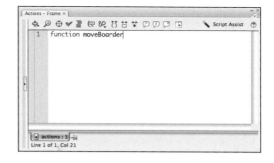

5 Directly after **moveBoarder**, type the following:

```
():void
```

Parentheses are required when you are defining a function. The word after the colon defines the return data type, which will be covered in detail in a future exercise. For now, you just need to know that **void** means the function will not be returning data.

6 Press **Enter** (Windows) or **Return** (Mac) to move to the next line, and type a left curly brace (**{**).

The information you'll type in the curly braces defines what happens in the **moveBoarder()** function.

7 Press **Enter** (Windows) or **Return** (Mac) to move to the next line, and type the following:

```
boarder_mc.y = 50;
```

Notice that the line automatically indents when you hit Enter (Windows) or Return (Mac) after the curly brace. This indicates this code resides "inside" the function. The code sets the Y position of the **boarder_mc** object to 50 (pixels from the top edge of the Stage). Remember that unlike a standard graph, Flash counts pixels starting from the top-left corner of the Stage.

Now you'll rotate the boarder.

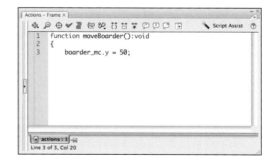

8 Press **Enter** (Windows) or **Return** (Mac) to move to the next line, and type the following:

```
boarder_mc.rotation = 45;
```

This code rotates the snowboarder by 45 degrees.

9 Press **Enter** (Windows) or **Return** (Mac) to move to the next line, and type a right curly brace (**}**).

Notice as soon as you type the right curly brace, the indent decreases. Now it looks as though you have a complete statement, but if you were to test the movie, nothing would happen. If you remember from the first example, properties were dragged inside the function block, but the **run function** button had to be clicked before anything would happen. You're not going to click a button, but you do need to run the function.

10 Press **Enter** (Windows) or **Return** (Mac) twice to move down two lines, and type the following:

moveBoarder();

The syntax of this statement is similar to what you use when you run a method, such as **stop();**. In this case, you've just defined a custom function beforehand.

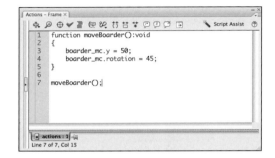

11 Move the **Actions** panel, and note where the snowboarder is on the **Stage**. Then press **Ctrl+Enter** (Windows) or **Cmd+Return** (Mac) to test the movie.

Notice that the snowboarder jumps to the top of the Stage and rotates slightly, just as you specified in the **moveBoarder()** function.

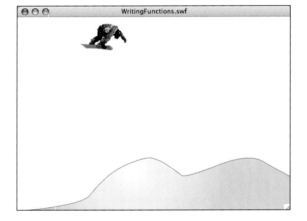

12 When you are finished, close the preview window, and then close **WritingFunctions.fla**. You don't need to save your changes.

Congratulations! You just wrote your first custom function. Now that you know how to write custom functions, you'll try making those functions more useful in the next exercise.

Understanding Modular Functions

ActionScript code is sometimes broken up into separate ActionScript files (**.as**) that reside outside of a Flash file. These **.as** files comprise a library of objects and functions that can be reused over and over again by linking them to various Flash files or Flash project files (**.flp**). This type of coding is called **modular coding**.

However, the term **modular coding** can also refer to how code is designed and managed in a single ActionScript or Flash file. When you make your code modular, you are making sure it is flexible and can be reused as many times as needed. Modular code cuts down on the need to repeat statements and the time it takes to edit those statements when you need to make a change. When you create a modular function, you do not specify the object on which the function should run.

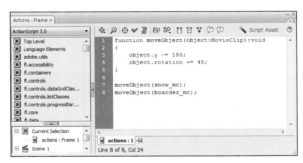

The illustration shown here is an example of a modular function. The other two illustrations to the right are from the **ModularFunctions.swf** file included in the **chap_03** exercise folder. The first one is a visual representation of this same function. The function is represented by the large block in the center of the Stage. The function changes the position and rotation properties of the **snow** and **boarder** movie clips.

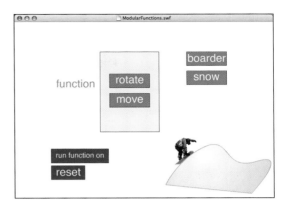

In the SWF file, you specify an object by selecting either **boarder** or **snow** from the right and clicking **run function on**. When you do that, the function runs on that object. Likewise, in the code, you must specify the object when you run the function.

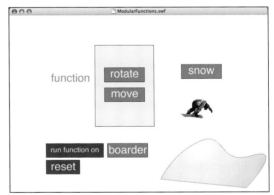

Designing functions this way makes the code a lot more useful. It also keeps the code more concise and less time-consuming to modify when you need to make a change. In the next exercise, you'll learn how to write the code in the illustration shown above.

3 | Making a Function Modular

In this exercise, you'll learn how to make a function **modular**, that is, reusable.

---

1 Choose **File > Open**, and open **Making_Modular.fla** from the **chap_03** exercise folder you copied to your desktop.

---

2 Select **Frame 1** on the **art** layer, and click and drag two instances of **mcBoarder** from the **Library** panel to the **Stage**. Place them as shown in the illustration here.

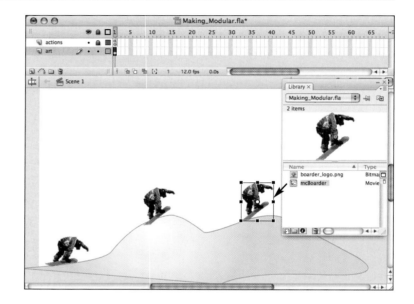

3 Select the **Free Transform** tool in the **Tools** panel. Rotate and move the two new **mcSnowboarder** instances so their boards are flush with the snow.

Note: The X and Y properties of your snowboarders may be different from mine, depending on where you initially place them.

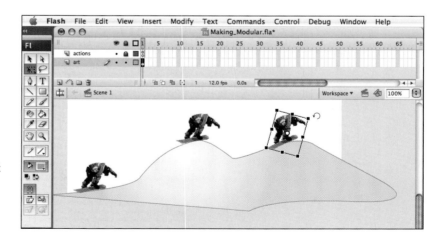

---

4 Select the **Selection** tool in the **Tools** panel, and select the middle snowboarder.

5 Go to the **Property inspector**, and type **boarder1_mc** as the instance name for the snowboarder.

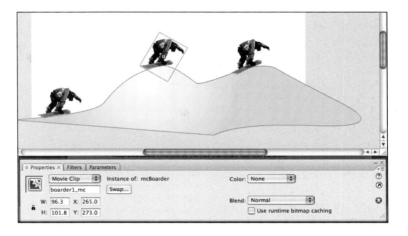

6 Select the snowboarder on the left, go to the **Property inspector**, and type **boarder2_mc** in the **Instance Name** field. Repeat for the snowboarder on the right; name it **boader3_mc**.

7 Select **Frame 1** on the **actions** layer, and press **F9** (Windows) or **Opt+F9** (Mac) to open the **Actions** panel.

The `moveBoarder()` function is the same one you wrote in Exercise 3. However, since you renamed the first instance of the snowboarder, the function won't have an object to run on if you don't change the name.

```
function moveBoarder():void
{
    boarder_mc.y = 50;
    boarder_mc.rotation = 45;
}

moveBoarder();
```

8 Change the object **boarder_mc** on the third and fourth lines to **boarder1_mc**.

9 Press **Ctrl+Enter** (Windows) or **Cmd+Return** (Mac) to test the movie.

The middle boarder, boarder1_mc, is 50 pixels from the top of the screen and rotated at a 45-degree angle. But what about the other two boarders? You could copy and paste the function another two times and change the object names, but that would make your ActionScript unnecessarily long. Instead, when you call the function, you will call the objects you want to run the function on as well.

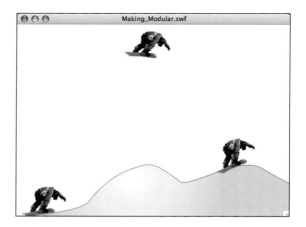

10 Close the preview window, and return to the **Actions** panel. Position your cursor between the parentheses on Line 7, and type the following:

boarder1_mc

moveBoarder(boarder1_mc); still runs the function, but now it also sends the function information about the object on which to run it.

```
1   function moveBoarder():void
2   {
3       boarder1_mc.y = 50;
4       boarder1_mc.rotation = 45;
5   }
6
7   moveBoarder(boarder1_mc);
```

actions : 1
Line 7 of 7, Col 24

11 Change the object **boarder1_mc** in Lines 3 and 4 back to just **boarder**.

boarder is the generic name for whatever type of object you want to move. You can choose whatever name you'd like. In fact, **boarder** is a variable, a generic term that is replaced by whatever you send into the function on Line 7 of the code.

Now in order to complete the code, you also need to set up the function itself to receive the data by defining the data type for the objects. In this case, the type of data is a movie clip.

```
1   function moveBoarder():void
2   {
3       boarder.y = 50;
4       boarder.rotation = 45;
5   }
6
7   moveBoarder(boarder1_mc);
```

actions : 1
Line 4 of 7, Col 9

12 Position your cursor between the parentheses on Line 1, and type the following:

boarder:

13 Notice that a code hint pops up. Type **Mov**. When the word **MovieClip** is highlighted, press **Enter** (Windows) or **Return** (Mac).

Now the function understands what type of data is being passed to it.

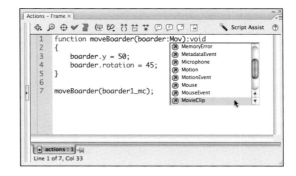

14 Press **Ctrl+Enter** (Windows) or **Cmd+Return** (Mac) to test the movie.

The function works the same as it did the last time you tested the movie. The middle boarder, boarder1_mc, flies in the air and rotates slightly. The difference is the function is now modular, which means it can be reused for the other two snowboarders on the Stage.

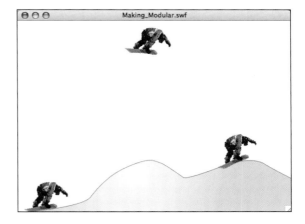

15 Close the preview window, and return to the **Actions** panel. Select the code on Line 7, and press **Ctrl+C** (Windows) or **Cmd+C** (Mac) to copy the code.

16 Position your cursor after the semicolon on Line 7, and press **Enter** (Windows) or **Return** (Mac) to move to the next line. Press **Ctrl+V** (Windows) or **Cmd+V** (Mac) to paste the code.

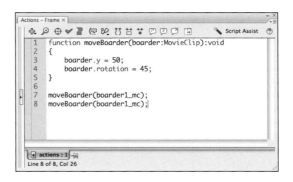

17 Press **Enter** (Windows) or **Return** (Mac) to move to the next line, and then press **Ctrl+V** (Windows) or **Cmd+V** (Mac) to paste the code again.

18 Go to Line 8, and change **boarder1_mc** to **boarder2_mc**. Go to Line 9, and change **boarder1_mc** to **boarder3_mc**.

Now the function will fun on all the snowboarders, starting with boarder1_mc on Line 7. Flash reads ActionScript from the top down, so the function will run on the first object, then the second, and then the third. You won't be able to see this, but it's important to note for future exercises.

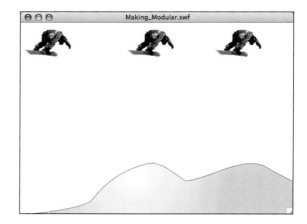

```
1  function moveBoarder(boarder:MovieClip):void
2  {
3      boarder.y = 50;
4      boarder.rotation = 45;
5  }
6
7  moveBoarder(boarder1_mc);
8  moveBoarder(boarder2_mc);
9  moveBoarder(boarder3_mc);
```

---

19 Press **Ctrl+Enter** (Windows) or **Cmd+Return** (Mac) to test the movie.

All three snowboarders are moved up and rotated 45 degrees to the left. Notice that they are uniform; they are all on the same Y axis and rotated the same way. Changing the Y position or the rotation of an object does not move an object relative to its current position but to an absolute position on the Stage. To move and rotate the boarders relative to their original locations, you need to change the function.

---

20 Close the preview window, and return to the **Actions** panel. Position your cursor before the **=** on Line 3, and press the **–** (minus) key. Change the Y position value from **50** to **150**.

The minus forces the function to subtract 150 pixels from the object's Y position value. Remember, subtracting will not make the snowboarder lower on the Stage, but higher. 0 on the Y axis is at the top of the Stage, not the bottom.

```
1  function moveBoarder(boarder:MovieClip):void
2  {
3      boarder.y -= 150;
4      boarder.rotation = 45;
5  }
6
7  moveBoarder(boarder1_mc);
8  moveBoarder(boarder2_mc);
9  moveBoarder(boarder3_mc);
```

Operators

In ActionScript, characters such as +, -, and = are considered operators. Specifically, they are called **mathematical operators** because they perform math such as addition and subtraction. You use operators with expressions, which can be numeric values, variables, or properties of an object. Other operators are comparison operators and logical or Boolean operators.

When you combine two or more operators, as in **+=**, it's called a **compound assignment operator**. It's not critical to remember these names. Just remember that to avoid confusion, it's best to avoid using these characters in variable, instance, or function names, since they serve a special purpose in ActionScript.

The following chart describes a selection of operators and compound assignment operators. I'll review operators in detail in Chapter 6, *"Decision Making and Repetition,"* and Chapter 7, *"Using Math—and Loving It!"*

Operators and Their Functions		
Operator	Example	Description
Mathematical		
=	`position = 6`	Assigns the value of the expression on the right side of the operator to the expression on the left
+	`position + 6`	Adds two expressions
++	`position++`	Increments the value of an expression by 1
-	`position - 6`	Subtracts one expression from another
--	`position--`	Decrements the value of an expression by 1
*	`position * .5`	Multiplies two expressions
/	`position / 2`	Divides one expression by another
+=	`boarder.y += 6`	Adds the value of one expression to the current value of another expression
Comparison		
==	`position == 6`	Tests whether two expressions are equal
>	`position > 6`	Tests whether the value of an expression on the left is greater than the value of the expression on the right

continues on next page

NOTE:

Operators *continued*

Operators and Their Functions *continued*		
Operator	Example	Description
Comparison *continued*		
<	`position < 6`	Tests whether the value of an expression on the left is less than the value of the expression on the right
Logical/Boolean		
&&	`(position = 6) && (boarder.y = 6)`	Checks whether both expressions are true
!	`!position = 6`	Inverts the value of an expression; usually used to check whether a statement is not true
II	`(position = 6) II (boarder.y = 6)`	Checks whether either value is true

21 Position your cursor before the = on Line 4, and press the **+** (plus) key.

```
function moveBoarder(boarder:MovieClip):void
{
    boarder.y -= 150;
    boarder.rotation += 45;
}

moveBoarder(boarder1_mc);
moveBoarder(boarder2_mc);
moveBoarder(boarder3_mc);
```

Actions – Frame ×

Script Assist

actions : 1

Line 4 of 9, Col 25

22 Press **Ctrl+Enter** (Windows) or **Cmd+Return** (Mac) to test the movie again.

Awesome! Now the snowboarders are all moved to different heights and are rotated at different angles.

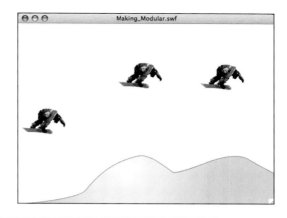

23 Close the preview window, and return to the **Actions** panel.

You have just created a reusable function! You could add another movie clip to your Library panel, add that instance to the Stage, and send it to the same function. Another way to make this function reusable is by sending different Y position and rotation values to it.

24 Position your cursor after the word **MovieClip** on Line 1, and type the following:

`, movement:Number, rotationAmt:Number`

Just like when you set up the boarder variable, you are creating variables for each of the properties in the function. **movement** will stand for the Y position value and **rotationAmt** for the rotation value. Number is the data type for the values, just as MovieClip is the data type for the objects.

```
1  function moveBoarder(boarder:MovieClip, movement:Number, rotationAmt:Number):void
2  {
3      boarder.y -= 150;
4      boarder.rotation += 45;
5  }
6
7  moveBoarder(boarder1_mc);
8  moveBoarder(boarder2_mc);
9  moveBoarder(boarder3_mc);
```

Line 1 of 9, Col 39

25 Position your cursor on Line 3. Replace **150** with the word **movement**.

```
1  function moveBoarder(boarder:MovieClip, movement:Number, rotationAmt:Number):void
2  {
3      boarder.y -= movement;
4      boarder.rotation += 45;
5  }
6
7  moveBoarder(boarder1_mc);
8  moveBoarder(boarder2_mc);
9  moveBoarder(boarder3_mc);
```

Line 3 of 9, Col 23

26 Position your cursor on Line 4. Replace **45** with the word **rotationAmt**.

The final step is to send in a `movement` value and a `rotation` value every time you run the function. If you don't send in values when you set up variables, the function won't work properly. The function is looking for a movie clip and two numbers. If it doesn't get them, it won't complete.

---

27 Position your cursor after the word **boader1_mc** on Line 7, and type the following:

, 150, 45

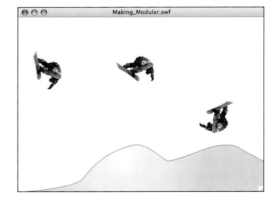

```
1   function moveBoarder(boarder:MovieClip, movement:Number, rotationAmt:Number):void
2   {
3       boarder.y -= movement;
4       boarder.rotation += rotationAmt;
5   }
6
7   moveBoarder(boarder1_mc, 150, 45);
8   moveBoarder(boarder2_mc);
9   moveBoarder(boarder3_mc);
```

---

28 Position your cursor after the word **boader2_mc** on Line 8, and type the following:

, 250, 90

---

29 Position your cursor after the word **boader3_mc** on Line 9, and type the following:

, 50, 180

---

30 Press **Ctrl+Enter** (Windows) or **Cmd+Return** (Mac) to test the movie again.

Now the snowboarders are moved to heights and rotated based on different values, each relative to their original position.

---

31 When you are finished, close the preview window. Close the **Actions** panel, and close **Making_Modular.fla**. You don't need to save your changes.

Modular functions can be complex, but ultimately, they can save you a lot of time and effort. You've learned how to create a modular function by sending in objects and values. In the next exercise, you'll learn how to get a function to return a value.

4 | Making a Function Return a Value

Functions, like trace statements, can actually return values. Unlike trace statements, the values that functions return do not show up in the **Output** panel, but they can be reused in other parts of the code. In this exercise, you'll learn how to make a function return a value.

1 Choose **File > Open**, and open **Returns.fla** from the **chap_03** exercise folder you copied to your desktop.

This file contains two instances of the snowboarder on a field of snow, one in the background and one in the foreground.

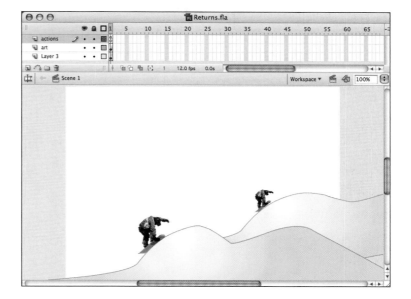

2 Select the **Selection** tool in the **Tools** panel. Select the snowboarder in the foreground, and go to the **Property inspector** to check the instance name.

boarder1_mc should appear in the Instance Name field in the Property inspector.

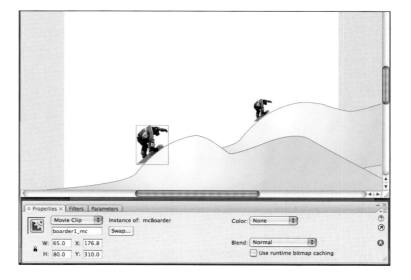

3 Select **Frame 1** on the **actions** layer, and press **F9** (Windows) or **Opt+F9** (Mac) to open the **Actions** panel.

The code contains a simple function that moves the object boarder1_mc up 150 pixels and scales it horizontally and vertically to be both twice as wide and twice as tall as the original.

4 Press **Ctrl+Enter** (Windows) or **Cmd+Return** (Mac) to test the movie.

The boarder in the foreground appears higher on the Stage and much larger. The boarder in the background stays the same. Now, what if you wanted these two objects to jump simultaneously but you don't want to resize the second snowboarder? You can't run the same function on him. This is where having a function return a value can come in handy.

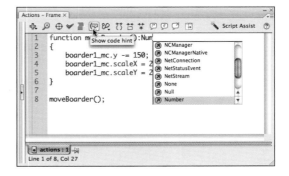

5 Close the preview window, and return to the **Actions** panel.

I promised you we were going to talk about the return data type, that **:void** following the function name, and now is the time. The return data type specifies what kind of data you want back from the function after it runs.

6 Position your cursor after the **:** (colon) on Line 1. Delete the word **void**, and type **Num**. Click the **Show Code Hint** button above the **Script** pane to show the **Code Hint** pop-up menu.

7 When the word **Number** is highlighted in the **Code Hint** pop-up menu, press **Enter** (Windows) or **Return** (Mac).

8 Position your cursor after the semicolon on Line 5, and press **Enter** (Windows) or **Return** (Mac) to insert a new line. Type the following:

```
return boarder1_mc.y;
```

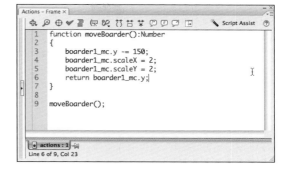

9 Press **Ctrl+Enter** (Windows) or **Cmd+Return** (Mac) to test the movie.

Nothing different happens to the movie, which is not to say the function is not returning a number— only that it doesn't have anything to do with it.

10 Close the preview window, and return to the **Actions** panel. Position your cursor in Line 9 before **moveBoarder**. Change the line so it reads as follows:

```
trace(moveBoarder());
```

Make sure you close both sets of parentheses.

11 Press **Ctrl+Enter** (Windows) or **Cmd+Return** (Mac) to test the movie.

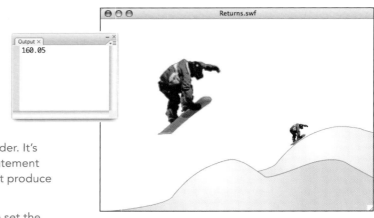

Now the Output panel opens, and you get 160.05. The trace statement runs the function and traces this number, from the last line of the function that returns the Y position of the first snowboarder. It's important to note that the trace statement *displays* the number, but it does not produce the number.

So now, you can use this number to set the position of the second boarder equal to that of the first.

---

12 Close the preview window, and return to the **Actions** panel. Press **Ctrl+Z** (Windows) or **Cmd+Z** (Mac) to undo the change to Line 9. Position your cursor in Line 9 before **moveBoarder**. Change the line so it reads as follows:

```
boarder2_mc.y = moveBoarder();
```

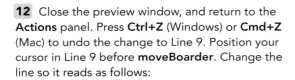

---

13 Press **Ctrl+Enter** (Windows) or **Cmd+Return** (Mac) to test the movie.

Now both snowboarders are in the same vertical position. They may look slightly different, but that's just because the snowboarders are aligned from the center and the second boarder is smaller than the first.

ActionScript 3.0 for Adobe Flash CS3 Professional : H·O·T

14 When you are finished, close the preview window. Close the **Actions** panel, and close **Returns.fla**. You don't need to save your changes.

That brings us to the end of this chapter. Now you know how to create regular functions, create modular functions, return values from functions, and more! These first few chapters will build the foundations for tackling more complicated projects in the future. In the next chapter, you'll focus on events and event handling.

4

Responding to Events

In this chapter, you'll learn how to write code that executes in response to an event. In Adobe Flash CS3 Professional, an event can be many different types of actions. Events can be initiated by users, such as by mouse clicks or by keystrokes, or when an action is initiated or completed, such as when a file finishes downloading, or even at a specific point in the **Timeline**. Event handlers execute a function in response to that event. You'll learn how to write event listeners first and then move on to event handlers and more complicated types of events.

Understanding Event Types

The illustration shown here is from the **UnderstandingEvents.swf** file included in the **chap_04** folder of the **exercise_files** folder, which is a visual representation of an event. The radio tower is continually broadcasting a signal, but the radio does not necessarily hear that broadcast. The radio needs to be tuned to, or be **listening** to, that particular station to hear what the station is broadcasting.

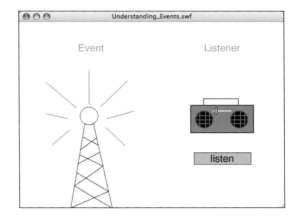

In this example, the tower broadcasting represents the event, and the radio is the event listener. When you click the **listen** button in the SWF file, the radio starts to listen to the broadcast and then plays it. The act of playing the broadcast is the function that the radio executes after it "hears" the event.

Now that you have a better understanding of events and event listeners, you'll practice writing them in the next exercise.

In this exercise, you'll set up an event listener to listen for a mouse click by the user.

---

1 Copy the **chap_04** folder from the **ActionScript HOT CD-ROM** to your desktop. Open **Listeners.fla** from the **chap_04** folder.

---

2 Select the **Selection** tool in the **Tools** panel, and select the snowboarder on the **Stage**. Go to the **Property inspector**, and examine the snowboarder's properties.

The snowboarder is a movie clip with the instance name of boarder_mc.

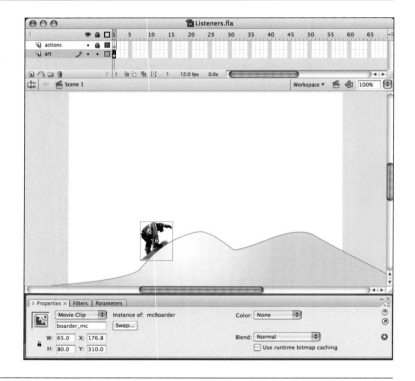

---

3 Select **Frame 1** on the **actions** layer, and choose **Window > Actions** or press **F9** (Windows) or **Opt+F9** (Mac) to open the **Actions** panel.

The first step when you add an event listener is to insert the object to which you are going to be listening.

---

4 Position your cursor on Line 1, and type the following:

`boarder_mc.`

Notice that the Code Hint menu pops up automatically.

---

5 Type **addEv**. When **addEventListener** is highlighted in the **Code Hint** menu, press **Enter** (Windows) or **Return** (Mac).

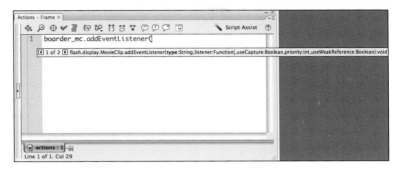

Notice that Flash automatically adds a left parenthesis to the end of the statement. A tool tip also pops up showing what other information Flash expects you to type in this statement. The next item it wants is in bold: **type**. Type is the event type.

---

6 After the left parenthesis, type the following:

`MouseEvent.CLICK`

A mouse click is a **CLICK** event of the type **MouseEvent** in ActionScript. Events are always capitalized. Now you'll specify a function that's going to run when the snowboarder is clicked.

---

7 After the word **CLICK**, type the following:

`, onClick);`

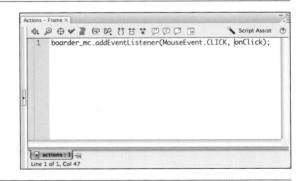

onClick is the name of a custom function you will write in the next exercise.

To review, to add an event listener, you type the object name first, followed by the method **addEventListener**, the event type, the event, and then the function you want to run.

8 Save and close **Listeners.fla**.

In the next exercise, you'll write the function that will execute when the user clicks the snowboarder.

---

2 | Writing Event Handlers

In this exercise, you'll learn how to write an event handler, something that will respond to the **CLICK** event you wrote in the previous exercise. An **event handler** is a function that responds to an event. Instead of triggering the function by calling it, using a `myFunction();` statement, it will be triggered by the event you specify.

---

1 Choose **File > Open**, and open **Handlers.fla** from the **chap_04** folder you copied to your desktop.

Remember to check the instance name of your object in the Property inspector before you start to write the ActionScript. The instance name of the snowboarder in this file is boarder_mc.

---

2 Select **Frame 1** on the **actions** layer, and press **F9** (Windows) or **Opt+F9** (Mac) to open the **Actions** panel.

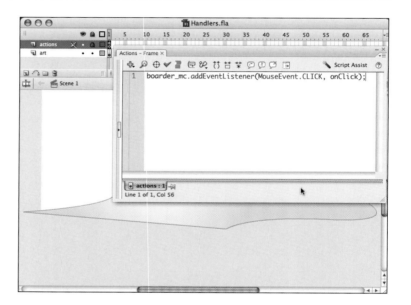

The first line of code is the same as what you wrote in the previous exercise. You added an event listener to boarder_mc, which is listening for a mouse click. Once the event happens, it will run the function called **onClick**. The event handler, you guessed it, will be called **onClick**.

---

3 Position your cursor at the end of Line 1, and press **Enter** (Windows) or **Return** (Mac) two times to go to the third line. Type the following:

```
function onClick(
```

Now if you typed a closed parenthesis, the function wouldn't run. You need to set it up to receive the event.

---

4 After the open parenthesis, type the following:

`event:MouseEvent):void`

event is the variable name representing the mouse event (**CLICK**) in the event listener in Line 1. The function isn't returning any information, so you used **void** as the return data type. Most event handlers do not return any type of data.

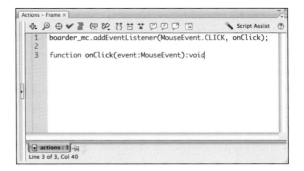

5 Press **Enter** (Windows) or **Return** (Mac), type **{** (a left curly brace), and then press **Enter** or **Return** a second time.

As you learned in Chapter 3, the information in the curly braces defines what the function does.

6 Type the following on the new line:

`trace("click!!!!!");`

You'll use this trace statement just to make sure the event listener and the event handler are both functioning properly.

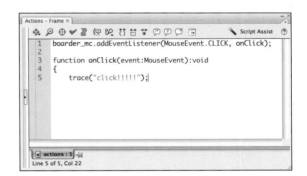

7 Press **Enter** (Windows) or **Return** (Mac), and type the right curly brace (**}**). Close the **Actions** panel.

8 Press **Ctrl+Enter** (Windows) or **Cmd+Return** (Mac) to test the movie. When the preview window opens, click the snowboarder once.

Perfect! Nothing happens on the Stage, but your text string, click!!!!!, appears in the Output panel when you click the snowboarder.

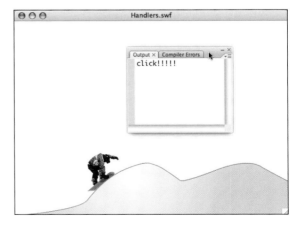

9 Click the snowboarder three more times, and watch what happens in the **Output** panel.

Notice that click!!!!! appears four times in the Output panel. The function will run exactly the same way every time a user clicks the snowboarder.

Now that you know your code is working properly, you can finesse it a little. You might have noticed there's nothing to indicate the snowboarder is an interactive element. You'll change this in the next step so that when you position your cursor over the boarder, it turns into a hand icon.

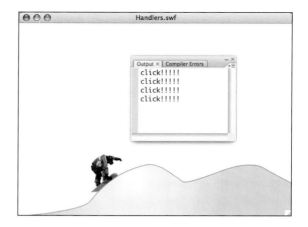

10 Close the preview window and the **Output** panel. Select **Frame 1** on the **actions** layer, and press **F9** (Windows) or **Opt+F9** (Mac) to open the **Actions** panel.

11 Position your cursor after the closing curly brace on Line 6, and press **Enter** (Windows) or **Return** (Mac) twice. On the new line, type the following:

`boarder_mc.buttonMode = true;`

buttonMode is a property of boarder_mc that tells Flash to use the hand icon if the object is listening for a mouse event.

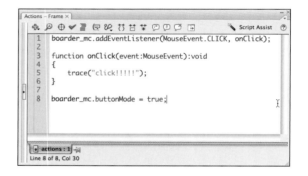

12 Press **Ctrl+Enter** (Windows) or **Cmd+Return** (Mac) to test the movie again. When the preview window opens, position your cursor over the snowboarder.

Now the hand icon appears, telling users the snowboarder is a clickable object.

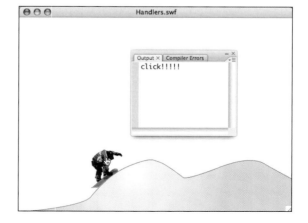

13 Close the preview window. Return to the **Actions** panel in Flash.

---

14 Position your cursor before the trace statement on Line 5, and type two slashes (//).

Since you've established that the code is working properly, you no longer need this trace statement. However, since it might come in handy if you make any changes to the code later, you have disabled the line instead of simply deleting it.

---

15 Position your cursor after the semicolon following the trace statement, press **Enter** (Windows) or **Return** (Mac), and type the following:

```
boarder_mc.y -= 15;
```

This line of code will move the boarder by subtracting 15 pixels from its current Y or vertical position, every time the boarder is clicked. The -= operator ensures that the boarder will not be moved 15 pixels from the top of the Stage but 15 pixels relative to its current position. You may remember working with this property and compound operators in Chapter 3.

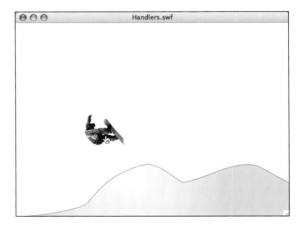

```
Actions - Frame ×
                                          Script Assist
1    boarder_mc.addEventListener(MouseEvent.CLICK, onClick);
2
3    function onClick(event:MouseEvent):void
4    {
5        //trace("click!!!!!");
6        boarder_mc.y -= 15;
7    }
8
9    boarder_mc.buttonMode = true;

   actions : 1
Line 6 of 9, Col 21
```

---

16 Press **Enter** (Windows) or **Return** (Mac), and type the following:

```
boarder_mc.rotation += 45;
```

This statement increments the snowboarder's rotation by 45 degrees every time the boarder is clicked.

---

17 Press **Ctrl+Enter** (Windows) or **Cmd+Return** (Mac) to test the movie. When the preview window opens, click the boarder several times.

Watch him fly. Again, the function runs every time it is triggered by the event.

Before you finish this exercise, I want to show you one more task you can do with event handlers. When the event listener calls the function, it passes information to the function, including information about what object was clicked. So instead of naming a specific object in a function, you could use the information passed by the event listener to target its object.

18 Close the preview window, and return to the **Actions** panel. Position your cursor at the beginning of Line 6, delete **boarder_mc**, and type **event.target**.

event is the variable name you assigned to the mouse click event in Line 3 of the event handler. **target** is the object in that event, specified in the **addEventListener** line of code. Now, if you wanted to apply an event listener to another object on the Stage, you could reuse both the event listener and the event handler. Using the generic **event.target** makes them much more reusable.

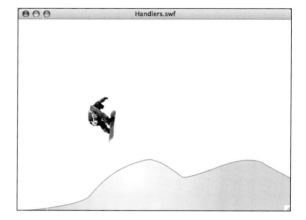

```
1  boarder_mc.addEventListener(MouseEvent.CLICK, onClick);
2
3  function onClick(event:MouseEvent):void
4  {
5      //trace("click!!!!!");
6      event.target.y -= 15;
7      boarder_mc.rotation += 45;
8  }
9
10 boarder_mc.buttonMode = true;
```

19 Press **Ctrl+Enter** (Windows) or **Cmd+Return** (Mac) to test the movie again. When the preview window opens, click the snowboarder several times.

There you have it. The snowboarder moves and rotates the same as when the object name was specified in the function. But now you have code that is much more useful.

20 Close the movie preview window. When you are finished, close **Handlers.fla**. You don't need to save your changes.

Now that you know how to write an event handler, in the next exercise you'll investigate other types of events, starting with other kinds of mouse events.

3 | Responding to Mouse Events

In this exercise, you'll learn about the various mouse events in Flash CS3 and how to respond to them.

---

1 Choose **File > Open**, and open **MouseEvents.fla** from the **chap_04** folder you copied to your desktop.

---

2 Select **Frame 1** on the **actions** layer, and press **F9** (Windows) or **Opt+F9** (Mac) to open the **Actions** panel, if it is not open.

The Script pane contains the code you have written up to this point in the chapter: the event listener, the event handler, and the change to the snowboarder's button mode that changes the cursor icon to a hand icon when a user positions the cursor over the snowboarder. Now you'll add listeners to check for when a user rolls over and rolls out from the snowboarder.

---

3 Position your cursor at the end of Line 1, and press **Enter** (Windows) or **Return** (Mac) to go to the second line. Type the following:

```
boarder_mc.addEventListener
```

Make sure the *E* and *L* in **addEventListener** are both capitalized.

---

4 Next, type the following:

(MouseEvent.ROLL_OVER, boarderOver);

Remember that events like **ROLL_OVER** are always capitalized. **boaderOver** is the name you're giving to the function that will run when the event happens. Next you'll write that function—the event handler—so that when the user moves their cursor over the boarder, it will become partially transparent. This is another good way to indicate that the boarder is an interactive element.

```
1  boarder_mc.addEventListener(MouseEvent.CLICK, onClick);
2  boarder_mc.addEventListener(MouseEvent.ROLL_OVER, boarderOver);
3
4  function onClick(event:MouseEvent):void
5  {
6      //trace("click!!!!!!!!");
7      event.target.y -= 15;
8      event.target.rotation += 45;
9  }
10
11 boarder_mc.buttonMode = true;
```

5 Position your cursor before Line 4. Press the **Shift** key, and drag down to Line 9 to select the entire **OnClick()** function statement. Press **Ctrl+C** (Windows) or **Cmd+C** (Mac) to copy the code.

6 Position your cursor at the end of Line 2. Press **Enter** (Windows) or **Return** (Mac) twice to go to the fourth line, and press **Ctrl+V** (Windows) or **Cmd+V** (Mac) to paste the function.

Now you just need to change the function name so it matches the one specified in your **ROLL_OVER** event.

7 Double-click the word **OnClick** on Line 4, and type **boarderOver**.

You don't need to change anything else on this line since **ROLL_OVER** is still a **MouseEvent** type event.

```
1  boarder_mc.addEventListener(MouseEvent.CLICK, onClick);
2  boarder_mc.addEventListener(MouseEvent.ROLL_OVER, boarderOver);
3
4  function boarderOver(event:MouseEvent):void
5  {
6      //trace("click!!!!!!!!");
7      event.target.y -= 15;
8      event.target.rotation += 45;
9  }
10
11 function onClick(event:MouseEvent):void
12 {
13     //trace("click!!!!!!!!");
14     event.target.y -= 15;
15     event.target.rotation += 45;
16 }
17
18 boarder_mc.buttonMode = true;
```

8 Select Lines 6 through 8, and press **Delete** to remove them. On the empty line between the curly braces, type the following:

```
event.target.alpha -= .5;
```

Again, here you are using **event.target** instead of boarder_mc to maximize the usability of this function. **alpha** is the property that controls transparency. When the user positions the cursor over boarder_mc, the opacity will be reduced by 50 percent.

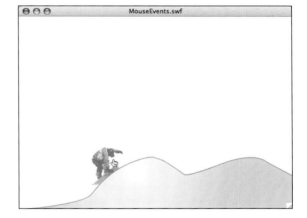

```
 1   boarder_mc.addEventListener(MouseEvent.CLICK, onClick);
 2   boarder_mc.addEventListener(MouseEvent.ROLL_OVER, boarderOver);
 3
 4   function boarderOver(event:MouseEvent):void
 5   {
 6       event.target.alpha -= .5;
 7   }
 8
 9   function onClick(event:MouseEvent):void
10   {
11       //trace("click!!!!!!!!");
12       event.target.y -= 15;
13       event.target.rotation += 45;
14   }
15
16   boarder_mc.buttonMode = true;
```

9 Press **Ctrl+Enter** (Windows) or **Cmd+Return** (Mac) to test the movie. When the preview window opens, position your cursor over the snowboarder.

As expected, the boarder becomes semitransparent. It's kind of a cool effect, but there are a few issues, as you'll see in the next steps.

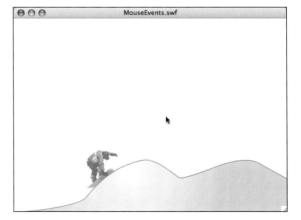

10 Move your cursor away from the snowboarder.

Notice that the transparency does not revert to normal.

11 Move your cursor over the snowboarder again.

Now the boarder completely disappears! Keep in mind that handlers continue to run as long as the event keeps happening. The first time you positioned your cursor over the boarder, the opacity was reduced by 50 percent. The second time you positioned your cursor over him, it reduced it by 50 percent again, resulting in a 0 percent opacity. This is not exactly the effect you want.

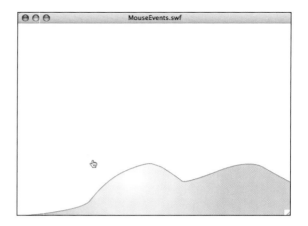

12 Close the preview window, and return to the **Actions** panel. Position your cursor before the equals sign on Line 6, and press **Delete** to remove the minus sign.

Now the snowboarder's opacity won't reduce every time a roll over event occurs. Better yet, you can add a rollout event so that when the user moves the cursor away from the snowboarder, it will return to full opacity.

13 Select Line 2, and press **Ctrl+C** (Windows) or **Cmd+C** (Mac) to copy the code.

14 Position your cursor on Line 3, and press **Enter** (Windows) or **Return** (Mac) to insert a new line. Press the **up arrow** key to return to Line 3, and press **Ctrl+V** (Windows) or **Cmd+V** (Mac) to paste the code.

15 Double-click `ROLL_OVER` in Line 3 to select it, and type `ROLL_OUT`. Change the `boarderOver` function name to `boarderOut`.

```
1   boarder_mc.addEventListener(MouseEvent.CLICK, onClick);
2   boarder_mc.addEventListener(MouseEvent.ROLL_OVER, boarderOver);
3   boarder_mc.addEventListener(MouseEvent.ROLL_OUT, boarderOut);
4
5   function boarderOver(event:MouseEvent):void
6   {
7       event.target.alpha = .5;
8   }
9
10  function onClick(event:MouseEvent):void
11  {
12      //trace("click!!!!!!!!");
13      event.target.y -= 15;
14      event.target.rotation += 45;
15  }
16
17  boarder_mc.buttonMode = true;
```

16 Select Lines 5–8, and press **Ctrl+C** (Windows) or **Cmd+C** (Mac). Position your cursor on Line 9, and press **Enter** (Windows) or **Return** (Mac) to insert a new line. Press **Ctrl+V** (Windows) or **Cmd+V** (Mac) to paste the code.

---

17 Double-click `boarderOver` in Line 10 to select it, and type `boarderOut` to change the function name.

---

18 Change the alpha value on Line 12 by changing **.5** to **1**.

```
Actions - Frame ×                                                    Script Assist
 1  boarder_mc.addEventListener(MouseEvent.CLICK, onClick);
 2  boarder_mc.addEventListener(MouseEvent.ROLL_OVER, boarderOver);
 3  boarder_mc.addEventListener(MouseEvent.ROLL_OUT, boarderOut);
 4
 5  function boarderOver(event:MouseEvent):void
 6  {
 7      event.target.alpha = .5;
 8  }
 9
10  function boarderOut(event:MouseEvent):void
11  {
12      event.target.alpha = 1;
13  }
14
15  function onClick(event:MouseEvent):void
16  {
17      //trace("click!!!!!!!!");
18      event.target.y -= 15;
19      event.target.rotation += 45;
20  }
21
22  boarder_mc.buttonMode = true;

actions : 1
Line 12 of 22, Col 21
```

---

19 Press **Ctrl+Enter** (Windows) or **Cmd+Return** (Mac) to test the movie. When the preview window opens, position your cursor over the snowboarder.

The snowboarder will still turn transparent.

---

20 Move your cursor away from the snowboarder, and move it back over him again.

Now the snowboarder returns to full opacity when the mouse is moved away from it, and it doesn't disappear when you move it over him again.

---

21 Click the snowboarder a couple of times to test the mouse click event.

Hooray! The animation still works! A few more mouse events exist that you can experiment with. For a full listing, choose Help > Flash Help, and search for *mouse events* in the Help index.

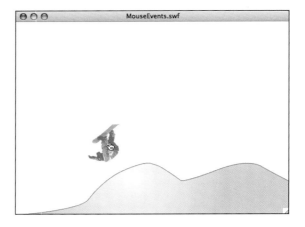

22 Close the movie preview window. When you are finished, close **MouseEvents.fla**. You don't need to save your changes.

In the next exercise, you'll learn how to write a different type of event called keyboard events.

4 | Responding to Keyboard Events

In this exercise, you'll learn how to capture and respond to **keyboard events**, in other words, when a user clicks a button or presses a key.

1 Choose **File > Open**, and open **KeyboardEvents.fla** from the **chap_04** folder you copied to your desktop.

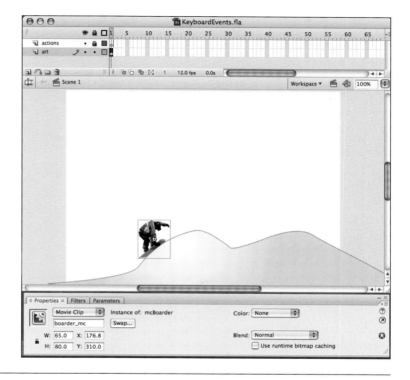

This file is similar to the other files you have been working with in this chapter. There are two layers in the file, one containing the actions and one containing the artwork. There is one instance of the movie clip mcBoarder on the Stage called boarder_mc.

2 Select **Frame 1** on the **actions** layer, and press **F9** (Windows) or **Opt+F9** (Mac) to open the **Actions** panel if it is not already open.

Keyboard events work a little differently than mouse events work. With mouse events, you apply the event listener directly to the object. With a keyboard event, you apply the listener to the entire Stage. If you were to apply the event listener to the object, the user would have to select the object before it would respond to a key press. When the listener is applied to the Stage, the entire movie is automatically active and receptive to that keyboard event.

3 Position your cursor after the first line of code, and type the following:

```
stage.addEventListener
```

stage is the object name you can use for the Stage in any movie.

4 Next type the following:

(KeyboardEvent.KEY_DOWN, jump);

Remember, event names are always capitalized. **jump** is the name of the event handler, which you will be writing next.

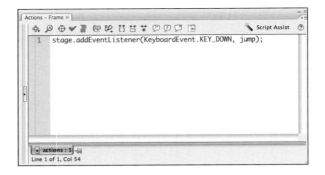

5 Press **Enter** (Windows) or **Return** (Mac) twice to go to the third line. Type the following:

function jump (event:KeyboardEvent):void

Just as you did with the mouse event handler in the previous exercise, in order to make the function listen for the event, you need to specify the event data type in between the parentheses.

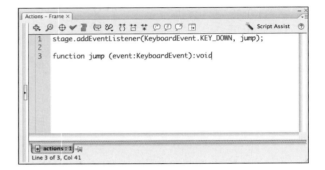

6 Press **Enter** (Windows) or **Return** (Mac) to go to the fourth line, and type an open curly brace ({). Press **Enter** (Windows) or **Return** (Mac) again, and type the following:

boarder_mc.y -= 50

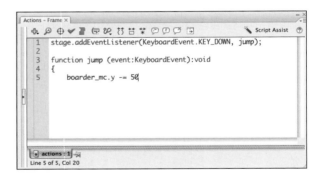

7 Press **Enter** (Windows) or **Return** (Mac) again, and type the closing curly brace (}).

8 Press **Ctrl+Enter** (Windows) or **Cmd+Return** (Mac) to test the movie. When the movie window opens, press the **spacebar** a couple of times.

Notice the snowboarder moves 50 pixels up every time you press the spacebar. You could press any key, in fact. The Stage is responding to any key down event. Next, you'll add an event listener for when a key is released.

9 Close the movie window, and return to the **Actions** panel.

10 Select the code on Line 1, and press **Ctrl+C** (Windows) or **Cmd+C** (Mac) to copy the code.

11 Deselect the code, and then press **Enter** (Windows) or **Return** (Mac) to insert a new line. Press **Ctrl+V** (Windows) or **Cmd+V** (Mac) to paste the code on the new line.

12 Select the event **KEY_DOWN** in Line 2, and change it to **KEY_UP**. Select the word **jump**, and change it to **land**.

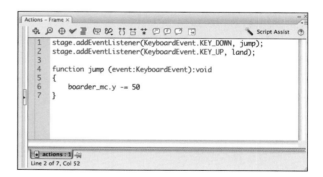

13 Select the code on Lines 4–7, and press **Ctrl+C** (Windows) or **Cmd+C** (Mac) to copy it. Position your cursor at the end of Line 7, press **Enter** (Windows) or **Return** (Mac) twice, and then press **Ctrl+V** (Windows) or **Cmd+V** (Mac) to paste the code on the new line.

14 Select the **jump** function name in Line 9, and change it to **land**. Select the minus sign in Line 11, and change it to a plus sign.

```
1   stage.addEventListener(KeyboardEvent.KEY_DOWN, jump);
2   stage.addEventListener(KeyboardEvent.KEY_UP, land);
3
4   function jump (event:KeyboardEvent):void
5   {
6       boarder_mc.y -= 50
7   }
8
9   function land (event:KeyboardEvent):void
10  {
11      boarder_mc.y += 50
12  }
```

15 Press **Ctrl+Enter** (Windows) or **Cmd+Return** (Mac) to test the movie. When the movie window opens, press the **spacebar** once.

Notice the snowboarder moves 50 pixels when you press the spacebar. As soon as you release the key, the boarder returns to his original position.

16 Press the **Shift** key once.

As I mentioned before, the event listeners are responding to any key press/release. Whether you press and release the spacebar, the Shift key, or any other key on the keyboard, the same thing happens to the boarder. However, you can specify a certain key as the event trigger. You can't use the key's corresponding character, though, such as P or Shift. You have to use **keyCode**, one of the properties of a keyboard event corresponding to a number that represents the key that was pressed. How do you find the key codes? I'll show you in the next steps.

17 Close the movie window, and return to the **Actions** panel.

18 Position your cursor after the curly brace on Line 5, and press **Enter** (Windows) or **Return** (Mac) to go to the next line. Type the following:

`trace(event.keyCode);`

This trace statement will return the **keyCode** of whatever key is pressed.

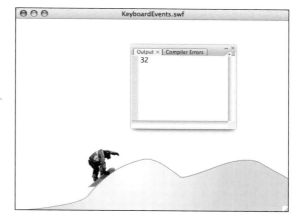

```
1   stage.addEventListener(KeyboardEvent.KEY_DOWN, jump);
2   stage.addEventListener(KeyboardEvent.KEY_UP, land);
3
4   function jump (event:KeyboardEvent):void
5   {
6       trace(event.keyCode);
7       boarder_mc.y -= 50
8   }
9
10  function land (event:KeyboardEvent):void
11  {
12      boarder_mc.y += 50
13  }
```

19 Press **Ctrl+Enter** (Windows) or **Cmd+Return** (Mac) to test the movie. When the movie window opens, press the **spacebar**, and hold it for a second before you release.

The Output panel will open containing a two-digit key code. Key codes are unique. Press the Shift key, and the Output panel would contain a different code, and so on. Using a trace statement, you can detect which key is pressed. However, you can't tell the function to run only when a key code is returned until you learn how to use something called conditional statements. I'll cover conditional statements in Chapter 7, *"Decision Making and Repetition."*

20 Close the movie preview window. When you are finished, close **KeyboardEvents.fla**. You don't need to save your changes.

5 | Creating a Link to a Web Site

In this exercise, you'll learn how to create a link to an external Web site in your Flash files. You'll add the link to a button, which will open the URL when it is clicked.

1 Choose **File > Open**, and open **Links.fla** from the **chap_04** folder you copied to your desktop.

2 Select the **Selection** tool in the **Tools** panel, and click the **click me** button on the **Stage**. Go to the **Property inspector** to verify the instance name.

This is a simple Flash file containing one instance, button_mc, of a movie clip consisting of a rectangle with the text, Click Me. This is the object you're going to convert to a link to a Web site.

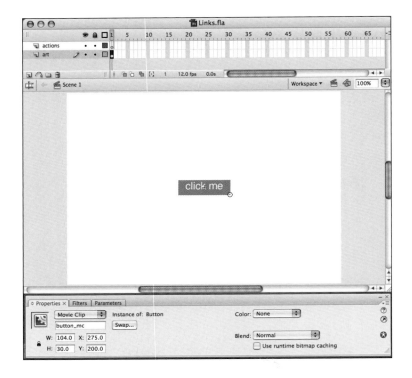

3 Select **Frame 1** on the **actions** layer, and press **F9** (Windows) or **Opt+F9** (Mac) to open the **Actions** panel, if it is not already open.

The first step is to add an event listener to the movie clip to listen for the user's click.

4 Position your cursor on the first blank line, and type the following:

```
button_mc.addEventListener(MouseEvent.CLICK,
onClick);
```

The next step is to create the **onClick()** event handler.

5 Press **Enter** (Windows) or **Return** (Mac) twice to go to the third line. Type the following:

```
function onClick(event:MouseEvent):void
{
}
```

Before you add the link, you might want to make sure the user knows the button is an interactive element. An easy way to do this is to change the appearance of the cursor, as you learned in Exercise 2.

6 Press **Enter** (Windows) or **Return** (Mac) to insert a new line after the closed curly brace, and type the following:

```
button_mc.buttonMode = true;
```

Now the pointer will turn into a hand when a user moves the cursor over the button.

It's time to add the link. In ActionScript 2.0, you would call the **getURL()** function to link to a Web site. However, ActionScript 3.0 works a little differently. You have to first create an **URLRequest** object that houses the URL and then use the **navigateToURL()** method to link to it. So in the next step, you'll create a new instance of the **URLRequest** class that you'll call **link**.

7 Position your cursor at the beginning of Line 1, and press **Enter** (Windows) or **Return** (Mac) twice to insert two new lines at the beginning of the code. Return to Line 1, and type the following:

`var link:URLRequest`

Notice you are creating a new instance of a class without adding it to the Stage via the Library panel. Interestingly, not every class or data type can be accessed in the Library panel. Some classes can be created only in ActionScript. `URLRequest` is one of these classes, sometimes called an abstract class.

```
1  var link:URLRequest
2
3  button_mc.addEventListener(MouseEvent.CLICK, onClick);
4
5  function onClick(event:MouseEvent):void
6  {
7
8  }
9  button_mc.buttonMode = true;
```

Line 1 of 9, Col 20

---

8 Directly after **URLRequest**, type a space, and then type the following:

`= new URLRequest("http://www.lynda.com");`

Notice that the URL is a string.

TIP: Strings can be contained within double or single quotation marks, as long as you use each consistently.

Now that you've specified the URL in the new variable `link`, you can use this variable in place of a string when you run the `navigateToURL()` method.

```
1  var link:URLRequest = new URLRequest("http://www.lynda.com");
2
3  button_mc.addEventListener(MouseEvent.CLICK, onClick);
4
5  function onClick(event:MouseEvent):void
6  {
7
8  }
9  button_mc.buttonMode = true;
```

Line 1 of 9, Col 62

---

9 Position your cursor between the curly braces on Line 7 (in the **onClick** function), and type the following:

`navigateToURL(link);`

```
1  var link:URLRequest = new URLRequest("http://www.lynda.com");
2
3  button_mc.addEventListener(MouseEvent.CLICK, onClick);
4
5  function onClick(event:MouseEvent):void
6  {
7      navigateToURL(link);
8  }
9  button_mc.buttonMode = true;
```

Line 5 of 9, Col 40

10 Press **Ctrl+Enter** (Windows) or **Cmd+Return** (Mac) to test the movie. When the movie window opens, click the button.

The lynda.com Web site will open in your default browser. When you create a link of your own, all you have to remember are these two steps: create a new `URLRequest` instance in a variable, and pass in the variable name to the `navigateToURL()` method in your function.

---

11 Close the movie preview window. When you are finished, close **Links.fla**. You don't need to save your changes.

Using the Enter Frame Event to Create Animation

In this exercise, you'll learn how to create a basic animation using a special event called ENTER_FRAME.

---

1 Choose **File > Open**, and open **Enter_Frame.fla** from the **chap_04** folder you copied to your desktop.

This file is similar to those you have been working with throughout this chapter. There is one instance of the snowboarder on the Stage, named boarder_mc.

---

2 Select **Frame 1** on the **actions** layer, and press **F9** (Windows) or **Opt+F9** (Mac) to open the **Actions** panel, if it is not already open.

The Actions panel contains the code you wrote in Exercise 4, the two keyboard events, and the functions **jump** and **land**.

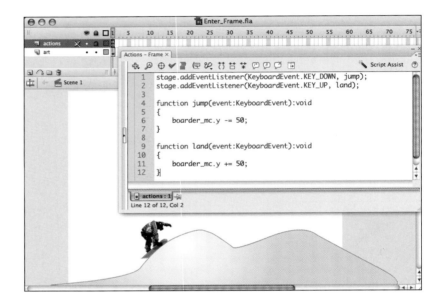

```
stage.addEventListener(KeyboardEvent.KEY_DOWN, jump);
stage.addEventListener(KeyboardEvent.KEY_UP, land);

function jump(event:KeyboardEvent):void
{
    boarder_mc.y -= 50;
}

function land(event:KeyboardEvent):void
{
    boarder_mc.y += 50;
}
```

---

3 Press **Ctrl+Enter** (Windows) or **Cmd+Return** (Mac) to test the movie. When the movie window opens, press and hold the **spacebar**.

Notice that the snowboarder jumps up into the air, off the Stage, but he never comes back down. By the end of this exercise, you'll make the boarder do a complete flip. First, though, you need to make sure he comes back down to Earth.

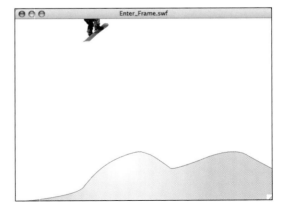

---

4 Close the movie window, and return to the **Actions** panel.

The reason why the snowboarder never comes down is because Flash keeps running the **jump** function as long as a key is being pressed. What you need to do is delay the running of the function until the key is let go.

---

5 Select Line 1, and press **Ctrl+C** (Windows) or **Cmd+C** (Mac) to copy it.

---

6 Position your cursor at the end of Line 6, inside the **jump** function, and press **Enter** (Windows) or **Return** (Mac) to insert a new line. Press **Ctrl+V** (Windows) or **Cmd+V** (Mac) to paste the event listener.

---

7 Select and replace **addEventListener** in Line 7 with **removeEventListener**.

This code tells the object that is listening for the event to stop listening for the **KEY_DOWN** event. (Remember it's the Stage that listens for keyboard events.) It also stops the **jump** function from executing. By embedding the statement in the function itself, it means the function will execute once and then stop.

```
Actions – Frame ×
                                              Script Assist
1   stage.addEventListener(KeyboardEvent.KEY_DOWN, jump);
2   stage.addEventListener(KeyboardEvent.KEY_UP, land);
3
4   function jump(event:KeyboardEvent):void
5   {
6       boarder_mc.y -= 50;
7       stage.removeEventListener(KeyboardEvent.KEY_DOWN, jump);
8   }
9
10  function land(event:KeyboardEvent):void
11  {
12      boarder_mc.y += 50;
13  }
```

actions : 1
Line 7 of 13, Col 14

---

8 Press **Ctrl+Enter** (Windows) or **Cmd+Return** (Mac) to test the movie. When the movie window opens, press and hold the spacebar.

Voila! The snowboarder jumps up 50 pixels, but he doesn't go any further because the Stage is no longer paying attention for a key down event.

---

9 Release the **spacebar**, and then press and release it again.

The first time you release the spacebar, the snowboarder returns to his original position. The second time you press the spacebar, he doesn't go up any further, but he does sink another 50 pixels. That's because the Stage has stopped listening for **KEY_DOWN** but still responds to the **KEY_UP** event when you release the spacebar. That's OK. All you need to do is ask it to start listening for **KEY_DOWN** again as soon as you release the key.

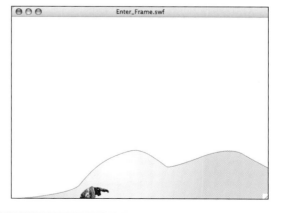

10 Close the movie window, and return to the **Actions** panel.

11 Select Line 1, and press **Ctrl+C** (Windows) or **Cmd+C** (Mac) to copy it again.

12 Position your cursor at the end of Line 12, and press **Enter** (Windows) or **Return** (Mac) to insert a new line. Press **Ctrl+V** (Windows) or **Cmd+V** (Mac) to paste the event listener.

You don't need to change anything this time. You're simply adding the `EventListener` back in so the Stage starts listening again after the key is released. Basically, you're suspending the listener immediately after the key is pressed until it is released, which keeps the function from running more than once at each event. Because Flash reads ActionScript from top to bottom, it allows you to respond to sequenced events in this manner.

```
Actions - Frame ×                                                    Script Assist
 1   stage.addEventListener(KeyboardEvent.KEY_DOWN, jump);
 2   stage.addEventListener(KeyboardEvent.KEY_UP, land);
 3
 4   function jump(event:KeyboardEvent):void
 5   {
 6       boarder_mc.y -= 50;
 7       stage.removeEventListener(KeyboardEvent.KEY_DOWN, jump);
 8   }
 9
10   function land(event:KeyboardEvent):void
11   {
12       boarder_mc.y += 50;
13       stage.addEventListener(KeyboardEvent.KEY_DOWN, jump);
14   }

  actions : 1
Line 2 of 14, Col 52
```

13 Press **Ctrl+Enter** (Windows) or **Cmd+Return** (Mac) to test the movie again. When the movie window opens, press and hold the **spacebar**.

Again, the snowboarder jumps up 50 pixels, but no further.

14 Release the **spacebar**, and then press and release it again.

The snowboarder drops down 50 pixels to his original position when you release the spacebar and then jumps up down again when you press and release the spacebar the second time. This may seem kind of academic, but it makes a big difference when you start to think about the user experience.

Now that you have that taken care of, let's move on to flipping the snowboarder. This is where `ENTER_FRAME` comes in. `ENTER_FRAME` listens to every frame in the Timeline of the movie. If your movie's frame rate is 12 frames per second, `ENTER_FRAME` will be triggered 12 times every second. `ENTER_FRAME` is often used to create a basic animation using ActionScript.

15 Close the movie window, and return to the **Actions** panel.

16 Position your cursor at the end of Line 2, and press **Enter** (Windows) or **Return** (Mac). On the new line, type the following:

```
stage.addEventListener(Event.ENTER_FRAME,
flip);
```

ENTER_FRAME is a non-object-oriented event (just like **KEY_UP** or **KEY_DOWN**) of the event type **Event**. Now you need to define the **flip()** event handler.

```
1  stage.addEventListener(KeyboardEvent.KEY_DOWN, jump);
2  stage.addEventListener(KeyboardEvent.KEY_UP, land);
3  stage.addEventListener(Event.ENTER_FRAME, flip);
4
5  function jump(event:KeyboardEvent):void
6  {
7      boarder_mc.y -= 50;
8      stage.removeEventListener(KeyboardEvent.KEY_DOWN, jump);
9  }
10
11 function land(event:KeyboardEvent):void
12 {
13     boarder_mc.y += 50;
14     stage.addEventListener(KeyboardEvent.KEY_DOWN, jump);
15 }
```

17 Position your cursor at the end of Line 15, press **Enter** (Windows) or **Return** (Mac) twice, and type the following:

```
function flip (event:Event):void
{
}
```

```
1  stage.addEventListener(KeyboardEvent.KEY_DOWN, jump);
2  stage.addEventListener(KeyboardEvent.KEY_UP, land);
3  stage.addEventListener(Event.ENTER_FRAME, flip);
4
5  function jump(event:KeyboardEvent):void
6  {
7      boarder_mc.y -= 50;
8      stage.removeEventListener(KeyboardEvent.KEY_DOWN, jump);
9  }
10
11 function land(event:KeyboardEvent):void
12 {
13     boarder_mc.y += 50;
14     stage.addEventListener(KeyboardEvent.KEY_DOWN, jump);
15 }
16
17 function flip (event:Event):void
18 {
19
20 }
```

18 Position your cursor between the curly braces on Line 19, and type the following:

```
boarder_mc.rotation += 45;
```

That's it. Since this movie uses the default frame rate of 12 frames per second, the boarder will rotate 45 degrees every frame.

```
Actions - Frame
                                                              Script Assist
 1   stage.addEventListener(KeyboardEvent.KEY_DOWN, jump);
 2   stage.addEventListener(KeyboardEvent.KEY_UP, land);
 3   stage.addEventListener(Event.ENTER_FRAME, flip);
 4
 5   function jump(event:KeyboardEvent):void
 6   {
 7       boarder_mc.y -= 50;
 8       stage.removeEventListener(KeyboardEvent.KEY_DOWN, jump);
 9   }
10
11   function land(event:KeyboardEvent):void
12   {
13       boarder_mc.y += 50;
14       stage.addEventListener(KeyboardEvent.KEY_DOWN, jump);
15   }
16
17   function flip (event:Event):void
18   {
19       boarder_mc.rotation += 45;
20   }

 actions : 1
Line 19 of 20, Col 28
```

19 Press **Ctrl+Enter** (Windows) or **Cmd+Return** (Mac) to test the movie.

Whoa! The snowboarder is definitely rotating. And he's not even in the air yet. That's because **ENTER_FRAME** event is tied to the movie; it's not triggered by any user action. To make sure this event is triggered only when the snowboarder is in the air, you need to remove the event listener and add it again, as you did with the **KEY_DOWN** event.

20 Select Line 3, and press **Ctrl+X** (Windows) or **Cmd+X** (Mac) to cut it.

21 Position your cursor at the end of Line 8, and press **Enter** (Windows) or **Return** (Mac) to add a new line. Press **Ctrl+V** (Windows) or **Cmd+V** (Mac) to paste the event listener.

This ensures the snowboarder will flip when the snowboarders jumps.

```
1    stage.addEventListener(KeyboardEvent.KEY_DOWN, jump);
2    stage.addEventListener(KeyboardEvent.KEY_UP, land);
3
4    function jump(event:KeyboardEvent):void
5    {
6        boarder_mc.y -= 50;
7        stage.removeEventListener(KeyboardEvent.KEY_DOWN, jump);
8        stage.addEventListener(Event.ENTER_FRAME, flip);
9    }
10
11   function land(event:KeyboardEvent):void
12   {
13       boarder_mc.y += 50;
14       stage.addEventListener(KeyboardEvent.KEY_DOWN, jump);
15   }
16
17   function flip (event:Event):void
18   {
19       boarder_mc.rotation += 45;
20   }
```

Line 8 of 20, Col 1

22 Position your cursor at the end of Line 15, and press **Enter** (Windows) or **Return** (Mac) to add a new line. Press **Ctrl+V** (Windows) or **Cmd+V** (Mac) to paste the event listener again in the **land** function. In the new line, select **addEventListener**, and change it to **removeEventListener**.

Now as soon as the boarder lands, he will stop rotating.

```
1    stage.addEventListener(KeyboardEvent.KEY_DOWN, jump);
2    stage.addEventListener(KeyboardEvent.KEY_UP, land);
3
4    function jump(event:KeyboardEvent):void
5    {
6        boarder_mc.y -= 50;
7        stage.removeEventListener(KeyboardEvent.KEY_DOWN, jump);
8        stage.addEventListener(Event.ENTER_FRAME, flip);
9    }
10
11   function land(event:KeyboardEvent):void
12   {
13       boarder_mc.y += 50;
14       stage.addEventListener(KeyboardEvent.KEY_DOWN, jump);
15       stage.removeEventListener(Event.ENTER_FRAME, flip);
16   }
17
18   function flip (event:Event):void
19   {
20       boarder_mc.rotation += 45;
21   }
```

Line 2 of 21, Col 52

23 Press **Ctrl+Enter** (Windows) or **Cmd+Return** (Mac) to test the movie again. When the movie window opens, press and hold the **spacebar**.

The snowboarder starts in a static position and starts rotating while he is suspended in midair.

24 When you're ready, release the **spacebar**.

Yikes. Sometimes he doesn't fly, he falls. Press and release the spacebar again to try to land the boarder flat on the snow. Building multiple, inter-dependent events like this introduces a lot of interactivity and variety into your animation, which are both important when you're building a more complex animation or even a game, as you'll do in Chapter 9, *"Creating a Memory Game."*

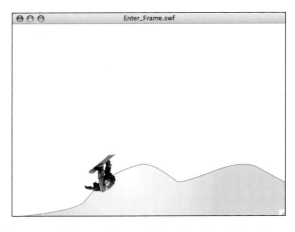

The next logical step, which you may be thinking already, would be to have the boarder jump from one slope to another. How would you do this using the pieces of code you've already learned? Well, the `ENTER_FRAME` event and the `flip()` event handler control the rotation, and they're already in place. You could simply add another statement to the function and take advantage of the existing setup. The property to modify in this statement, of course, would be the X position.

---

25 Close the movie window, and return to the **Actions** panel.

---

26 Position your cursor at the end of Line 20, in the **flip()** function, and press **Enter** (Windows) or **Return** (Mac) to add a new line. Then type the following:

`boarder_mc.x += 20;`

Twenty pixels might not seem like a lot, but remember, the snowboarder will move 20 pixels for every frame the spacebar is held down.

```
Actions - Frame ×
1   stage.addEventListener(KeyboardEvent.KEY_DOWN, jump);
2   stage.addEventListener(KeyboardEvent.KEY_UP, land);
3
4   function jump(event:KeyboardEvent):void
5   {
6       boarder_mc.y -= 50;
7       stage.removeEventListener(KeyboardEvent.KEY_DOWN, jump);
8       stage.addEventListener(Event.ENTER_FRAME, flip);
9   }
10
11  function land(event:KeyboardEvent):void
12  {
13      boarder_mc.y += 50;
14      stage.addEventListener(KeyboardEvent.KEY_DOWN, jump);
15      stage.removeEventListener(Event.ENTER_FRAME, flip);
16  }
17
18  function flip (event:Event):void
19  {
20      boarder_mc.rotation += 45;
21      boarder_mc.x += 20;
22  }
```

actions : 1
Line 21 of 22, Col 21

27 Press **Ctrl+Enter** (Windows) or **Cmd+Return** (Mac) to test the movie again. When the movie window opens, press and hold the spacebar. When you're ready, release the **spacebar**.

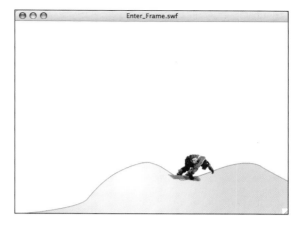

The boarder starts in a static position and starts rotating and moving to the right while he is suspended in midair. He lands when you release your mouse. Pretty cool! Feel free to change any of the values in the ActionScript to change the height of the jump, the rotation amount, or even the distance the boarder moves each frame.

---

28 Close the movie preview window. When you are finished, close **Enter_Frame.fla**. You don't need to save your changes.

In the next exercise, you'll learn about one more function you can use to create animations, called a timer.

---

7 | Using the Timer Event to Control Animation

In this exercise, you'll learn about a different technique in ActionScript called a timer. A **timer** is something that doesn't automatically execute with the frame rate of the movie like **ENTER_FRAME** but at an interval you specify or a certain number of times in a movie, or a combination of both.

---

1 Choose **File > Open**, and open **Timer.fla** from the **chap_04** folder you copied to your desktop.

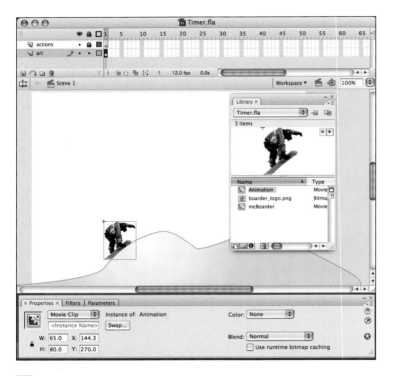

2 Select the snowboarder on the **Stage**. Choose the **Property inspector**, and look at the properties of this movie clip. Choose **Window > Library** to open the project's **Library** panel.

Here you have another instance of a snowboarder on the Stage, but in this case, the mcBoarder movie clip is nested in another movie clip called Animation.

---

3 Double-click the snowboarder to open it in symbol editing mode. Choose the **Property inspector**, and look at the properties of the nested movie clip.

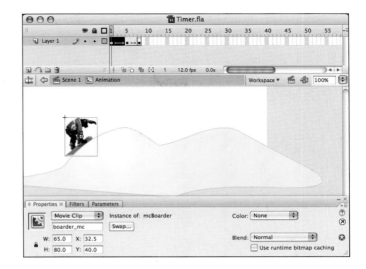

Here's the mcBoarder movie clip you've been working with throughout this chapter. The instance name for the clip is boarder_mc. Notice that the Timeline contains eight frames. Remember this is the Timeline of the Animation movie clip, not mcBoarder. The Timeline contains three distinct keyframes and two motion tweens.

4 Scrub the playhead in the **Timeline** forward to preview the animation.

The boarder stays in the same horizontal position, but he jumps up and comes back down. This was created with tweens rather than ActionScript.

5 Press **Ctrl+Enter** (Windows) or **Cmd+Return** (Mac) to test the movie.

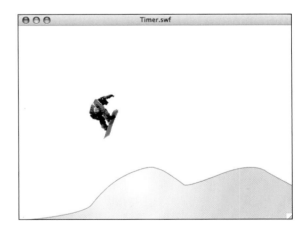

Unlike previous movies you've worked on in this chapter, the snowboarder jumps up and down over and over again automatically, instead of in response to an event. You'll stop the movie from playing automatically by adding a **stop()** action next.

6 Close the movie window. Click the **Insert Layer** button, and name the new layer **actions**.

Make sure you are adding the new layer to the Animation Timeline, not the main Timeline. The edit bar should say Scene 1 > Animation.

7 Select **Frame 1** on the **actions** layer, and press **F9** (Windows) or **Opt+F9** (Mac) to open the **Actions** panel. On the first line, type the following:

```
stop();
```

---

8 Press **Ctrl+Enter** (Windows) or **Cmd+Return** (Mac) to test the movie.

The boarder should stay in place.

---

9 Close the movie window, and then close the **Actions** panel.

---

10 Click **Scene 1** in the **edit bar** to return to the main **Timeline**.

---

11 Select **Frame 1** on the **actions** layer in the main **Timeline**, and press **F9** (Windows) or **Opt+F9** (Mac) to open the **Actions** panel.

Now you'll add the timer to the main Timeline. Timer is an abstract class, similar to a **URLRequest**. You'll learn more about classes in Chapter 5, *"Understanding Classes."*

---

12 On the first line in the **Actions** pane, type the following:

```
var jumpTimer:Timer = new Timer
```

As with **URLRequest**, to create a new **Timer** instance, you create a variable, specify a name of your choosing, specify the class/data type, use the keyword **new**, and then call the class. Next you need to specify two things for your new **Timer** instance: the delay (in milliseconds) and the repeat count. The repeat count is optional.

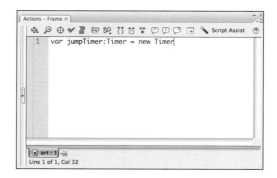

13 After the word `Timer`, type the following:

`(5000);`

Remember the delay is calculated in milliseconds; 5000 here is equal to 5 seconds in the movie.

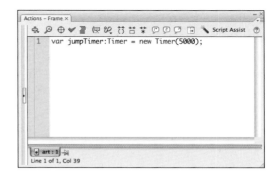

---

14 Press **Enter** (Windows) or **Return** (Mac), and type the following:

`jumpTimer.addEventListener(TimerEvent.TIMER, jump);`

This time you're adding the event listener to the timer itself, not the Stage or a movie clip. `TIMER` is a special type of event which is triggered whenever the timer runs, in this case, every 5 seconds. `jump` will be the event handler that is executed.

---

15 Press **Enter** (Windows) or **Return** (Mac) twice to insert another two new lines, and type the following:

```
function jump(event:TimerEvent):void
{
}
```

Next you will decide what you want the function to do. However, since you want to target the snowboarder, you need to first give it an instance name.

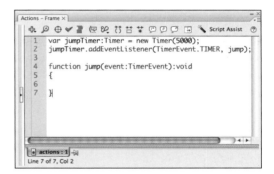

---

16 Minimize the **Actions** panel, and select the snowboarder on the **Stage**.

Remember, the snowboarder is an instance of the Animation movie clip symbol, not mcBoarder.

17 Choose the **Property inspector**, and type **animation_mc** in the **Instance Name** field.

18 Select **Frame 1** on the **actions** layer in the main **Timeline**, and maximize the **Actions** panel. Position your cursor on Line 6, and type the following:

```
animation_mc.play();
```

This function instructs the movie clip instance animation_mc to play when the timer runs. However, if you were to test the movie right now, nothing would happen. Why? Well, you need to start the timer.

---

19 Position your cursor after the curly brace on Line 7, press **Enter** (Windows) or **Return** (Mac) twice to inset two new lines, and type the following:

```
jumpTimer.start();
```

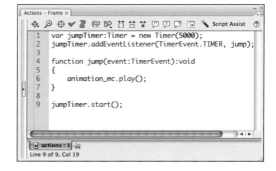

---

20 Press **Ctrl+Enter** (Windows) or **Cmd+Return** (Mac) to test the movie.

Wait 5 seconds, and the snowboarder will jump up and down once. He'll jump every 5 seconds from the start of the movie. If you want him to jump only once 5 seconds into the movie, you need to specify how many times the timer will repeat.

---

21 Close the movie window, and return to the **Actions** panel. Position your cursor after 5000 on Line 1, type a comma, and type **1**.

1 is the **repeat count**, or how many times the timer will run.

22 Press **Ctrl+Enter** (Windows) or **Cmd+Return** (Mac) to test the movie.

After 5 seconds, the snowboarder will jump up and down once. Wait another 5 seconds, and he'll just stay in place.

`TIMER` is similar to `ENTER_FRAME`. It's determined not by the user, but by you, the author. You can trigger it as often as you need. The `TIMER` event requires a little more code than `ENTER_FRAME`, but it also gives you a little more control. You can run it at a pace separate from the frame rate or only a certain number of times.

---

23 When you are finished, close the movie window, and close **Timer.fla**. You don't need to save your changes.

That's another chapter under your belt! In the next one, you'll get a better understanding of classes such as `Timer` and `URLRequest` and even learn how to create custom classes of your own.

5

Understanding Classes

In this chapter, you'll learn about classes: what they are, what they do, why they're important, and how to code them in ActionScript 3.0. Classes determine how an object acts, how it animates, and, to some extent, how it looks. If objects are the foundation of ActionScript, think of classes as the blueprint. Classes can be prebuilt or user-defined. User-defined, or custom, classes are created in external ActionScript (**.as**) files, which you'll work with for the first time in this chapter. You'll also learn to link custom classes to existing objects in the **Library** panel in order to bring an instance of the class to the **Stage,** and how to assign a document class. You'll learn about packages, the display list, and public versus private properties and methods. I know that seems like a lot of material to cover in one chapter, but don't worry—it will all come together for you in the end.

Understanding Classes

What are classes? A **class** is like a blueprint for how the objects in that class are constructed. A class contains a predefined collection of properties and methods. Instances of a class may look different on the surface, but they all act the same way. ActionScript 2.0 first introduced classes, but ActionScript 3.0 makes them more consistent and offers significant performance improvements.

You should already have a concept of classes if you've worked with symbols in Adobe Flash. The illustration shown here is a visual representation of three types of symbols. Each symbol is a different type of class that has its own particular properties and behaviors.

A movie clip is a type of class, and a button is a type of class. You can change the look and feel of these objects, but you can't change their inherited properties.

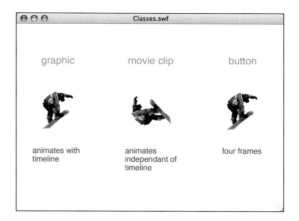

graphic	movie clip	button
animates with timeline	animates independant of timeline	four frames

VIDEO: **symbolclasses.mov**

To learn more about symbols and how their classes determine their behavior, check out **symbolclassses.mov** in the **videos** folder on the **ActionScript HOT CD-ROM**.

1 | Writing a Custom Class

In this exercise, you'll create a custom class in an external ActionScript (**.as**) file. External **.as** files are a great way to make your code modular and reusable.

---

1 Copy the **chap_05** folder from the **ActionScript HOT CD-ROM** to your desktop. Start Flash CS3. On the **Welcome Screen**, click **ActionScript File** in the **Create New** section.

You build custom classes in external ActionScript files. In this exercise, you'll be building one from scratch.

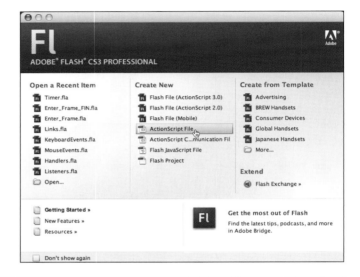

2 Save your new file by choosing **File > Save**. Navigate to the **chap_05/5-2** folder, and type **CustomClass** for the file name.

Names are not only significant when it comes to ActionScript, specifically for instances and variables, but also when it comes to file names. When you are building a custom class, the name of your ActionScript file becomes the name of your class. If you use a different

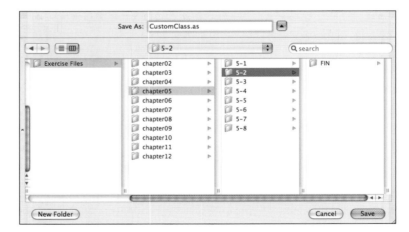

naming convention, including the date or time, for example, you'll have to write slightly different, and more difficult, code. Also, remember class names must start with a capital letter.

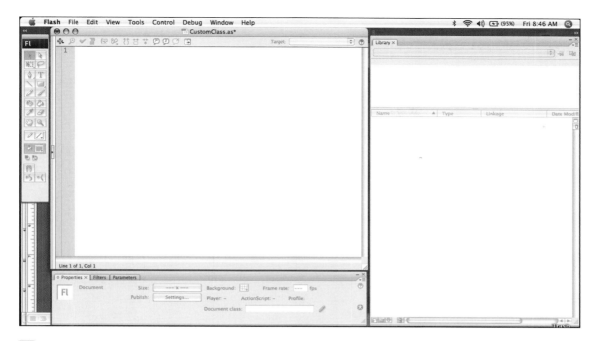

3 Click **Save**.

The Flash interface should look like the one shown in the illustration. Because you are working with an .as file, which contains only code and no content, the Stage and Timeline disappear and the Actions panel is maximized.

---

4 Position your cursor on Line 1, and type the following:

```
package
{

}
```

Make sure to leave an empty line between the two curly braces. All the rest of the code for this class will fit between them.

You may not realize it, but you've just created your first package. A **package** is a group of classes with related functionality. Although ActionScript 2.0 users might not recognize them, packages aren't new. ActionScript 2.0 didn't require you to specify packages in the code, but they were inferred by the directory structure. Packages are required in ActionScript 3.0; therefore, every custom class needs to be wrapped in a package. You can specify a package name, such as `package flash.display`, or simply use the top-level package, `package`.

The next step is to define your class, which is similar to defining a function or a variable.

---

5 Position your cursor on Line 3 between the curly braces, and type the following:

```
class CustomClass
{

}
```

Again, make sure to press Enter (Windows) or Return (Mac) after each line, and insert an empty line between the curly braces.

class is the keyword you use to define a new class in ActionScript, similar to **var** or **function**. Note your class name must be the same as the ActionScript file name.

```
1  package
2  {
3      class CustomClass
4      {
5
6      }
7  }
```

Line 6 of 7, Col 3

6 Position your cursor on Line 5 after the left curly brace, and type the following:

```
function CustomClass()
{

}
```

Here **CustomClass** defines a constructor function. Specifically, it's a method, since you are defining it in the class. A **constructor function** is a function that runs when an instance of the class is first created. For example, if you were to call this ActionScript file at Frame 54 in your animation, when the movie was exported, an instance of the custom class would be created, and the function would automatically run on Frame 54.

Constructor functions always use the same name as the class. You never use a return data type with a constructor function.

7 Position your cursor on Line 7 after the left curly brace, and type the following:

```
trace("The custom class is working!"};
```

The trace statement will run when the function is executed or the next time an instance of the new class is created in Flash.

And that's all there is to creating a custom class! First, specify the package. Second, define your class, making sure to use the same name as the file. Third, create the constructor function, using the same name again.

```
1   package
2   {
3       class CustomClass
4       {
5           function CustomClass()
6           {
7               trace("The custom class is working!");
8           }
9       }
10  }
```

Line 7 of 10, Col 42

8 Choose **File > Save**, and leave **CustomClass.as** open for the next exercise.

In the next exercise, you'll learn how to take some of the guesswork out of creating a custom class by building on the properties and methods of an existing class using the **extends** keyword.

2 | Extending an Existing Class

In this exercise, you'll learn how to take an existing class, such as **MovieClip**, and extend it. When you create a custom class, you're building from the ground up. When you extend a class, it's like renovating an existing object. You keep the basic framework and just make the changes where you want or need them. Extending a class is referred to as **inheritance** in ActionScript.

1 If you just completed Exercise 1, **CustomClass.as** should still be open. If it's not, complete Exercise 1, and then return to this exercise.

2 Position your cursor at the end of Line 3 after the word **CustomClass**, and press the **spacebar** to insert a space. Then type the following:

extends MovieClip

This might not seem like a lot of code, but it does a lot of work for you, the author. Rather than creating a Timeline for the class, creating the methods for positioning and animating the instances, specifying how they animate in relationship to the Timeline, and so on and so forth, you can use all the predefined attributes of another class, such as **MovieClip**, and modify them as you want. Extending a class is a huge time-saver.

Extending a class also builds more integrity into your code, since you know the class you're extending (called the **base class**) has been thoroughly tested. Inheritance is a popular form of reusing code.

But you're not done yet. As is, this code is not going to run properly. You still need to import the class.

3 Position your cursor at the end of Line 2, and press **Enter** (Windows) or **Return** (Mac) two times to go to the fourth line. Press the **up arrow** key to return to Line 3, and type the following:

import flash.display.MovieClip;

The **import** statement imports all the information about movie clips, their methods, their properties, and so on, into the new class. Without this statement, Flash will not recognize **MovieClip** when you try to extend the class.

You may be asking yourself, why do I have to use import now? I didn't have to use it in my Flash file. That's because when code is in the Flash Timeline, prebuilt packages are automatically imported at compile time. When you specify packages and classes in an external ActionScript file, Flash doesn't do this work for you. You have to explicitly direct the ActionScript compiler to the classes.

N O T E :

Custom Methods

What are custom methods? Well, you've already worked with methods in this book. Methods are nothing more than functions attached to a specific class of object. In the statement `Timer.start()`, `start()` is a method of the object `Timer`.

To write a custom method, you simply write a function in a custom class in an external ActionScript file. To add a method to the class `CustomClass`, you would add a function statement right after the constructor function.

The difference between a custom method and a custom function you write in the **Timeline** (like you wrote in Chapter 3, "*Using and Writing Functions*") is that the method can be executed only on `CustomClass`. You couldn't run the method on a movie clip or any other object, unless you assigned them to `CustomClass`.

4 Position your cursor at the end of Line 10, and press **Enter** (Windows) or **Return** (Mac) twice. Type the following:

```
function myCustomMethod()
{
  trace("This method is working!")
}
```

Now, this custom class is still not written quite properly. When you define a custom class by creating an entirely new class or extending another class, you need to also define whether the class methods and properties are known only to the class, a.k.a. **private**, or whether they can be called and modified outside the class, a.k.a. **public**.

```
CustomClass.as*
                                              Target:
1   package
2   {
3       import flash.display.MovieClip;
4
5       class CustomClass extends MovieClip
6       {
7           function CustomClass()
8           {
9               trace("The custom class is working!");
10          }
11
12          function myCustomMethod()
13          {
14              trace("This method is working!")
15          }
16      }
17  }

Line 15 of 17, Col 4
```

5 Position your cursor on Line 5 before the word `class`, and type `public`.

Defining the class as public allows you to use the class anywhere and anytime you want. The `public` keyword is not required for the class since ActionScript 3.0 does not support private classes, but it's considered best practice to specify a custom class as `public`. Again, `public` means you can create an instance of this class on any frame on the main Timeline or in a nested Timeline in any Flash file to which you link the ActionScript file.

6 Position your cursor on Line 7 before the word `function`, and type `public`.

7 Position your cursor on Line 12 before the word `function`, and type `private`.

Adding `private` to this function means you will be able to run it only inside the CustomClass.as file. You'll see how this works in the next exercise.

```
package
{
    import flash.display.MovieClip;

    public class CustomClass extends MovieClip
    {
        public function CustomClass()
        {
            trace("The custom class is working!");
        }

        private function myCustomMethod()
        {
            trace("This method is working!")
        }
    }
}
```
Line 12 of 17, Col 11

8 Position your cursor on Line 6 after the right curly brace, and press **Enter** (Windows) or **Return** (Mac) twice. Press the **up arrow** key to return to Line 7, and type the following:

`private _myVar:String;`

Here you have defined a property, or variable, that extends the original class, `MovieClip`. You've assigned the data type String to this variable. Just like custom class methods, custom class properties can be either public or private, using the previous syntax. Starting the custom class variable name with an underscore is not necessary, but it's common practice among Flash developers.

```
package
{
    import flash.display.MovieClip;

    public class CustomClass extends MovieClip
    {
        private _myVar:String;

        public function CustomClass()
        {
            trace("The custom class is working!");
        }

        private function myCustomMethod()
        {
            trace("This method is working!")
        }
    }
}
```
Line 7 of 19, Col 25

9 Save your changes, and close **CustomClass.as**.

In the next exercise, you'll put a custom class to practical use by linking the .as file to an existing object in a Flash project.

In this exercise, you'll learn how to take an existing object on the **Timeline** and connect with a custom class. By changing the object's **Linkage** properties, you will switch the object's class for another while preserving its appearance.

1 Choose **File > Open**, and navigate to the **chap_05/5-6** folder you copied to your desktop. Select **Button.fla**, press **Ctrl** (Windows) or **Cmd** (Mac), select **FunButton.as**, and then click **Open**.

Button.fla contains three instances of the movie clip symbol mcBoarder. I've applied different tints and transformed the instances, but they don't have any instance names yet.

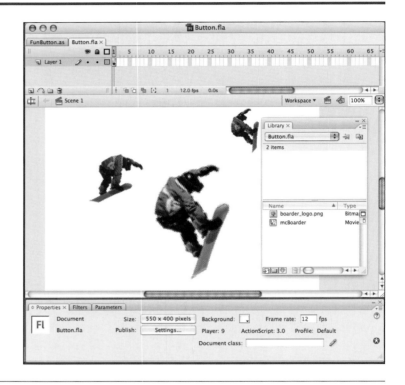

2 Click the **FunButton.as** tab above the **Timeline** to display the file.

You already know that when you work with an ActionScript file, the Flash interface changes slightly. The Tools panel and the other Flash panels are dimmed. However, notice that at the top of the Actions panel, a new Target field allows you to link the ActionScript file to any currently open Flash files. The open file, Button.fla, is selected by default.

```
package
{
    import flash.display.Sprite;

    public class FunButton extends Sprite
    {
        public function FunButton()
        {

        }
    }
}
```

The code in this file defines a custom class named **FunButton**, which extends the class **Sprite**. You'll use this class to add some rollover and rollout effects on the mcBoarder instances.

3 Position your cursor on Line 9 between the curly braces of the constructer function, and type the following:

```
this.addEventListener(
```

this is a keyword referring to the root object in an ActionScript or Flash file. In this case, it means any instance of the **FunButton** class. Once you connect **FunButton** to an object on the Timeline, this will refer to any instance you select.

Now you need to add the event for which you want to listen. You'll add **ROLL_OVER** first.

---

4 Next, type the following:

```
MouseEvent.ROLL_OVER, grow);
```

grow will be the name of the function that runs when the user moves the cursor over the instance.

```
package
{
    import flash.display.Sprite;

    public class FunButton extends Sprite
    {
        public function FunButton()
        {
            this.addEventListener(MouseEvent.ROLL_OVER, grow);
        }
    }
}
```

Line 9 of 12, Col 54

---

5 Select the code on Line 9, and press **Ctrl+C** (Windows) or **Cmd+C** (Mac) to copy the code.

---

6 Position your cursor at the end of Line 9. Press **Enter** (Windows) or **Return** (Mac) to go to the next line, and press **Ctrl+V** (Windows) or **Cmd+V** (Mac) to paste the code.

---

7 Double-click the word **ROLL_OVER** on Line 10, and type **ROLL_OUT**.

Remember that events use all capital letters.

8 Double-click the word **grow** on Line 10, and type **shrink**.

I bet you can tell what the behavior of the event handlers is going to be already. But you have one more important aspect to add before you continue. Remember how you have to use an **import** statement to import a class when you extend it, like on Line 3? Well, you also have to import **MouseEvent**. Whenever you are working in an external ActionScript file, you need to import events so Flash will understand them at compile time (when you export your movie).

```
1   package
2   {
3       import flash.display.Sprite;
4
5       public class FunButton extends Sprite
6       {
7           public function FunButton()
8           {
9               this.addEventListener(MouseEvent.ROLL_OVER, grow);
10              this.addEventListener(MouseEvent.ROLL_OUT, shrink);
11          }
12      }
13  }
```

Line 10 of 13, Col 53

9 Position your cursor at the end of Line 3, and press **Enter** (Windows) or **Return** (Mac) to go to the next line. Type the following:

```
import flash.events.MouseEvent;
```

Now you just need to define the **grow()** and **shrink()** event handlers.

10 Position your cursor at the end of Line 12 after the right curly brace, and press **Enter** (Windows) or **Return** (Mac) twice to insert two new lines. Type the following:

```
private function grow
(Event:MouseEvent):void
{
  this.scaleX = 1.5;
  this.scaleY = 1.5;
}
```

You're defining **grow()** as a private method because you'll never be calling it outside the **FunButton** class. This function will cause the object to get 50 percent larger whenever the user moves the cursor over it.

```
5
6       public class FunButton extends Sprite
7       {
8           public function FunButton()
9           {
10              this.addEventListener(MouseEvent.ROLL_OVER, grow);
11              this.addEventListener(MouseEvent.ROLL_OUT, shrink);
12          }
13
14          private function grow (Event:MouseEvent):void
15          {
16              this.scaleX = 1.5;
17              this.scaleY = 1.5;
18          }
19      }
20  }
```

Line 18 of 20, Col 4

11 Select Lines 14–18, and press **Ctrl+C** (Windows) or **Cmd+C** (Mac) to copy the event handler.

12 Position your cursor at the end of Line 18. Press **Enter** (Windows) or **Return** (Mac) twice to go to the next line, and press **Ctrl+V** (Windows) or **Cmd+V** (Mac) to paste the code.

13 Double-click the word `grow` on Line 20, and change it to `shrink`.

14 Select **1.5** on Line 22, and change it to **1**. Change the value on Line 23 to **1** as well.

This function causes the object to return to its original size once the user moves their cursor away from it.

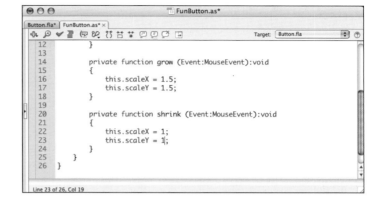

15 Press **Ctrl+S** (Windows) or **Cmd+S** (Mac) to save **FunButton.as**.

TIP:

To Save or Not to Save?

In the best-case scenario, everyone would save their documents on a regular basis every time they made a change. But, hey, we're only human. Luckily, Flash CS3 offers a visual cue when a document has not been saved since the last change. An asterisk will appear next to the file name on the document tab. Flash will also prompt you to save a file when you close it without saving.

16 Click the **Button.fla** document tab to switch files.

Ordinarily, if you knew you were going to call objects on the Stage with ActionScript, the first step you would take, and should take, is to give them instance names. However, you'll use a slightly different approach here.

17 If the **Library** panel is not open, press **Ctrl+L** (Windows) or **Cmd+L** (Mac) to open it.

18 **Right-click** (Windows) or **Ctrl-click** (Mac) the **mcBoarder** item, and choose **Linkage** in the contextual menu.

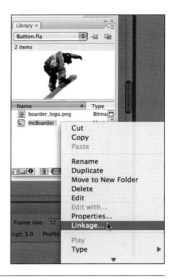

19 In the Linkage Properties dialog box, select Export for ActionScript.

Choosing Export for ActionScript displays the class name and base class for the movie clip. Remember that the base class is what the class is *extended* from, or where it inherits its properties and methods.

Notice that Linkage is turned off. Flash assumes that not every Library item is going to be used on the Stage, and since exporting (especially exporting a symbol for use in ActionScript) adds to your file size, it turns Linkage off by default.

20 Change the class name from **mcBoarder** to **FunButton**. Change **Base class** to **flash.display.Sprite**, and click **OK** to close the **Linkage Properties** dialog box.

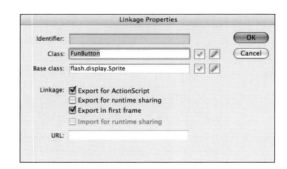

21 Press **Ctrl+Enter** (Windows) or **Cmd+Return** (Mac) to test the movie. When the preview window opens, move your cursor over each of the snowboarders.

The snowboarders get bigger when you move your cursor over the buttons and get smaller when you move your mouse away. This is all without adding any ActionScript to the Flash file!

Move the preview window to the left or right so you can see the Stage. Notice that although the snowboarders are all different sizes in the original Flash file, once you roll away from them, they return to the size of the original movie clip symbol. You need to make the `grow` and `shrink` functions relative to the instances' original sizes.

---

22 Close the preview window, and return to Flash. Click the **FunButton.as** document tab.

Since the snowboarders do not have instance names, you'll have to capture the x and y scales in variables before the functions run.

---

23 Position your cursor after the left curly brace on Line 7 (after the left curly brace of **public class FunButton extends Sprite**), and press **Enter** (Windows) or **Return** (Mac) twice to insert two new lines. Press the **up arrow** key to move up one line. Type the following:

```
private var _origXScale:Number;
```

`_origXScale` is a placeholder that will represent the width of objects. The data type is Number.

```
1  package
2  {
3      import flash.display.Sprite;
4      import flash.events.MouseEvent;
5
6      public class FunButton extends Sprite
7      {
8          private var _origXScale:Number;
9
10         public function FunButton()
11         {
12             this.addEventListener(MouseEvent.ROLL_OVER, grow);
13             this.addEventListener(MouseEvent.ROLL_OUT, shrink);
14         }
15
16         private function grow (Event:MouseEvent):void
```

Line 8 of 28, Col 34

---

24 Press **Enter** (Windows) or **Return** (Mac) to go to the next line, and type the following:

```
private var _origYScale:Number;
```

Now, you'll make the variables equal to the original x and y scale of the objects. You'll place this code in the constructor function.

25 Position your cursor after the left curly brace that appears after the public function **FunButton()** (on Line 12), and press **Enter** (Windows) or **Return** (Mac) to insert a new line. Type the following:

```
_origXScale = this.scaleX;
_origYScale = this.scaleY;
```

Now you can use a compound assignment operator to make the **grow()** and **shrink()** functions execute relative to each object's original x and y scale (**_origXScale** and **_origYScale**) properties.

```
                                          FunButton.as*
Button.fla  FunButton.as* ×
                                                              Target:  Button.fla
 1  package
 2  {
 3      import flash.display.Sprite;
 4      import flash.events.MouseEvent;
 5
 6      public class FunButton extends Sprite
 7      {
 8          private var _origXScale:Number;
 9          private var _origYScale:Number;
10
11          public function FunButton()
12          {
13              _origXScale = this.scaleX;
14              _origYScale = this.scaleY;
15              this.addEventListener(MouseEvent.ROLL_OVER, grow);
16              this.addEventListener(MouseEvent.ROLL_OUT, shrink);
17          }
18
Line 14 of 31, Col 4
```

---

26 Position your cursor before the first equals sign in the private function **grow()** (on Line 21), and add an asterisk (*).

The asterisk tells Flash to multiply the current x scale property by one and a half, or 150 percent, no matter what its current size.

```
                                                              Target:  Button.fla
10
11          public function FunButton()
12          {
13              _origXScale = this.scaleX;
14              _origYScale = this.scaleY;
15              this.addEventListener(MouseEvent.ROLL_OVER, grow);
16              this.addEventListener(MouseEvent.ROLL_OUT, shrink);
17          }
18
19          private function grow (Event:MouseEvent):void
20          {
21              this.scaleX *= 1.5;
22              this.scaleY = 1.5;
23          }
24
25          private function shrink (Event:MouseEvent):void
26          {
27              this.scaleX = 1;
Line 21 of 31, Col 17
```

---

27 Position your cursor before the second equals sign in the private function **grow()** (on Line 22), and add an asterisk (*).

---

28 Position your cursor on Line 27 in the **shrink** function, and replace **1** with **_origXScale**. Replace **1** on Line 28 with **_origYScale**.

This returns the object not to mcBoarder's original size but to its original x scale.

```
                                                              Target:  Button.fla
16              this.addEventListener(MouseEvent.ROLL_OUT, shrink);
17          }
18
19          private function grow (Event:MouseEvent):void
20          {
21              this.scaleX *= 1.5;
22              this.scaleY *= 1.5;
23          }
24
25          private function shrink (Event:MouseEvent):void
26          {
27              this.scaleX = _origXScale;
28              this.scaleY = _origYScale;
29          }
30      }
31  }
Line 28 of 31, Col 29
```

29 Press **Ctrl+S** (Windows) or **Cmd+S** (Mac) to save **FunButton.as**. Click the **Button.fla** document tab.

30 Press **Ctrl+Enter** (Windows) or **Cmd+Return** (Mac) to test the movie. When the preview window opens, move your cursor over each of the snowboarders.

Sweet! Now the snowboarders get bigger and smaller relative to their original scales.

Before you finish with this file, I want to show you one more trick that will demonstrate the power of classes.

31 Close the preview window, and return to Flash. Make sure **Button.fla** is still active.

32 Select the **Rectangle** tool in the **Tools** panel, and draw a rectangle in the lower-left corner of the **Stage**.

The rectangle can be any size or color.

33 Select the **Selection** tool in the **Tools** panel, and draw a selection area around the rectangle on the **Stage**. Press **F8** to open the **Convert to Symbol** dialog box. Type **rectangle** for the symbol name, select **Movie clip** for **Type**, and click **OK**.

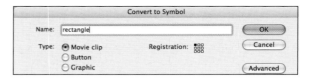

34 In the **Library** panel, right-click the **rectangle** symbol. Choose **Linkage** in the contextual menu.

35 In the **Linkage Properties** dialog box, choose **Export for ActionScript**. Change **Class** to **FunButton** and **Base class** to **flash.display.Sprite**, and click **OK**.

Whoops. An error message pops up. Flash says you must type a unique class name that is not associated with other symbols in the Library panel. Hmmm. How do you work around this? Well, the base class *can* be associated with multiple objects. If you use `FunButton` as the base class, you can then name the class whatever you want.

36 Click **OK** to close the warning dialog box. Type **FunButton** in the **Base class** field. Type **rectangle** in the **Class** field, and click **OK**.

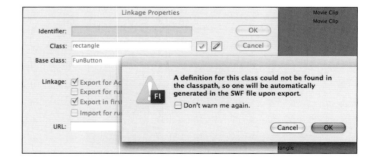

Another warning message! This one says a definition could not be found for the class `rectangle`, so one will be generated on export. In a nutshell, this means since there is no ActionScript file defining rectangle.as, Flash will create a definition using the base class, FunButton.as, when the movie is exported. Perfect!

37 Click **OK** to close the warning dialog box. Press **Ctrl+Enter** (Windows) or **Cmd+Return** (Mac) to test the movie. When the preview window opens, move your cursor over the rectangle.

Pretty cool, isn't it? Flash translates the behavior of `FunButton` to `rectangle` so it grows 50 percent larger when you move your cursor over the shape, and returns to its original size when you move your cursor away.

You may notice the rectangle is scaling from the top-left corner, whereas the snowboarders are scaling from the center. This is simply because the registration point for the rectangle is set to the top left by default. The registration points for the snowboarders are in the center of the objects, so they appear to scale differently. Return to Flash, and use the Free Transform tool to move the registration point if you want to change the registration and the way the symbol instance scales.

---

38 Close the preview window, and close **Button.fla** and **FunButton.as**. You don't need to save your changes.

That's how you add a custom class to the Timeline of your movie! You can see how useful classes are when you connect them to multiple objects. In the next exercise, you'll learn how to define a class for your entire document, which runs automatically without having to connect it to any objects on the Stage.

---

4 | Defining a Document Class

In this exercise, you'll learn how to set up a document class. In previous versions of Flash, the main **Timeline**, or main class, of the Flash movie was a movie clip. In Flash CS3, you can define any class for the document. A document class is no different from any other class file, except you use the **Property inspector** to add it to the document, rather than using the **Linkage** feature to connect it to a single object. Document classes also run automatically when you export the SWF file.

---

1 Choose **File > Open**, and open **Button.fla** and **ButtonClass.as** in the **5-7** folder of the **chap_05** folder you copied to your desktop.

---

2 Select the **Button.fla** document tab. Select the **Selection** tool in the **Tools** panel, and drag a selection area around all three snowboarders on the **Stage**. Press the **Delete** key to remove them from the **Stage**.

These objects were created by dragging instances of mcBoarder directly from the Library to the Stage. In this exercise, you'll re-create them using an external ActionScript file.

The first step is to add code to the file you'll be using for the document class, ButtonClass.as.

NOTE: | ## Why Use a Document Class?

The document class is a new feature of ActionScript 3.0 in Flash CS3 that allows you to associate a class file with the root level of your document, in other words, the main **Timeline**. The inclusion of a document class allows you to keep ActionScript code out of frames in the **Timeline** and make your code more modular and reusable.

---

3 Click the **ButtonClass.as** document tab to display the ActionScript file. In the first line of the file, type the following:

```
package
{
public class ButtonClass extends MovieClip
    {
    }
}
```

Remember that the class name must be the same as the name of the file in which it is defined.

Now you need to import the `MovieClip` class so Flash understands what you are extending.

4 Position your cursor after the left curly brace on Line 2, and press **Enter** (Windows) or **Return** (Mac) twice to insert two new lines. Press the **up arrow** key once to go to the previous empty line. Type the following:

```
import flash.display.MovieClip
```

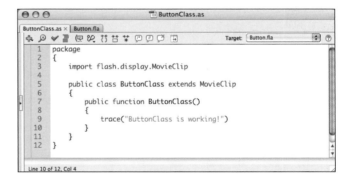

5 Position your cursor after the left curly brace on Line 6, press **Enter** (Windows) or **Return** (Mac), and type the following:

```
public function ButtonClass()
```

Remember when you add a function with the same name as new class, it's called a **constructor function**.

Since it is a public function, you will be able to run `ButtonClass()` outside the ActionScript file. To establish that the class has been added to the Timeline and the method is working properly, you'll add a trace statement to this function.

6 Press **Enter** (Windows) or **Return** (Mac) to go to the next line, and type the following:

```
{
    trace("ButtonClass is working!")
}
```

7 Press **Ctrl +S** (Windows) or **Cmd+S** (Mac) to save **ButtonClass.as**.

8 Return to **Button.fla**. Choose **Window > Properties > Properties** to open the **Property inspector**, if it is not already open.

In the bottom-right corner of the Property inspector, there is a Document class field. If you don't see this field, click the **gray** area outside the Stage so you are looking at the document properties.

9 Type **ButtonClass** in the **Document class** field.

10 Press **Ctrl+Enter** (Windows) or **Cmd+Return** (Mac) to test the movie.

The movie window will be empty when it opens, but the Output panel should contain your trace statement, "ButtonClass is working!" If you don't get this message, check your work in Steps 2–9.

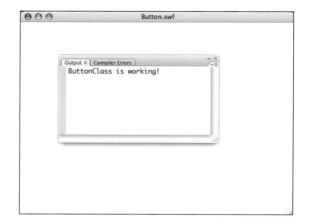

11 Close the movie window and the **Output** panel, and return to **Button.fla**.

12 Choose the **Library** panel, and **right-click** (Windows) or **Ctrl-click** (Mac) **mcBoarder**. Choose **Linkage** in the contextual menu.

13 In the **Linkage Properties** dialog box, choose **Export for ActionScript**.

mcBoarder is the class name, and **flash.display.MovieClip** is the base class. As you learned in the previous exercise, you can change the class or base class of an object to your custom class. I recommend changing the base class because you can use the same base class for multiple objects.

14 Change **Base class** to **FunButton**.

FunButton is the custom class you created in the previous exercise. I put a copy in the 5-7 folder so that Flash will be able to find it. Flash uses what's called a **classpath** to locate files. By default, the classpath is defined as the folder in which the ActionScript file is saved. If the ActionScript file were in a different folder, you'd have to use a special technique to reference it. You'll learn more about classpaths in the next exercise.

15 Click **OK** to close the **Linkage Properties** dialog box. When the warning message appears letting you know Flash will create a new class on export, click **OK**.

Nothing exciting has happened yet. You still have to add mcBoarder, now part of the **FunButton** class, to the Stage.

---

16 Click the **ButtonClass.as** document tab. Insert you cursor at the end of Line 3 after the **import** statement, press **Enter** (Windows) or **Return** (Mac) to go to the next line, and type the following:

```
import mcBoarder
import FunButton
```

Here you are importing the class and the new base class for the object so that Flash has a definition for these objects.

```
package
{
    import flash.display.MovieClip
    import mcBoarder
    import FunButton

    public class ButtonClass extends MovieClip
    {
        public function ButtonClass()
        {
            trace("ButtonClass is working!")
        }
    }
}
```

---

17 Position your cursor after the left curly brace on Line 8 inside the public class **ButtonClass**, and press **Enter** (Windows) or **Return** (Mac) twice. Press the **up arrow** key to go to Line 9, and type the following:

```
private var _boarder:mcBoarder;
```

This code creates a new variable called **boarder** of the data type mcBoarder. Remember, the variable does not create the instance. The variable is just a placeholder.

---

18 Position your cursor in the curly braces of the **ButtonClass()** function, and delete the trace statement. On the same line, type the following:

```
_boarder = new mcBoarder();
```

This code creates a new instance of the **mcBoarder** class. However, if you were to test this movie, you wouldn't be able to see the instance on the Stage. You still need to add the object to the display list. The display list is a new concept, but it is something you'll be working with throughout the rest of this book. See the *"What Is the Display List?"* sidebar for more information on the display list in Flash.

```
package
{
    import flash.display.MovieClip
    import mcBoarder
    import FunButton

    public class ButtonClass extends MovieClip
    {
        private var _boarder:mcBoarder;

        public function ButtonClass()
        {
            _boarder = new mcBoarder();
        }
    }
}
```

NOTE:

What Is the Display List?

The **display list** is ActionScript's way of managing and organizing all the visible elements in the movie. It has a built-in hierarchy. The **Stage** is the base container for all display objects. Certain display objects, such as movie clips, can contain other display objects, or children, which makes them display object containers. Where an object falls in this hierarchy determines the order in which it is drawn on the **Stage**. You can add display objects to the **Stage** using the `addChild()` method and remove them using `removeChild()`.

If you're familiar with ActionScript 2.0, this might seem revolutionary. Previously, all objects were added to the **Stage** through a movie clip, which is still a display object in ActionScript 3.0. However, now you can add text, graphics, and bitmaps to the **Stage** without using a movie clip, through another type of container called a **sprite**. Sprites are new to Flash CS3. A sprite does not have its own **Timeline** or some of the other movie clip properties, which can lead to more efficient rendering and smaller file sizes. For now, just keep in mind that when you add an object to the **Stage**, you also need to include it in the display list so it will be visible when you export your movie.

---

19 Press **Enter** (Windows) or **Return** (Mac) to insert a new line, and type the following:

```
addChild(_boarder);
```

This code will add **boarder** to the display list of **ButtonClass**.

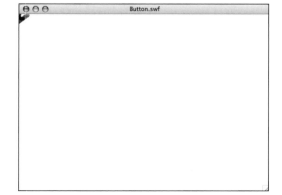

---

20 Choose **File > Save** to save **ButtonClass.as**. Click the **Button.fla** document tab, and press **Ctrl+Enter** (Windows) or **Cmd+Return** (Mac) to test your work.

Yikes! The snowboarder is added to the Stage, but he's stuck in the upper-left corner of the screen. You can still move your cursor over him to get the scale effect, but it is not the most aesthetically pleasing composition. Let's change the snowboarder's x and y properties.

21 Close the movie window, and return to Flash. Click the **ButtonClass.as** document tab. Position your cursor at the end of Line 14 after **addChild(_boarder);**, press **Enter** (Windows) or **Return** (Mac) to insert a new line, and type the following:

```
_boarder.x = 200;
_boarder.y = 200;
```

```
1   package
2   {
3       import flash.display.MovieClip
4       import mcBoarder
5       import FunButton
6
7       public class ButtonClass extends MovieClip
8       {
9           private var _boarder:mcBoarder;
10
11          public function ButtonClass()
12          {
13              _boarder = new mcBoarder();
14              addChild(_boarder);
15              _boarder.x = 200;
16              _boarder.y = 200;
17          }
18      }
19  }
```

Line 16 of 19, Col 21

22 Choose **File > Save** to save **ButtonClass.as**. Press **Ctrl+Enter** (Windows) or **Cmd+Return** (Mac) to test your work.

I haven't mentioned it before, but you can test the movie from within your open ActionScript file, provided the FLA file is also open.

And there you have it. The snowboarder is in a much better position.

23 Close the preview window, and close **Button.fla** and **ButtonClass.as**. You don't need to save your changes.

In this exercise, you used some of the knowledge from the previous exercise, linking a Library item to an external custom class file, but you also added a document class to the Flash file. Keep in mind a document class is like any other ActionScript file, except you call it in the Property inspector and it runs automatically when the SWF file is exported. In the next exercise, you'll see what happens when the link to a class file is broken and then how to correct it.

5 | Setting Up a Classpath

In this exercise, you'll learn about an amazing tool in Flash that you can use to organize your classes. If you have a lot of ActionScript files, wouldn't it be nice to have a designated location on your hard drive to save them rather than copying and pasting them into the same folders as the FLA files you'd like to use them with? Well, in Flash CS3 you can. Using ActionScript, you can specify a folder where Flash will look for classes and import them into the SWF file at run time.

1 Choose **File > Open**, and open **Button.fla** and **ButtonClass.as** from the **5-8** folder in the **chap_05** folder you copied to your desktop. Examine the two files' document settings.

Notice these files are the same as the ones you created in the previous exercise.

---

2 Open **Windows Explorer** (Windows) or **Finder** (Mac). Navigate to your desktop, **right-click** (Windows) or **Ctrl-click** (Mac), and choose **New Folder** in the contextual menu. Name the new folder **AS3 Classes**. Double-click **AS3 Classes** to open it, **right-click** (Windows) or **Ctrl-click** (Mac) in the folder, and choose **New Folder** again. Name this new folder **classes**.

This folder will represent your classes folder, where Flash will look for class files. You can name and organize this folder in any way you want. You can even add subfolders, as you did here.

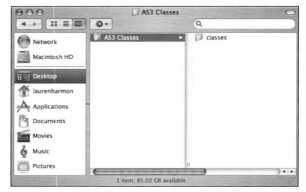

3 In **Windows Explorer** (Windows) or **Finder** (Mac), navigate to the **5-8** folder. Move **FunButton.as** to the **AS3Classes/ classes** folder on your desktop by either dragging or cutting and pasting the file.

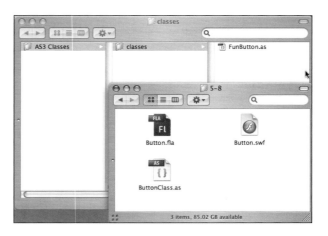

4 Return to Flash. Press **Ctrl+Enter** (Windows) or **Cmd+Return** (Mac) to test the movie.

Yikes! The Output panel opens with all kinds of error messages. Because you moved FunButton.as, Flash can't find the document class, and the movie doesn't run properly. You'll need to direct Flash to the location of the file in order to access the class.

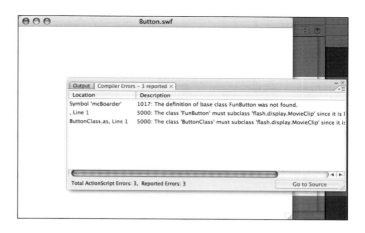

---

5 Close the movie window and the **Output** panel. Choose **Window > Properties > Properties** to open the **Property inspector**, if it is not already open. Click the **Publish : Settings** button.

The Publish Settings dialog box will open. You can also access this dialog box by choosing File > Publish Settings or by pressing Ctrl+Shift+F12 (Windows) or Cmd+Shift+F12 (Mac).

---

6 Click the **Flash** button at the top of the dialog box. Click the **Settings** button.

The ActionScript 3.0 Settings dialog box will open. At the bottom of the window, notice there is a Classpath area. This area defines the classpath (or classpaths) where Flash will look to find all your external ActionScript files. The area appears blank, but the default setting is to look in the same folder as the .fla file.

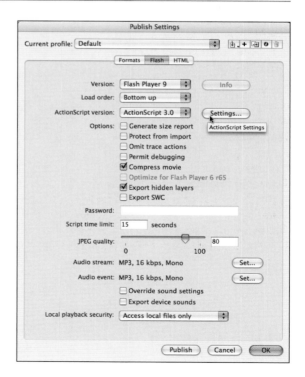

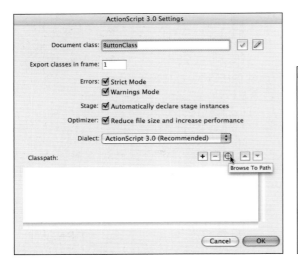

7 Click the **Browse to Path** button to open the **Choose a Folder** (Mac) or **Browse for Folder** (Windows) dialog box. Navigate to and select the **AS3 Classes** folder you created on your desktop, and click **Choose** or **OK**.

I mentioned the folder could be named and organized in any way you want, but you should also know that you can place it anywhere on your hard drive. For simplicity's sake, you put the folder on your desktop for this exercise.

8 Click **OK** to close the **ActionScript 3.0 Settings** dialog box, and click **OK** again to close the **Publish Settings** dialog box.

9 Choose **File > Save** to save **Button.fla**. Press **Ctrl+Enter** (Windows) or **Cmd+Return** (Mac) to test the movie.

Hmm. You're still getting error messages. Let's review each of the issues. First, the definition of mcBoarder's base class, FunButton, cannot be found.

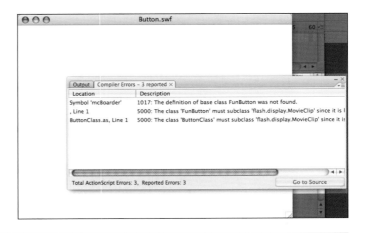

10 Close the movie window and the **Output** panel, and in the **Library** panel, **right-click** (Window) or **Ctrl-click** (Mac) **mcBoarder**. Then choose **Linkage** in the contextual menu.

11 In the **Linkage Properties** dialog box, check to make sure **Export for ActionScript** is selected and the **Base class** name is **FunButton**. Click **OK**.

Now a warning message appears. The **FunButton** classpath could not be found.

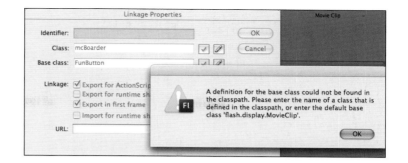

12 Click **OK** to close the warning dialog box. Delete **FunButton** from the **Base class** field, and type **classes.FunButton**. Click **OK** to close the **Linkage Properties** dialog box.

Sweet. No error messages! Unlike when you link to a document class using the Property inspector, when you link an object to a class file, Flash cannot navigate subfolders to find a class file. You need to spell out the classpath, separating subfolders by periods.

The new classpath also needs to be outlined in any class files that import the class. In the next step, you'll change the `import` statement in ButtonClass.as to reflect the new location of FunButton.as.

13 Click the **ButtonClass.as** document tab. Position your cursor on Line 5, and change **import FunButton;** to **import classes.FunButton;**. Select **Button.fla**. Choose **File > Save All** to save **Button.fla** and **ButtonClass.as**.

```
package
{
    import flash.display.MovieClip;
    import mcBoarder;
    import classes.FunButton;

    public class ButtonClass extends MovieClip
    {
        private var boarder:mcBoarder;

        public function ButtonClass()
        {
            boarder = new mcBoarder();
            addChild(boarder);
            boarder.x = 200;
            boarder.y = 200;
        }
    }
}
```

14 Press **Ctrl+Enter** (Windows) or **Cmd+Return** (Mac) to test the movie.

You're still getting errors in the Output panel. For one, the definition of base class **FunButton** cannot be found. Let me show you what the problem is.

15 Close the movie window and the **Output** panel, and return to Flash.

---

16 Choose **File > Open**. In the **Open** dialog box, navigate to **AS3 Classes/classes**, and select **FunButton.as**. Click **Open**.

---

17 Position your cursor at the end of the first line in **FunButton.as**. Press the **spacebar** once, and type the following:

classes

When you bury an ActionScript file in one or more folders, you need to specify the path in the package area of the file itself. This lets you communicate with this file from within any other Flash file anywhere on your hard drive.

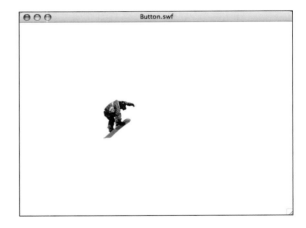

```
package classes
{
    import flash.display.MovieClip;
    import flash.events.MouseEvent;

    public class FunButton extends MovieClip
    {
        private var _origXScale:Number;
        private var _origYScale:Number;

        public function FunButton()
        {
            _origXScale = this.scaleX;
            _origYScale = this.scaleY;
            this.addEventListener(MouseEvent.ROLL_OVER, grow);
            this.addEventListener(MouseEvent.ROLL_OUT, shrink);
        }

        private function grow(event:MouseEvent):void
        {
```

18 Choose **File > Save** to save **FunButton.as**. Verify that the other two open files are saved, and then press **Ctrl+Enter** (Windows) or **Cmd+Return** (Mac) to test the movie.

Ta-da! The boarder should appear on the Stage. Move your cursor over and away from the snowboarder, and he should get bigger and smaller in accordance with the functions you created previously in this chapter in the **FunButton** class.

Creating a separate folder for your ActionScript classes may seem like a little more work initially, but it pays off in the end. The folder serves as a veritable library of custom ActionScript files that you can call on for a variety of projects, without having to copy and paste or move them around.

To summarize, remember these four tips when you set up a new classpath:

- Specify the classpath in Publish Settings.
- Type the full classpath when you link movie clips to classes.
- Type the full classpath in your **import** statements.
- Type the classpath in the class file itself, after the word *package*.

VIDEO: | **usefulclasses.mov**

The key to creating ActionScript classes is making them useful. By *useful*, I mean reusable. The **FunButton** class you created in this chapter is a useful class. You can apply it any object to have the object get bigger and smaller as the user moves the cursor over and away from the object. Another example of a useful class would be a scroll bar. You could use it to control a text field, as a volume slider, or even to control the playback of a movie.

For more information about useful classes and how to organize them, see **usefulclasses. mov** in the **videos** folder on the **ActionScript HOT CD-ROM**.

19 Close the preview window, and choose **File > Close All** to close any open files.

In the next chapter, you'll learn about using conditional statements to control under what circumstances functions execute and also how to use loops to repeat actions.

6

Decision Making and Repetition

In this chapter, you'll learn how to make Adobe Flash CS3 Professional perform repetitive tasks and make decisions for you. Having Flash perform repetitive tasks can save you loads of time writing code, so you can spend more time enjoying life! Using Flash to make decisions for you gives Flash the ability to think for itself so you can create more interactive applications. In fact, many of the questions you've probably had up to this point that begin with "How do I...?" will be answered in this chapter. So let's get started!

Understanding Conditional Statements

You may not know it, but you already have a concept of conditional statements from programming the functions in the other chapters in this book. You may think of functions as simple cause-and-effect reactions, but there is a different perspective in which you can consider functions.

The illustration shown here is from the **Understanding.swf** file included in the **chap_06** exercise folder. This movie is a visual representation of a function that operates on the object **boarder**, which you might recognize from Chapter 3, *"Using and Writing Functions."* Add **boarder**, **rotate**, and **move** to the function, and then run the function. The instance of the snowboarder will jump up in the air and rotate. 1, 2, 3, presto, magic!

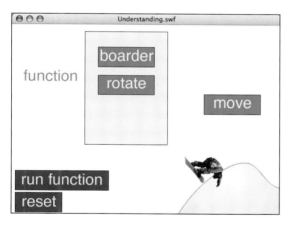

In fact, a lot of internal checks and balances are working behind the scenes to make sure the code runs properly. If something doesn't check out, it won't run at all. Code is like a well-oiled machine. Add the object and the properties you want to change, and start the engine (the function). You'll get a reaction. However, if you were to remove one of these things, nothing happens. You don't go anywhere. The function works on an implied condition, an **if/then** scenario.

You can specify **if/then** directly in a **conditional statement**. A conditional statement tests whether conditions are met, or what the result of another action is, and performs an action based on the test results.

Conditional statements, functions, and loops, which you'll explore later in this chapter, are related elements in ActionScript. Adobe refers to them as **flow-control elements**. You use these elements to control when and how actions are performed.

1 | Writing a Conditional Statement

In this exercise, you'll write a conditional statement using the keyword **if**.

1 Copy the **chap_06** folder from the **ActionScript HOT CD-ROM** to your desktop. Open **Writing.fla** from the **chap_06** folder.

This file contains artwork on the Stage, an instance of mcBoarder, which you should be intimately familiar with now, and as you can see from the small a in Frame 1 of the actions layer, some ActionScript is embedded in the Timeline.

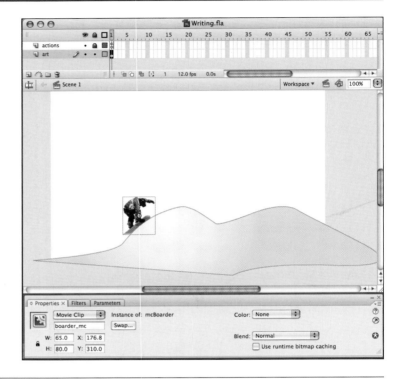

2 Select **Frame 1** on the **actions** layer, and choose **Window > Actions** to open the **Actions** panel.

To start with, you have an event listener added to boarder_mc, listening for a mouse click, and you have an event handler, onClick. The **buttonMode** of boarder_mc is set to **true**, which will turn the user's cursor into a hand icon when the user moves the cursor over the snowboarder.

```
1   boarder_mc.addEventListener(MouseEvent.CLICK, onClick);
2
3   function onClick(event:MouseEvent):void
4   {
5
6   }
7
8   boarder_mc.buttonMode = true;
```

3 Position your cursor on Line 5 inside the event handler, and type the following:

```
event.target.y -= 100;
```

Remember that *target* refers to the target of the event listener, boarder_mc.

```
 1   boarder_mc.addEventListener(MouseEvent.CLICK, onClick);
 2
 3   function onClick(event:MouseEvent):void
 4   {
 5       event.target.y -= 100;
 6   }
 7
 8   boarder_mc.buttonMode = true;
```

4 Press **Ctrl+Enter** (Windows) or **Cmd+Return** (Mac) to test the movie. When the preview window opens, click the snowboarder two or three times.

The snowboarder moves up 100 pixels every time you click him, but he never comes back down. Rather than setting up another event listener and event handler to move him back down, what if you could set up the function so that he would move up and then down every other click, depending on whether he was in the air? Well, you can! This is where the conditional statement comes into play.

5 Close the movie window, and return to the **Actions** panel. Position your cursor at the beginning of Line 1, and press **Enter** (Windows) or **Return** (Mac) twice to insert two new lines. Press the **up arrow** key to return to Line 1, and type the following:

```
var jumping
```

This variable is going to hold a **true/false** value that will tell the rest of the code whether the snowboarder is in the air or on the ground.

You may be wondering why you're always placing the variables at the top of your code. Well, Flash reads ActionScript files from the top down, so it's best practice to insert variables that you are going to be using throughout your code at the top. Also, it's good to keep your code organized and consistent. I always place variables at the top of my code so I always know where to find them if I need to make a change.

6 After **jumping**, type the following:

:Boolean = false;

Boolean is a data type, like Number or String, but the only values a Boolean variable can contain are **true** or **false**. The initial value is **false**, since the snowboarder starts on the ground.

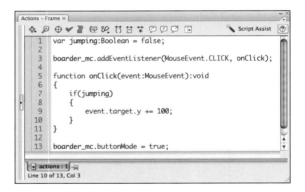

---

7 Select the code on Line 7 (**event.target.y -= 100;**), press **Delete** to erase the code, and then type the following:

if(jumping)

When you start a conditional statement, you use the word **if**. The code in the parentheses is the condition, an expression that produces either a **true** value or a **false** value. Usually, you write an expression using an operator, such as **boarder_mc.height > 2**. However, variables of the Boolean data type, such as **jumping**, also fall into this category. By typing just the variable name, Flash assumes you want to test whether it is true and you don't need to use **jumping = true**.

Also note, it is important to understand that an **if** statement will execute only when the condition is the parentheses is true.

---

8 Press **Enter** (Windows) or **Return** (Mac) to go to the next line, and type the following:

```
{
    event.target.y += 100;
}
```

This code determines what happens if the condition is true. So if **jumping** is equal to true, the event target (boarder_mc) will jump down 100 pixels.

---

9 Position your cursor at the end of Line 9, and press **Enter** (Windows) or **Return** (Mac) to go to the next line. Type the following:

jumping = false;

This line of code sets the jumping variable back to **false** after the **if** statement has executed.

---

10 Position your cursor at the end of Line 11 (after the closed curly brace of the **if** statement), and press **Enter** (Windows) or **Return** (Mac) to go to the next line. Type the following:

```
else
```

An **else** statement is another type conditional statement, but it can follow an **if** statement only.

You don't have to specify the condition for **else** in parentheses. **else** uses the same condition as the preceding **if** statement, but unlike **if**, it executes only if the condition is *not* true.

11 Press **Enter** (Windows) or **Return** (Mac) to go to the next line, and type the following:

```
{
    event.target.y -= 100;
    jumping = true;
}
```

When the initial condition is **false** (the snowboarder is not jumping), Flash will bypass the **if** statement and run the **else** statement. When the **else** statement is executed, the condition is set back to **true**.

```
Actions - Frame ×                                          Script Assist  ?
 1   var jumping:Boolean = false;
 2
 3   boarder_mc.addEventListener(MouseEvent.CLICK, onClick);
 4
 5   function onClick(event:MouseEvent):void
 6   {
 7       if(jumping)
 8       {
 9           event.target.y += 100;
10           jumping = false;
11       }
12       else
13       {
14           event.target.y -= 100;
15           jumping = true;
16       }
17   }
18
19   boarder_mc.buttonMode = true;

  actions : 1
Line 16 of 19, Col 3
```

12 Press **Ctrl+Enter** (Windows) or **Cmd+Return** (Mac) to test the movie. When the preview window opens, click the snowboarder two or three times.

Click once, and the snowboarder jumps up 100 pixels. Click again, and he jumps down. Click to your heart's content!

13 Close the preview window, and close **Writing.fla**. You don't need to save your changes.

That's how to write a conditional statement. You don't always need an **else**; you can use **if** on its own, but it's great to be able to have an alternate set of instructions if the condition turn out not to be true.

In the next exercise, you'll build on these concepts by working with conditional operators. Conditional operators help you evaluate whether an expression is true.

2 | Using Conditional Operators

In this exercise, you'll write a conditional statement using conditional operators. Conditional operators are used to compare one expression with another and determine which is true. Operators become conditional when you use comparison or logical operators within conditional statements. You saw a brief overview of operators in Chapter 3, *"Using and Writing Functions,"* but this exercise will allow you to explore these kinds of operators in detail.

1 Choose **File > Open**, and open **Using_Operators.fla** from the **chap_06** folder.

In this exercise, you'll use a conditional operator to compare the larger instance of mc_Boarder to the smaller instance. The larger snowboarder already has an instance name, boarder_mc, but the smaller one doesn't. Before you dive into the ActionScript, you'll want to change this.

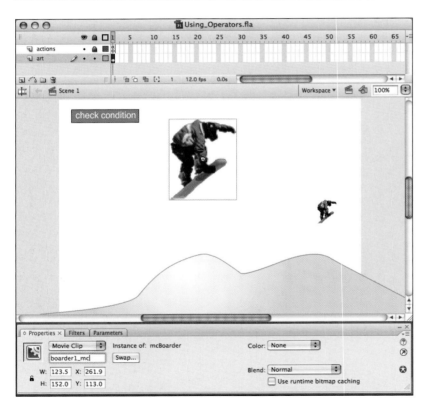

2 Choose **Window > Properties > Properties** to open the **Property inspector**, if it is not already open. Select the **Selection** tool in the **Tools** panel, and click the smaller snowboarder. In the **Property inspector**, type **boarder2_mc** in the **Instance Name** field. Click the larger snowboarder on the **Stage**, and change the instance name to **boarder1_mc**.

3 Select **Frame 1** on the **actions** layer, and press **F9** (Windows) or **Opt+F9** (Mac) to open the **Actions** panel.

This code contains an event listener that is listening to the other object on the Stage, the button called check_mc. There is an event handler, but it doesn't do anything yet.

```
1   check_mc.addEventListener(MouseEvent.CLICK, onClick);
2
3   function onClick(event:MouseEvent):void
4   {
5
6   }
7
8   check_mc.buttonMode = true;
```

actions : 1
Line 8 of 8, Col 28

---

4 Position your cursor on Line 5 (between the curly braces of the **onClick()** function), press the **Tab** key once to indent the line, and type the following:

```
if(boarder1_mc.height > boarder2_mc.height)
{
   trace("Boarder1 is taller than boarder2!")
}
```

Here you are using an **if** statement to evaluate whether the condition in the parentheses is true. The greater than sign is the conditional operator. This operator returns a true value if expression 1 (the expression on the left side of the statement) is greater than expression 2 (the expression on the right). If the condition is true, the trace statement will run.

```
1   check_mc.addEventListener(MouseEvent.CLICK, onClick);
2
3   function onClick(event:MouseEvent):void
4   {
5       if(boarder1_mc.height > boarder2_mc.height)
6       {
7           trace("Boarder1 is taller than boarder2!")
8       }
9   }
10
11  check_mc.buttonMode = true;
```

actions : 1
Line 8 of 11, Col 3

Height, by the way, means the height of the object, not its y position on the Stage.

---

5 Press **Ctrl+Enter** (Windows) or **Cmd+Return** (Mac) to test the movie. When the movie window opens, click the **check condition** button.

As soon as you click the button, the Output panel will open with your message, "Boarder1 is taller than boarder2!" No surprise there, but at least you know the **if** statement is working.

Now you'll add an **else** statement.

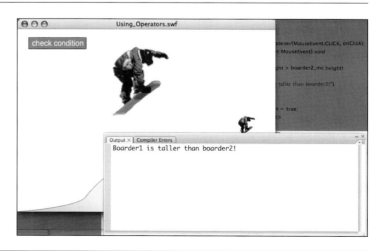

6 Close the movie window and the **Output** panel, and return to Flash. In the **Actions** panel, position your cursor at the end of Line 8 (after the closed curly brace), press **Enter** (Windows) or **Return** (Mac) to insert a new line, and type the following:

```
else
{
    trace("Condition is not true.");
}
```

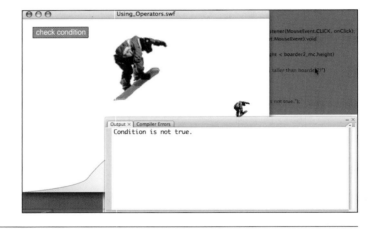

```
1    check_mc.addEventListener(MouseEvent.CLICK, onClick);
2
3    function onClick(event:MouseEvent):void
4    {
5        if(boarder1_mc.height > boarder2_mc.height)
6        {
7            trace("Boarder1 is taller than boarder2!")
8        }
9        else
10        {
11            trace("Condition is not true.");
12        }
13    }
14
15    check_mc.buttonMode = true;
```

Line 12 of 15, Col 3

---

7 Select the greater than sign (>) on Line 5, and change it to a less than sign (<).

Now you can test the **else** statement. If you were to test the movie without changing the operator, the **if** trace statement would still show up because the condition would still be true!

---

8 Press **Ctrl+Enter** (Windows) or **Cmd+Return** (Mac) to test the movie. When the movie window opens, click the **check condition** button.

As soon as you click the button, the Output panel will open with your other message, "Condition is not true." Now you know the **else** statement is working.

Let's try a different operator.

---

9 Close the movie window and the **Output** panel, and return to Flash. In the **Actions** panel, position your cursor in the condition on Line 5, and change both instances of the word **height** to **rotation**. Change the less than sign to **==** (two equals signs).

If you recall, neither of the snowboarders is rotated. This conditional statement will check whether the rotation is equal. Remember to use two equal signs, which compares the values, not a single equals sign. A single equals sign actually makes the values equal, which wouldn't make much sense in the context of this conditional statement.

```
1    check_mc.addEventListener(MouseEvent.CLICK, onClick);
2
3    function onClick(event:MouseEvent):void
4    {
5        if(boarder1_mc.rotation == boarder2_mc.rotation)
6        {
7            trace("Boarder1 is taller than boarder2!")
8        }
9        else
10        {
11            trace("Condition is not true.");
12        }
13    }
14
15    check_mc.buttonMode = true;
```

Line 5 of 15, Col 49

10 Change the trace statement on Line 7 to read as follows:

```
trace("The rotation is the same.")
```

11 Press **Ctrl+Enter** (Windows) or **Cmd+Return** (Mac) to test the movie. When the movie window opens, click the **check condition** button.

As soon as you click the button, the Output panel will open with the new message, "The rotation is the same."

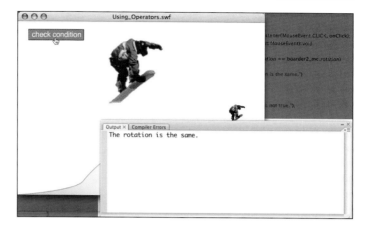

12 Close the movie window and the **Output** panel, and return to Flash. Minimize the **Actions** panel. Select the **Free Transform** tool in the **Tools** panel, and rotate **boarder1_mc**.

13 Select **Frame 1** on the **actions** layer, and maximize the **Actions** panel.

As is, the code still works. If the snowboarders' rotations are the same, a message will pop up to that effect. If they are not the same, the **else** statement will run, and a message will pop up saying the condition is not true. Let's have the snowboarders actually do something.

14 Position your cursor after the trace statement on Line 11, press **Enter** (Windows) or **Return** (Mac), and type the following:

```
boarder1_mc.rotation = boarder2_mc.rotation;
```

So if the rotation of the boarders is different, you'll still get the "not true" message in the Output panel, but then the rotation of the first snowboarder will change to match boarder2_mc.

15 Press **Ctrl+Enter** (Windows) or **Cmd+Return** (Mac) to test the movie. When the movie window opens, click the **check condition** button.

As soon as you click the button, the Output panel will open with the message "Condition is not true," and boarder1_mc rights himself.

---

16 Close the preview window, and close **Using_Operators.fla**. You don't need to save your changes.

And that's how to write a conditional statement using operators. There are plenty more to choose from.

In the next exercise, you'll set up another type of conditional statement, one that contains alternate conditions.

VIDEO: | **operators.mov**

For a list and description of all the different conditional operators, check out **operators.mov** in the **videos** folder on the **ActionScript HOT CD-ROM**.

3 | Setting Up Alternate Conditions

In this exercise, you'll learn how to set up a conditional statement to check for alternate conditions. Basically, checking alternate conditions just means checking if more than one condition is true.

1 Choose **File > Open**, and navigate to the **chap_06** folder you copied to your desktop. Select **Alternate.fla**, and click **Open**.

Alternate.fla is similar to the file you started with in the previous exercise, Using_Operators.fla. It has two instances of mcBoarder on the Stage, named boarder1_mc and boarder2_mc, along with a check condition button. In this file, boarder1 is rotated.

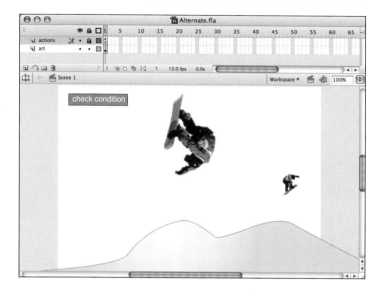

2 Select **Frame 1** in the **actions** layer, and press **F9** (Windows) or **Opt+F9** (Mac) to open the **Actions** panel, if it is not already open.

This is the same code you started with in the previous exercise: an event listener, an empty event handler, and a statement that changes the button's **ButtonMode** to **true**.

3 Position your cursor on Line 5 between the curly braces of the event handler, and type the following:

```
if(boarder1_mc.rotation ==
boarder2_mc.rotation)
{
   trace("Condition 1 is true.");
}
```

This will check whether boarder1's rotation is equal to boarder2's. If the condition is true, the trace statement will run. Now you'll add a second, or alternate, condition.

```
check_mc.addEventListener(MouseEvent.CLICK, onClick);

function onClick(event:MouseEvent):void
{
    if(boarder1_mc.rotation == boarder2_mc.rotation)
    {
        trace("Condition 1 is true.");
    }
}

check_mc.buttonMode = true;
```

4 Press **Enter** (Windows) or **Return** (Mac) to insert a new line, and type the following:

```
else if(boarder1_mc.alpha ==
boarder2_mc.alpha)
{
    trace("Condition 2 is true.");
}
```

else if instructs Flash to check whether the second condition is true. Unlike **else**, **else if** requires that you enter a condition.

If the **else if** condition is true, the second trace message will run.

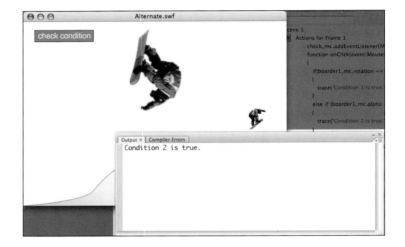

5 Press **Ctrl+Enter** (Windows) or **Cmd+Return** (Mac) to test the movie. When the preview window opens, click the **check condition** button.

The Output panel opens with the message "Condition 2 is true." So now you know the alpha values, or the transparency of these objects, are equal.

6 Close the movie window and the **Output** panel. In the **Actions** panel, change the == operator after the word **alpha** on Line 9 to the **!=** operator.

!= is the operator for "not equal to." So if boarder1's alpha is not equal to boarder2's, then the condition is true.

7 Position your cursor after the closed curly brace on Line 12, press **Enter** (Windows) or **Return** (Mac) to insert a new line, and type the following:

```
else if(boarder1_mc.y < boarder2_mc.y)
{
  trace("Condition 3 is true.");
}
```

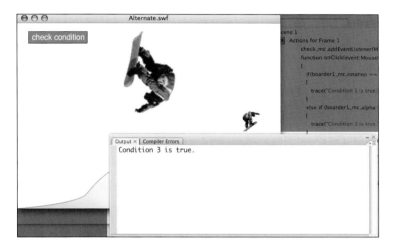

8 Press **Ctrl+Enter** (Windows) or **Cmd+Return** (Mac) to test the movie. When the preview window opens, click the **check condition** button.

The Output panel opens with the message "Condition 3 is true." So now you know that the Y value of boarder 1 is less than boarder2. It's kind of confusing, since boarder1 is actually higher, but remember that the Y value is measured from the top of the Stage, not the bottom.

Only one of the conditions is true and it happens to be the last condition. But the thing about using **else if** to check for alternate conditions is that once it finds a true condition, it stops checking. If you wanted to check for multiple true conditions, you'd have to use compound conditions. There's more about compound conditions in the next exercise.

For now, let's stick with alternate conditions. Now, a situation might arise when you have alternate conditions, but you want to check for the condition that is false. For example, let's say you want to compare different properties of the two snowboarders and be alerted only when one of the expressions was not equal. Remember you can check for (and act on) a false condition using the **else** conditional statement.

9 Close the movie window and the **Output** panel. In the **Actions** panel, select the less than sign (<) on Line 13, and change it to a greater than sign (>).

Now none of the conditions is true.

10 Position your cursor at the end of Line 16 after the closed curly brace, and press **Enter** (Windows) or **Return** (Mac) to insert a new line. Type the following:

```
else
{
  trace("No conditions are
true.");
}
```

By adding the statement at the end of the list of alternate conditions, Flash will check them all before running the **else** trace statement.

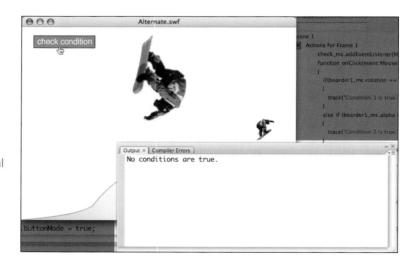

```
1   check_mc.addEventListener(MouseEvent.CLICK, onClick);
2
3   function onClick(event:MouseEvent):void
4   {
5       if(boarder1_mc.rotation == boarder2_mc.rotation)
6       {
7           trace("Condition 1 is true.");
8       }
9       else if (boarder1_mc.alpha != boarder2_mc.alpha)
10      {
11          trace("Condition 2 is true.");
12      }
13      else if(boarder1_mc.y > boarder2_mc.y)
14      {
15          trace("Condition 3 is true.");
16      }
17      else
18      {
19          trace("No conditions are true.");
20      }
21  }
22
23  check_mc.buttonMode = true;
```

Line 20 of 23, Col 3

11 Press **Ctrl+Enter** (Windows) or **Cmd+Return** (Mac) to test the movie. When the preview window opens, click the **check condition** button.

The Output panel opens with the message "No conditions are true." This is just an example, but you can see how useful alternate conditions can be. You can set functions to execute or change properties exactly when and where you need to by checking as many conditions as you need.

No conditions are true.

12 Close the preview window, and close **Alternate.fla**. You don't need to save your changes.

4 | Writing Compound Conditions

In this exercise, you'll learn how to write compound conditional statements.

---

1 Choose **File > Open**, and open **Compound.fla** from the **chap_06** folder you copied to your desktop.

To understand a compound conditional statement, first you have to understand the anatomy of a conditional statement.

---

2 Select **Frame 1** on the **actions** layer, and press **F9** (Windows) or **Opt+F9** (Mac) to open the **Actions** panel, if it is not already open.

This file contains code similar to what you have been working with in the previous several exercises. Lines 5–8 contain an **if** conditional statement. The condition is contained in the parentheses. The condition uses the operator == to test whether the two properties are equal.

However, let's say you wanted to run the

```
Actions - Frame ×
                                                    Script Assist
 1    check_mc.addEventListener(MouseEvent.CLICK, onClick);
 2
 3    function onClick(event:MouseEvent):void
 4    {
 5        if(boarder1_mc.rotation == boarder2_mc.rotation)
 6        {
 7            trace("condition is true");
 8        }
 9    }
10
11    check_mc.buttonMode = true;
```

```
actions : 1
Line 11 of 11, Col 28
```

trace statement in this code not only when the snowboarders' rotations were equal but when both their rotation and opacity values were equal. All conditions would have to be true before the trace statement would run. Using alternate conditions to do this would require a lot of fancy footwork. In this case, it would be a lot easier to use a compound conditional statement.

A compound conditional statement is nothing more than a conditional statement that contains more than one expression in the condition. You use AND operators and OR operators to put more than one expression in a condition. The conditional statement checks whether all expressions are true before running a function.

---

3 Position your cursor in the expression on Line 5 directly after **boarder2_mc.rotation**, and press **Enter** (Windows) or **Return** (Mac) to insert a new line.

Note: You do not have to insert new lines to write compound conditional statements, but it does make the code easier to read.

---

4 Enter two ampersands (**&&**) on Line 6.

&& is the symbol for the AND operator.

---

5 Press the **spacebar** once, and type the following:

```
boarder1_mc.alpha == boarder2_mc.alpha
```

These two lines of code mean that if the first expression is true *and* the second expression is true, then the result of the condition will equal true. Now you'll type a statement describing what happens if this condition is false.

```
1   check_mc.addEventListener(MouseEvent.CLICK, onClick);
2
3   function onClick(event:MouseEvent):void
4   {
5       if(boarder1_mc.rotation == boarder2_mc.rotation
6          && boarder1_mc.alpha == boarder2_mc.alphd)
7       {
8           trace("condition is true");
9       }
10  }
11
12  check_mc.buttonMode = true;
```

Line 6 of 12, Col 46

6 Position your cursor at the end of Line 9 after the closed curly brace, and press **Enter** (Windows) or **Return** (Mac) to go to the next line. Type the following:

```
else
{
  trace("Condition is false.");
}
```

```
1   check_mc.addEventListener(MouseEvent.CLICK, onClick);
2
3   function onClick(event:MouseEvent):void
4   {
5       if(boarder1_mc.rotation == boarder2_mc.rotation
6          && boarder1_mc.alpha == boarder2_mc.alpha)
7       {
8           trace("condition is true");
9       }
10      else
11      {
12          trace("Condition is false.");
13      }
14  }
15
```

Line 13 of 16, Col 3

7 Press **Ctrl+Enter** (Windows) or **Cmd+Return** (Mac) to test the movie. When the movie window opens, click the **check condition** button.

The Output panel will open with the message "Condition is false." The reason you get this message is because although the alpha values of the two snowboarders are equal, the rotation values are different.

ActionScript 3.0 for Adobe Flash CS3 Professional : H·O·T

8 Close the movie window and the **Output** panel.

The other way to write a compound condition is using the OR operator.

---

9 Select the two ampersands on Line 6, and press **Delete**. In their place, type two pipes (||).

|| is the symbol for the OR operator. To create the pipes, hold the Shift key, and press the backslash key twice. This condition now means if the first expression is true OR the second expression is true, then the result of the condition will equal true.

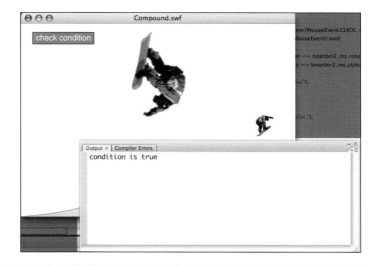

```
Actions - Frame ×
                                                    Script Assist
1   check_mc.addEventListener(MouseEvent.CLICK, onClick);
2
3   function onClick(event:MouseEvent):void
4   {
5       if(boarder1_mc.rotation == boarder2_mc.rotation
6           || boarder1_mc.alpha == boarder2_mc.alpha)
7       {
8           trace("condition is true");
9       }
10      else
11      {
12          trace("Condition is false.");
13      }
14  }
15
```

actions : 1
Line 6 of 16, Col 7

---

10 Press **Ctrl+Enter** (Windows) or **Cmd+Return** (Mac) to test the movie. When the movie window opens, press the **check condition** button.

The Output panel will open with your first trace statement, "condition is true." The reason you get this message is because even though the rotation is different, the alpha values of the two snowboarders are the same. Only one expression needs to be true when you use the OR operator.

---

11 Close the movie window and the **Output** panel. Save and close **Compound.fla**.

That's how to write compound conditions. In the next exercise, you'll create a code loop.

Understanding Loops

The illustration shown here is from a movie I created in Flash. It's just a static image with multiple instances of the snowboarder placed at regular intervals across the **Stage**, tracing a jump from the left side of the **Stage** to the right. Each instance of the snowboarder is slightly more opaque than the last.

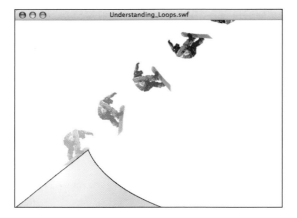

If you were to create this movie using the design mode in Flash, you'd have to drag an instance on the **Stage**, reduce the alpha in the **Property**

inspector, rotate it using the **Free Transform** tool, then drag another instance to a different location, reduce the alpha, change the rotation, and so on, and so forth. You might make it a little easier on yourself by copying and pasting, but you'd still have to manually increment the properties of each boarder and adjust the spacing. It would be very tedious to re-create this file in design mode.

I avoided all that by creating a loop that automates the spacing, the alpha, and the rotation changes of the snowboarders for me. A **loop** is a function in ActionScript that runs as many times as you specify. In this loop, changes to the snowboarders are incremented the same amount each time, relative to the last instance of the snowboarder. A loop allows me to control exactly how many times the function runs, so I can easily go back and make a simple change to my ActionScript to add or subtract snowboarders. Loops are powerful tools that make repetitive tasks such as these, which would be monotonous in design mode, a snap.

In the next exercise, you'll learn how to write a loop of your own.

5 | Creating a Code Loop

In this exercise, you'll learn how to create a code loop.

---

1 Choose **File > New**, and choose **Flash File (ActionScript 3.0)**.

---

2 Double-click the first layer in the new document, and rename it **actions**. Click the dot underneath the **lock** icon to lock the **actions** layer.

The Library panel will be empty. But don't worry; you'll get to that.

---

3 Select **Frame 1** on the **actions** layer, and press **F9** (Windows) or **Opt+F9** (Mac) to open the **Actions** panel, if it is not already open.

---

4 Position your cursor on Line 1, and type the word **for**.

There are different kinds of loop statements, but **for** is the keyword you'll use most often to write a loop statement.

---

5 After **for**, type the following:

(var i:Number = 0;

This should look familiar to you. You're just creating a new variable, or placeholder, named **i** that is the data type Number. You are declaring the initial value of **i** to be 0.

i stands for index. Index is the number of times the loop will run. When you start to look at other authors' code, you'll notice that **i** is often used for the index variable in loops. You don't have to use **i**, but it is common practice among ActionScript developers.

---

6 Next type:

i < 20;

i < 20 is kind of like a condition. It means the loop will run as long as **i** is less than 20. Now you'll write what will happen as long as this condition is true.

---

7 Type the following:

i++)

++ is a mathematical operator that means to increment the value of a variable or number by 1. So when this code runs the first time, **i** will equal 0. Because **i** is still less than 20, it will run again, and after the second time it runs, **i** will be equal to 1. The third time it runs, **i** will be equal to 2, and so on, all the way up to 19. At that point, it cannot run again because otherwise the condition would be false.

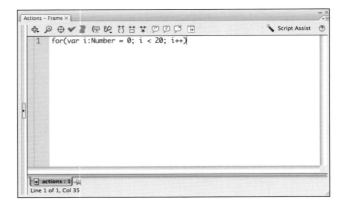

Now, by itself the loop doesn't do anything but increment the index variable. You still need write the code to make something happen when the loop runs.

---

8 Press **Enter** (Windows) or **Return** (Mac) to insert a new line, and type the following:

```
{
   trace(i);
}
```

You are telling Flash that every time the codes run, trace the value of **i**. The trace statement will run over and over again until the loop condition, **i < 20**, is no longer true.

Make sure not to enter any quotation marks in the trace statement. You use quotation marks only around strings.

---

9 Press **Ctrl+Enter** (Windows) or **Cmd+Return** (Mac) to test the movie.

The results of the trace statement should appear in the Output panel. The numbers 0–19 appear, indicating that the code ran once at 0 and over and over again until i was equal to 19. At that point, the code stopped.

That's a way to write a simple **for** loop statement. You can change the index to run any number of times you want by changing the value in the condition. Replace the trace statement with a function, and you can run that function as many times as you want.

In the next exercise, you'll use your knowledge of loop statements to drag instances of a symbol from the Library panel and to the Stage at run time.

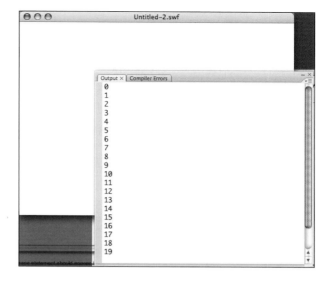

10 Close the preview window, and close the Flash file. You don't need to save your changes.

6 | Using a Loop to Generate Instances of a Class

In this exercise, you'll use a code loop to drag instances of a class into your movie at run time.

---

1 Choose **File > Open**, and navigate to the **chap_06** folder you copied to your desktop. Select **Generating_Instances.fla**, and click **Open**.

Before you get started coding, you have to take a couple of steps to set up your Flash file in order to drag symbol instances to the Stage.

---

2 Choose **Window > Library** to open the **Library** panel. **Right-click** (Windows) or **Ctrl-click** (Mac) **mcBoarder**, and choose **Linkage** in the contextual menu.

---

3 In the **Linkage Properties** dialog box, select **Export for ActionScript**. Click **OK** to close the dialog box.

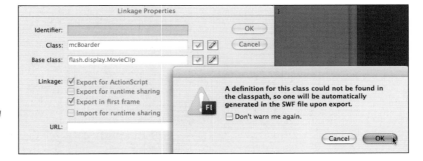

As you learned in the previous chapter, *"Understanding Classes,"* if you don't have an instance of the class already on the Stage, you need to make sure to export the class at run time in order to communicate with it via ActionScript. The class name, `mcBoarder`, will be the name you will use to call the object out of your Library panel.

After you click OK, a message will appear letting you know that Flash will write the class definition for you.

---

4 Click **OK** to close the warning dialog box.

---

5 Select **Frame 1** on the **actions** layer, and press **F9** (Windows) or **Opt+F9** (Mac) to open the **Actions** panel, if it is not already open.

You're going to create the **for** loop, but first you need to create a new variable to hold the mcBoarder class.

---

6 On the first line of the **Actions** pane, type the following:

`var _boarder:mcBoarder;`

boarder will be the placeholder name for the instances of mcBoarder you'll create in the loop. Notice that instead of one of the prebuilt data types, you used the class name as the data type for this variable.

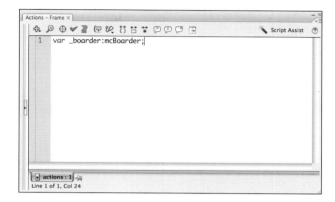

---

7 Press **Enter** (Windows) or **Return** (Mac) twice, and type the following:

`for(var i:Number = 0; i < 6; i++)`

This is the same syntax you used in the previous exercise. The only difference is that this code will run six times, instead of twenty. Now you'll write the function that runs when the **i < 6** condition is true.

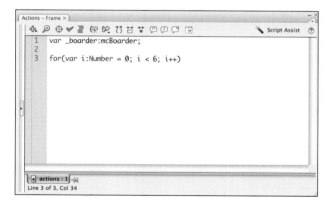

---

8 Press **Enter** (Windows) or **Return** (Mac) to insert a new line, and type the following:

```
{
    _boarder = new mcBoarder();
```

This statement will create a new instance of mcBoarder every time the loop runs.

If you recall from the previous chapter, although you've created the instance, it won't be visible until you add it to the movie's display list. To add an object to the display list, you use the `addChild()` function.

---

9 Press **Enter** (Windows) or **Return** (Mac) to insert a new line, and type the following:

```
    addChild(_boarder);
}
```

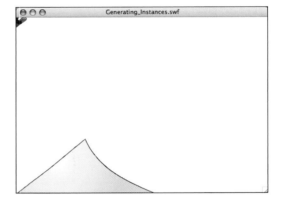

10 Press **Ctrl+Enter** (Windows) or **Cmd+Return** (Mac) to test the movie.

See the snowboarders? There's one floating in the top-left corner of the Flash Player window. Where are the rest? Here's a neat little trick to check your work.

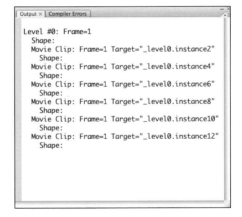

11 Without closing the player window, go to Flash, and choose **Debug > List Objects**.

The Output panel will open with the results of the debug report. As you can see, there are six instances of your class. Because you didn't specify positioning, all six instances were added to the 0,0 position on the Stage.

The Output panel also lists the instance name for each boarder. Because you didn't specify instance names, Flash creates generic ones for you.

12 Close the player window and the **Output** panel. Save your changes, and leave **Generating_Instances.fla** open for the next exercise.

Now that you know how to use a loop to drag multiple instances of a class out of your Library panel, you can work on finessing the position and appearance of those instances. In the next exercise, you'll do just that!

7 | Placing Instances Created by a Loop

In this exercise, you'll use a code loop to drag instances of a class into your movie at run time.

---

1 If you just completed Exercise 6, **Generating_Instances.fla** should still be open. If not, complete Exercise 6, and return to this exercise. Make sure the **Actions** panel is open.

The code you have written thus far starts with a **for** loop that creates six instances of `mcBoarder` and adds them to the movie's display list. However, it doesn't specify how or where they are placed in the movie. As you saw in the previous exercise, Flash places them on top of each other in the default location in the upper-left corner of the movie. This is not quite the effect you want.

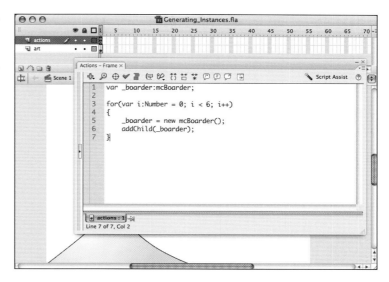

In the following steps, you'll modify the X and Y properties of the snowboarders so you can see the six instances.

---

2 Position your cursor at the end of Line 6 (after `addChild();`), press **Enter** (Windows) or **Return** (Mac) to insert a new line, and type the following:

`_boarder.x = i * 75;`

Using the `i` variable in this expression allows you to place the instances dynamically. I will be using a different value every time the codes runs, starting at 0 and ending at 5. So, the first time, x will be equal to 0 times 75, or 0. The second time it runs, x will be equal to 1 times 75, and so on.

3 Press **Ctrl+Enter** (Windows) or **Cmd+Return** (Mac) to test the movie.

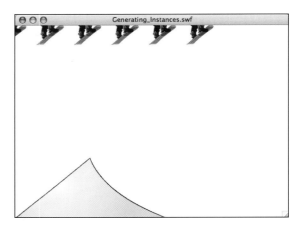

Ta-da! Now you can distinguish between each of the six instances of the snowboarder on the Stage. Flash has spaced the instances 75 pixels apart on the X axis.

Now let's make the snowboarder jump the slope. This is slightly more complicated. If you used the same formula to modify the snowboarders' Y properties, you'd end up with only one snowboarder on the Stage. The rest of them would be up in the air, above the player window. The first question to ask is, how do you determine the first boarder's starting position? The fastest and easiest way is to simply drag an instance from the Library panel.

---

4 Close the movie window, and return to Flash. Minimize the **Actions** panel.

---

5 Select **Frame 1** on the **art** layer in the **Timeline**. Click and drag an instance of **mcBoarder** from the **Library** panel to the **Stage**. Place the snowboarder on the top of the slope, as shown in the illustration here.

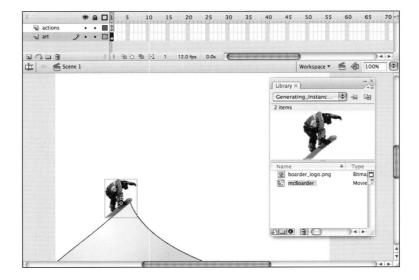

ActionScript 3.0 for Adobe Flash CS3 Professional : H•O•T

6 Choose **Window >
Properties > Properties** to open
the **Property inspector**, if it's not
already open. Select the snowboarder on the **Stage**, and note
the X and Y values of the instance.

Write down the values if you need to do so. It's important to get them correct in the ActionScript,
although they don't have to be exact. Round up to the nearest pixel for simplicity's sake (for example,
267.1 should just be 267).

---

7 Select the snowboarder, and press **Delete** to remove it from the Stage.

The snowboarder was just a ruler to check your initial X and Y values. Now you'll enter them in your
code.

Instead of defining the *x* and *y* starting positions in the loop, you'll need to create variables to define
these properties for the entire class. These variables should be grouped with the boarder variable at the
top of the code, outside the loop. Then you can increment the properties however you want in the loop.

---

8 Maximize your **Actions** panel. Position your
cursor after Line 1, press **Enter** (Windows) or
Return (Mac) to insert a new line, and type the
following:

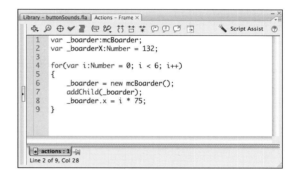

```
var _boarderX:Number = 132;
```

132 was the X value of the boarder instance
I placed on my Stage in Step 5. Yours may
be different.

---

9 Press **Enter** (Windows) or **Return** (Mac) to insert a new line, and type the following:

```
var _boarderY:Number = 267;
```

Now you'll use the new variables, **boarderX** and **boarderY**, instead of **i** to increment the *x* and *y* position
values in the loop.

---

10 Select Line 9 of your code, and change it so it reads as follows:

```
_boarder.x = _boarderX;
```

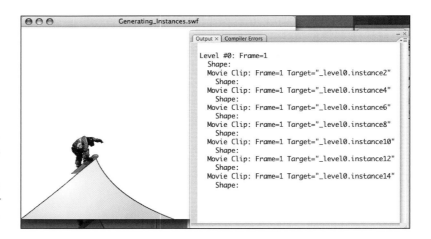

```
1    var _boarder:mcBoarder;
2    var _boarderX:Number = 132;
3    var _boarderY:Number = 267;
4
5    for(var i:Number = 0; i < 6; i++)
6    {
7        _boarder = new mcBoarder();
8        addChild(_boarder);
9        _boarder.x = _boarderX;
10   }
```

Line 9 of 10, Col 25

11 Press **Enter** (Windows) or **Return** (Mac) to insert a new line, and type the following:

```
_boarder.y = _boarderY;
```

12 Press **Ctrl+Enter** (Windows) or **Cmd+Return** (Mac) to test the movie. Choose **Debug > List Objects** to confirm six instances of **mcBoarder** have been created.

There you go. All the boarders are positioned at the top of the slope. Now, to increment their x and y positions, all you have to do is add pixels every time the loop runs.

```
Generating_Instances.swf

Output | Compiler Errors

Level #0: Frame=1
    Shape:
    Movie Clip: Frame=1 Target="_level0.instance2"
    Shape:
    Movie Clip: Frame=1 Target="_level0.instance4"
    Shape:
    Movie Clip: Frame=1 Target="_level0.instance6"
    Shape:
    Movie Clip: Frame=1 Target="_level0.instance8"
    Shape:
    Movie Clip: Frame=1 Target="_level0.instance10"
    Shape:
    Movie Clip: Frame=1 Target="_level0.instance12"
    Shape:
    Movie Clip: Frame=1 Target="_level0.instance14"
    Shape:
```

13 Close the movie window, and return to the **Actions** panel. Position your cursor at the end of Line 10, press **Enter** (Windows) or **Return** (Mac) to insert a new line, and type the following:

```
_boarderX += 75;
_boarderY -= 75;
```

Using the plus and minus operators before the equals sign adds or subtracts 75 from the current values.

```
1    var _boarder:mcBoarder;
2    var _boarderX:Number = 132;
3    var _boarderY:Number = 267;
4
5    for(var i:Number = 0; i < 6; i++)
6    {
7        _boarder = new mcBoarder();
8        addChild(_boarder);
9        _boarder.x = _boarderX;
10       _boarder.y = _boarderY;
11       _boarderX += 75;
12       _boarderY -= 75;
13   }
```

Line 3 of 13, Col 28

14 Press **Ctrl+Enter** (Windows) or **Cmd+Return** (Mac) to test the movie again.

Now each instance of the boarder is 100 pixels above and to the right of the previous instance. You can use whatever increment you want in your own code; 75 just seems to work with the dimensions of the movie window.

But why stop here? Let's make the snowboarder do a back flip. First you need to create a new variable to hold the **rotation** property.

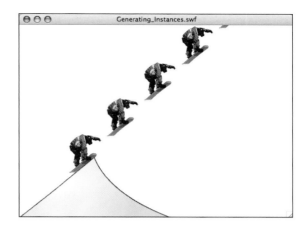

15 Close the movie window, and return to the **Actions** panel. Position your cursor at the end of Line 3, press **Enter** (Windows) or **Return** (Mac) to insert a new line, and type the following:

```
var _boarderR:Number = 0;
```

You start with 0 because the first time the code runs, you don't want the snowboarder to rotate at all. He's still on the ground, after all, and that would be a fall, not a flip. Now to add the rotation to the loop.

```
1   var _boarder:mcBoarder;
2   var _boarderX:Number = 132;
3   var _boarderY:Number = 267;
4   var _boarderR:Number = 0;
5
6   for(var i:Number = 0; i < 6; i++)
7   {
8       _boarder = new mcBoarder();
9       addChild(_boarder);
10      _boarder.x = _boarderX;
11      _boarder.y = _boarderY;
12      _boarderX += 75;
13      _boarderY -= 75;
14  }
```

16 Position your cursor at the end of Line 11, press **Enter** (Windows) or **Return** (Mac) to insert a new line, and type the following:

```
_boarder.rotation = _boarderR;
```

As is, the boarder's rotation won't change, because you've already defined it as 0. You need to add or subtract something from it.

```
1   var _boarder:mcBoarder;
2   var _boarderX:Number = 132;
3   var _boarderY:Number = 267;
4   var _boarderR:Number = 0;
5
6   for(var i:Number = 0; i < 6; i++)
7   {
8       _boarder = new mcBoarder();
9       addChild(_boarder);
10      _boarder.x = _boarderX;
11      _boarder.y = _boarderY;
12      _boarder.rotation = _boarderR;
13      _boarderX += 75;
14      _boarderY -= 75;
15  }
```

17 Position your cursor at the end of Line 14, press **Enter** (Windows) or **Return** (Mac) to insert a new line, and type the following:

```
_boarderR -= 45;
```

You're subtracting 45, degrees that is, so that the snowboarder will flip backward.

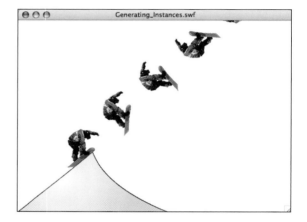

```
Library - buttonSounds.fla   Actions - Frame ×
1   var _boarder:mcBoarder;
2   var _boarderX:Number = 132;
3   var _boarderY:Number = 267;
4   var _boarderR:Number = 0;
5
6   for(var i:Number = 0; i < 6; i++)
7   {
8       _boarder = new mcBoarder();
9       addChild(_boarder);
10      _boarder.x = _boarderX;
11      _boarder.y = _boarderY;
12      _boarder.rotation = _boarderR;
13      _boarderX += 75;
14      _boarderY += 75;
15      _boarderR -= 45;
16  }
```

actions : 1
Line 15 of 16, Col 18

18 Press **Ctrl+Enter** (Windows) or **Cmd+Return** (Mac) to test the movie again.

Each instance of the boarder is now rotated -45 degrees from the last instance. If you wanted to modify the alpha, the scale, or any other property of the class, you'd use the same format. First create a variable to hold the initial value of the property, and then, inside the loop, define the property as equal to the variable. Last, create a statement that increases or decreases the value of the variable, using a compound assignment operator (+, −, /, or * plus the equal sign). That's how easy it is to place and modify multiple instances of a class using ActionScript.

Generating_Instances.swf

19 Close the preview window and the **Output** panel, and close **Generating_Instances.fla**. You don't need to save your changes.

Congratulations! You have completed another chapter, which means you're already halfway through this book and that much further on your way to programming ActionScript. In the next chapter, appropriately titled, *"Using Math—and Loving It,"* you'll learn how your high school algebra skills come in handy when you're writing ActionScript.

7

Using Math—and Loving It!

Are you one of those people who rolled their eyes during math class and asked, "When am I *ever* going to use this?" Then this chapter is for you. You're not alone. A lot of people don't like math. Luckily, Adobe Flash CS3 Professional makes math easy, practical, and, well, fun. In this chapter, you'll learn all about how to use the **Math** class, how to use mathematical operators, how to generate random numbers, and also how to round numbers. Then, you'll pool all these techniques and build a dice game in Flash.

Understanding the Math Class

The Math class is a built-in ActionScript class. The Math class simplifies a lot of the tasks you have learned in previous chapters by shortening and simplifying the code. It contains methods representing common mathematical functions, such as log, max/min, and round, and it contains properties representing mathematical constants, such as pi (3.14159… you get the idea). The Math class is in some ways a lot easier to code than other classes in ActionScript. Take the following code, for example:

```
var myInstance:MyClass = new myClass();
```

This code creates a variable named myInstance that is equal to a new instance of the class myClass. Creating a new instance of the Math class (that is, a number) is far simpler. To create a new instance of a random number, you simply type the following:

```
Math.random();
```

That's it! You can follow this with any one of the predefined methods or constants and perform calculations instantly. You'll dive into this in more detail in the next couple exercises.

1 | Using Basic Math Operators

In this exercise, you'll learn how to perform some basic math operations using—what else?—operators.

1 Choose **File > New**, and click **Flash File (ActionScript 3.0)** to start a new document.

2 Double-click the first layer in the new document, and rename it **actions**. Click the dot underneath the **lock** icon to lock the **actions** layer.

3 Select **Frame 1** on the **actions** layer, and press **F9** (Windows) or **Opt+F9** (Mac) to open the **Actions** panel, if it is not already open. Position your cursor on the first line, and type the following:

```
trace (2 + 4);
```

For simplicity's sake, you'll use trace statements to trace the results of the math in this exercise.

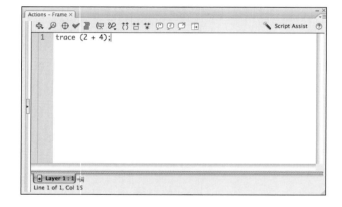

4 Press **Ctrl+Enter** (Windows) or **Cmd+Return** (Mac) to test the movie.

The Output panel will contain the result of your trace statement, 6. Note that Flash actually adds the values in the statement together at run time.

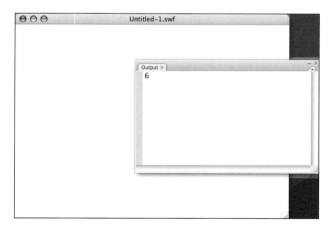

5 Close the movie window, and return to the **Actions** panel. Change the plus sign on Line 1 to an asterisk so that it reads as follows:

```
trace (2 * 4);
```

An asterisk is the sign for multiplication in ActionScript.

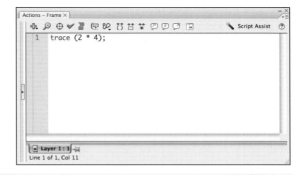

6 Press **Ctrl+Enter** (Windows) or **Cmd+Return** (Mac) to test the movie.

Now the Output panel contains the number 8. Flash multiplied the values in the statement.

7 Close the movie window, and return to the **Actions** panel. Change the plus sign on Line 1 to a slash so that it reads as follows:

```
trace (2 / 4);
```

A slash is the sign used for division in ActionScript.

8 Press **Ctrl+Enter** (Windows) or **Cmd+Return** (Mac) to test the movie again.

Now the Output panel contains the number 0.5. Flash divided the values in the statement. As you can see, math operations are not very complicated to code.

9 Close the movie window, and return to the **Actions** panel. Position your cursor after the 4 on Line 1, press the **spacebar**, and type **+ 1**.

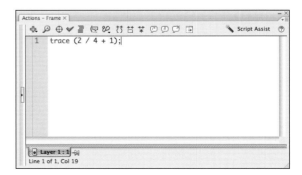

10 Press **Ctrl+Enter** (Windows) or **Cmd+Return** (Mac) to test the movie again.

Now the Output panel contains 1.5. Flash divides 2 by 4 before adding 1. Notice that Flash follows the typical math order of operations. If you need to brush up on the order of operations, check out the "Math Order of Operations" sidebar following this exercise.

11 Close the movie window, and return to the **Actions** panel. Close the file. You don't need to save your changes.

TIP:

Math Order of Operations

Flash follows the standard order of operations for arithmetic operations, used by grade-school students and mathematicians alike to ensure that everyone arrives at the same answer. There are four rules to the order of operations:

First, solve the operations inside parentheses, such as ().

Second, solve the exponents, such as 2^2.

Next, perform the multiplication and division operations, working from the left to the right side of the equation.

Last, perform any addition or subtraction, also working from left to right.

2 | Generating Random Numbers

In this exercise, you'll use a method of the `Math` class to generate a random number, called, appropriately enough, the `random()` method.

---

1 Choose **File > New**, and choose **Flash File (ActionScript 3.0)**.

---

2 Double-click the first layer in the new document, and rename it **actions**. Click the dot underneath the **lock** icon to lock the **actions** layer.

---

3 Select **Frame 1** on the **actions** layer, and press **F9** (Windows) or **Opt+F9** (Mac) to open the **Actions** panel, if it is not already open. Position your cursor on the first line, and type the following:

```
trace(Math.random());
```

You'll use another trace statement to check the results of the `Math` class's `random()` function.

---

4 Press **Ctrl+Enter** (Windows) or **Cmd+Return** (Mac) to test the movie.

The Output panel will open and contain a randomly generated number, between zero and 1, up to 1. Random numbers can contain, theoretically, an infinite number of decimal places, but they will never reach 1.0.

To generate more numbers, press Ctrl+Enter (Windows) or Cmd+Return (Mac) while the Flash Player is still open, and the results will appear in the Output panel.

Random numbers are great for generating random patterns or effects, such as the direction and speed of individual snowflakes in a snowstorm. These decimal digits aren't quite as useful as whole numbers, though. To generate a whole random number, you simply multiply the random method by 10.

---

5 Close the movie window and the **Output** panel, and return to Flash. In the **Actions** panel, position your cursor between the first and last closed curly brace on Line 1, and type *** 10**.

Now this statement will generate a random number between 0 and (but not including) 10.

6 Press **Ctrl+Enter** (Windows) or **Cmd+Return** (Mac) to test the movie.

The Output panel will open and contain a randomly generated whole number between 0 and 10. If your numbers don't match the ones in the illustrations shown here, don't worry—they shouldn't. Flash generates a string of numbers of indeterminate length, starting with a random "seed" number, and performs some complicated calculations to then further randomize the result. The chances that your number and mine would match are slim. Very, very slim. However, if they do match, send me a picture! That's one for the record books.

7 Close the preview window, and close the Flash file. You don't need to save your changes.

In the next exercise, you'll learn how to round a number up or down and about different rounding techniques.

3 | Rounding Numbers

In this exercise, you'll create a dice game using some of the math concepts you've learned throughout this chapter. You'll also learn a few new techniques for rounding numbers in ActionScript. You may be thinking, why would I want to round numbers in ActionScript? Let's say you wanted to generate a random number between 1 and 6 that you could paste on the face of a die like the one in this game. You could use the random number generator and multiply it by 10, but you would get a number between 0 and 9, not 1–6. To narrow your results, you would need to use a rounding technique. So let's get "rolling!"

1 Copy the **chap_07** folder from the **ActionScript HOT CD-ROM** to your desktop. Choose **File > Open**, and navigate to the **chap_07** folder you copied to your desktop. Select **Rounding.fla**, and click **Open**.

This file contains an instance of a movie clip representing a game die as well as a button called mc_Random labeled random.

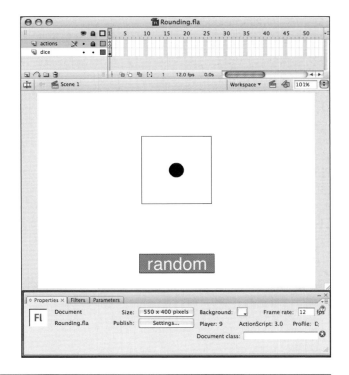

2 Select **Frame 1** on the **actions** layer, and press **F9** (Windows) or **Opt+F9** (Mac) to open the **Actions** panel, if it is not already open.

This code contains an event listener for the button random_mc and an empty event handler.

```
random_mc.addEventListener(MouseEvent.CLICK, onClick);

function onClick(event:MouseEvent):void
{
}
```

3 Press **Ctrl+Enter** (Windows) or **Cmd+Return** (Mac) to test the movie. When the preview window opens, click the **random** button.

The die "rolls" or changes faces automatically when the movie loads. The random button doesn't do anything yet.

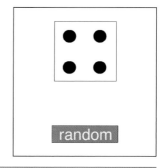

4 Close the player window, and minimize the **Actions** panel. Select the die on the **Stage**, and press **Delete** to remove it.

You'll add the die back once you've found a solution to generate a single number between 1 and 6.

5 Select **Frame 1** on the **actions** layer, and maximize the **Actions** panel. Position your cursor on Line 5 inside the event handler, and type the following:

```
trace(Math.random() * 6);
```

There are six sides to dice, right? By using 6 instead of 10 as the multiplier, the trace statement will generate a number between 0 and 6 (not including 6).

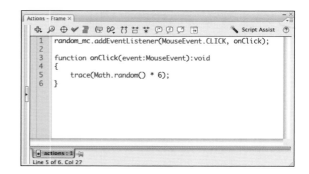

6 Press **Ctrl+Enter** (Windows) or **Cmd+Return** (Mac) to test the movie again. When the preview window opens, click the **random** button.

When you click the random button, the Output panel opens and shows the random number that was generated. Click the random button a couple more times to see how the results will vary.

These numbers have a couple of problems. Notice that numbers less than 1 are popping up. Also, I've never seen a die labeled 0.03859462345, have you?

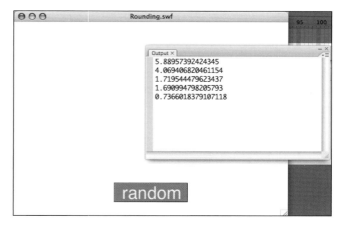

One way to resolve this is by adding 1 to the random function.

But this still leaves the problem of the trailing decimal. Other than the labeling issue this presents (how do you create 1.53 dots?), the design of this dice-rolling game calls for a `gotoAndStop()` function that stops the movie on the frame corresponding to the roll of the die. You can't stop a movie on Frame 1.03859432345 no more than you can stop it at 0.03859432345. So, you'll need to round the random number to a whole number. The first rounding technique you'll use is `Math.round()`.

7 Close the movie window and the **Output** panel. In the **Actions** panel, position your cursor on Line 5, and modify the trace statement so it reads as follows:

```
trace(Math.round(Math.random() * 6));
```

`Math.round()` uses the "nearest" rounding technique for rounding numbers up and down. Decimals from .0 to .4 are rounded down; decimals from .5 to .9 are rounded up.

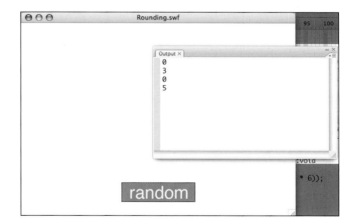

8 Press **Ctrl+Enter** (Windows) or **Cmd+Return** (Mac) to test the movie again. When the preview window opens, click the **random** button.

Excellent! The number that appears in the Output panel should be a whole number. Click the button a few more times to see how the results will vary.

If you click the button enough times, you'll notice that the range is between 0 and 6. Because 0 won't work, let's try a different technique.

9 Close the movie window and the **Output** panel. In the **Actions** panel, position your cursor on Line 5, and change the word **round** to **floor**.

`Math.floor()` uses the "round down" technique for rounding numbers. Decimals are rounded to the nearest whole number; for example, both 5.4 and 5.8 are rounded to 5.

10 Press **Ctrl+Enter** (Windows) or **Cmd+Return** (Mac) to test the movie again. When the preview window opens, click the **random** button at least 10 times.

The number that appears in the Output panel should still be a whole number, but you'll notice that the range is between 0 and 5. It looks like you need to round the other way. And what's the opposite of floor? Ceiling, of course.

11 Close the movie window and the **Output** panel. In the **Actions** panel, position your cursor on Line 5, and change the word **floor** to **ceil**.

Flash shortens ceiling to ceil. **Math.ceil()** uses the "round up" technique for rounding numbers. Decimals are rounded up to the nearest whole number; for example, both 5.4 and 5.8 are rounded to 6.

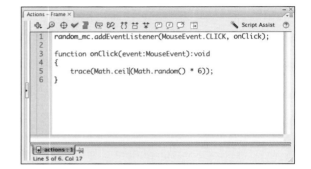

12 Press **Ctrl+Enter** (Windows) or **Cmd+Return** (Mac) to test the movie. When the preview window opens, click the **random** button at least 10 times.

You'll notice that the range is now between 1 and 6. It looks like we found a winning combination here.

13 Close the movie window and the **Output** panel. Minimize the **Actions** panel, and choose **Window > Library** to open the **Library** panel, if not already open.

14 Select **Frame 1** on the **dice** layer, and drag an instance of the **dice** movie clip from the **Library** panel to the **Stage**.

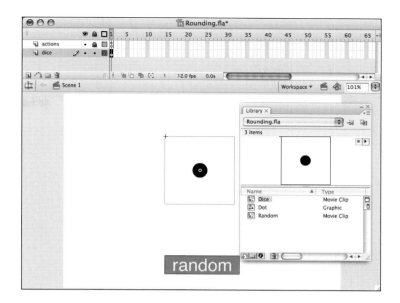

15 With the die still selected, choose the **Property inspector**, and type **die1_mc** in the **Instance Name** field.

16 Select **Frame 1** on the **actions** layer, and maximize the **Actions** panel. Select the word **trace** on Line 5, and replace it with the following:

die1_mc.gotoAndStop

You don't need to add any parentheses after the function because you're just replacing the **trace** keyword in this statement.

```
1  random_mc.addEventListener(MouseEvent.CLICK, onClick);
2
3  function onClick(event:MouseEvent):void
4  {
5      die1_mc.gotoAndStop(Math.ceil(Math.random() * 6));
6  }
```

Note the die move clip contains an embedded Timeline. On each of the first six frames of the movie clip Timeline, there are a different number of dots inside the die. Now when you click the random button, Flash will go to and stop at a random frame, and the corresponding number of dots will appear on the die.

17 Press **Ctrl+Enter** (Windows) or **Cmd+Return** (Mac) to test the movie. When the movie window opens, click the **random** button several times.

Cool! A random number will appear on the die every time you click the button. Now, in most games, don't you roll two dice? In the next step, you'll add another die to the game.

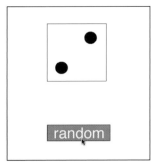

18 Close the movie window, and minimize the **Actions** panel. Select the **dice** layer on the **Timeline**, and then drag another instance of the **dice** movie clip from the **Library** panel to the **Stage**.

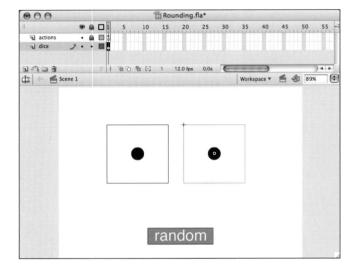

19 Align the new die with the first. Go to the **Property inspector**, and type **die2_mc** in the **Instance Name** field.

20 Select **Frame 1** on the **actions** layer, and maximize the **Actions** panel. Select the code on Line 5 (make sure to get the complete statement), and press **Ctrl+C** (Windows) or **Cmd+C** (Mac) to copy the code.

21 Position your cursor at the end of Line 5, and press **Enter** (Windows) or **Return** (Mac) to insert a new line. Press **Ctrl+V** (Windows) or **Cmd+V** (Mac) to paste the code.

22 Change **die1_mc** on Line 6 to **die2_mc**.

Now you'll get a random number for die1 and a second random number for die2.

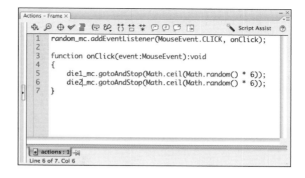

23 Press **Ctrl+Enter** (Windows) or **Cmd+Return** (Mac) to test the movie. When the movie window opens, click the **random** button.

What did you roll? If you get the same number on both die, don't worry. Just click the random button again. Since the range is smaller, the chances are far greater that both random functions will produce the same number. It's just like rolling the dice in real life!

24 Close the movie window. Save and close **Rounding.fla**.

That's how to write random number generators and manipulate the results using a combination of rounding and basic math operators. I hope this chapter was slightly more fun than the last math class you took! In the next chapter, you'll learn how to create and even style text fields using ActionScript.

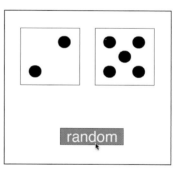

8

Using Text and Arrays

In this chapter, you will learn how to create, style, and scroll text fields using ActionScript. You will also learn about **arrays**, a special kind of data that can hold multiple variables. Then, you will use everything you have learned so far to create a word game.

1 | Creating a Text Field

In this exercise, you'll draw a text field using ActionScript. You may be thinking, why create a text field in ActionScript when I can just as easily use Adobe Flash's tools to draw one on the **Stage**? In fact, that is an excellent question. You shouldn't always use ActionScript to draw a text field. But sometimes the user might not want or need to see the text field. For example, when you create a game in Flash, you might display a message when the user wins the game. But if the user never wins, the message shouldn't appear. You could make the text field transparent, but why take up space, and resources, when you could create it dynamically when and if the user wins the game? ActionScript allows you to do just that. Otherwise, if the text field is going to be visible for a standard amount of time, create it in design mode.

---

1 Choose **File > New**, and click **Flash File (ActionScript 3.0)**. Double-click the name of the first layer, and rename it **actions**.

---

2 Select **Frame 1**, and press **F9** (Windows) or **Opt+F9** (Mac) to open the **Actions** panel.

---

3 On the first line of the **Actions** pane, type the following:

```
var myText:TextField = new TextField();
```

This code creates a variable, of the TextField data type, equal to a new instance of the **TextField** class. To see this text field, you need to add it to the display list. If you recall from Chapter 5, *"Understanding Classes,"* you add an object to the display list through the **addChild()** method.

---

4 Press **Enter** (Windows) or **Return** (Mac) to insert a new line, and type the following:

```
addChild(myText);
```

The text field still won't appear in the movie until you add some text.

5 Press **Enter** (Windows) or **Return** (Mac) to insert a new line, and type the following:

`myText.text = "This is some text in my brand new text field.";`

The **text** property of **TextField** accepts a string. You can insert any combination of numbers and letters in the quotation marks.

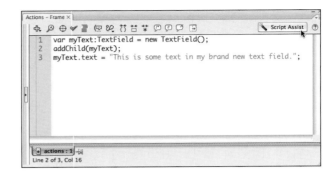

6 Press **Ctrl+Enter** (Windows) or **Cmd+Return** (Mac) to test your movie.

Notice that although the text appears, at least partially, the text field isn't wide enough to display the whole string. Select the text with your cursor to see the last half of the string.

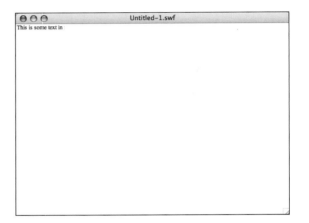

7 Close the Flash Player window, and return to the **Actions** panel. Press **Enter** (Windows) or **Return** (Mac) to insert a new line, and type the following:

`myText.width = 250;`

8 Press **Ctrl+Enter** (Windows) or **Cmd+Return** (Mac) to test your movie again.

There you go. Now the entire text string displays.

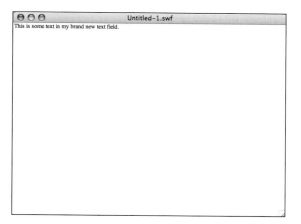

9 Close the Flash Player window, and return to the **Actions** panel. Select the keyword **TextField** on Line 1 of your code, and choose **Help > Flash Help** to open the **Help** menu.

Flash automatically takes you to the definition for the **TextField** object. The definition contains a complete list of the **TextField** properties, such as border and background. You can use these properties to style a text field. However, in the next exercise, you'll use a different method for styling text; you'll use the **TextField** class.

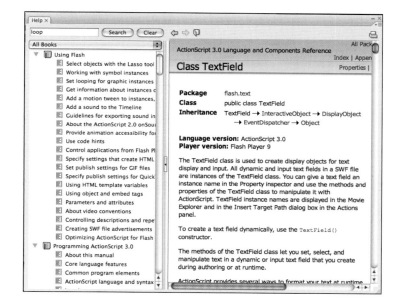

10 Close your Flash document. You don't need to save your changes.

2 | Styling a Text Field

In this exercise, you'll learn how to style a text field by changing the font face, font color, and font size through ActionScript using a **TextFormat** object.

---

1 Choose **File > Open**, and open **Styling.fla** from the **chap_08** folder on your desktop.

Notice that Frame 1 contains a small *a*, indicating there is ActionScript in this frame.

---

2 Select **Frame 1** on the **actions** layer, and press **F9** (Windows) or **Opt+F9** (Mac) to open the **Actions** panel, if it is not already open.

The Actions panel contains the same code you wrote in the previous exercise. The first line creates a new instance of the **TextField** object, the second line adds it to the display list, the third line defines the text string, and the last line modifies the width of the field so the entire string fits.

```
1  var myText:TextField = new TextField();
2  addChild(myText);
3  myText.text = "Here's some text in my brand new text field!!!";
4  myText.width = 250;
```

To style this text field, you need to perform three steps. The first step is to create a **TextFormat** object. Creating a **TextFormat** object is kind of like creating a style sheet for your text field. You define all the formatting in a single object, which can then be linked to as many text fields as you want. You can modify some of the **TextField** attributes directly, using properties such as **textColor** and **textHeight**, but since one of the goals in coding ActionScript is to keep the code as reusable as possible, I prefer to use **TextFormat** objects.

---

3 Position your cursor at the beginning of Line 2, and press **Enter** (Windows) or **Return** (Mac) twice to insert two new lines. Press the **up arrow** key to go to Line 2, and type the following:

```
var myFormat:TextFormat = new
TextFormat();
```

Remember to group your variables at the top of your code to make the code easier to read. This variable defines a new instance of the **TextFormat** class. The next step is to define the **TextFormat** properties.

```
1  var myText:TextField = new TextField();
2  var myFormat:TextFormat = new TextFormat();
3
4  addChild(myText);
5  myText.text = "Here's some text in my brand new text field!!!";
6  myText.width = 250;
7
```

---

4 Press **Enter** (Windows) or **Return** (Mac) twice to insert two new lines, and type the following:

`myFormat.font = "Helvetica";`

The **font** property accepts a string. If you don't have Helvetica installed on your machine, pick another font (such as Arial). Just remember to enclose it in quotation marks.

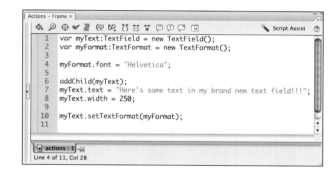

If you were to test the movie now, the text font would not update. You need to perform the third and final step to apply this formatting to the text field; you have to **associate**, or build a relationship between, the two objects.

---

5 Position your cursor after the last line of code, and press **Enter** (Windows) or **Return** (Mac) twice to insert two new lines. Type the following:

`myText.setTextFormat(myFormat);`

Here you are passing the formatting to the text field by specifying the `TextFormat` object's name in the parentheses.

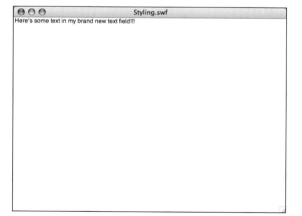

---

6 Press **Ctrl+Enter** (Windows) or **Cmd+Return** (Mac) to test the movie.

Now your text is styled in Helvetica (or the font you specified) instead of the default font, Times New Roman. Make a note that when you're formatting your text object, the most likely place to make an error is to neglect to associate `TextFormat` with the text field. Now let's modify a few more properties of the text.

7 Close the player window, and return to the **Actions** panel. Position your cursor after Line 4, where you specified the font face, and press **Enter** (Windows) or **Return**. Type the following:

`myFormat.color`

The **color** property accepts a number, a hexadecimal value. A **hexadecimal color value** is a six-digit number representing the RGB (**R**ed, **G**reen, and **B**lue) values that make up a hue. Hexadecimal digits start at 0 and go up to 9 and then go from A to F. The lowest is 0; the highest is F. Letters can be written as uppercase or lowercase. The first two digits represent the red value, the second two represent green, and the last two are the blue value. When coding a color value, you always write 0x before the hexadecimal.

---

8 To finish the statement, type a space and then type:

`= 0xFF0000;`

```
1   var myText:TextField = new TextField();
2   var myFormat:TextFormat = new TextFormat();
3
4   myFormat.font = "Helvetica";
5   myFormat.color = 0xFF0000;
6
7   addChild(myText);
8   myText.text = "Here's some text in my brand new text field!!!";
9   myText.width = 250;
10
11  myText.setTextFormat(myFormat);
```

---

9 Press **Ctrl+Enter** (Windows) or **Cmd+Return** (Mac) to test the movie.

Now your text is red! Once you have set up the **TextFormat** object and associated it with your text field, you can change as many properties of the text field as you want. You don't need to create another **TextFormat** object for each new property. Now let's change the text size.

Styling.swf

Here's some text in my brand new text field!!!

---

10 Close the player window, and return to the **Actions** panel. Position your cursor after the font color statement, and press **Enter** (Windows) or **Return** (Mac) to go to the next line. Type the following:

`myFormat.size = 24;`

```
1   var myText:TextField = new TextField();
2   var myFormat:TextFormat = new TextFormat();
3
4   myFormat.font = "Helvetica";
5   myFormat.color = 0xFF0000;
6   myFormat.size = 24;
7
8   addChild(myText);
9   myText.text = "Here's some text in my brand new text field!!!";
10  myText.width = 250;
11
12  myText.setTextFormat(myFormat);
13
```

Line 6 of 13, Col 20

TIP:

Typing a Hexadecimal Value

Most coders don't have the hexadecimal value for every color committed to memory. After all, there are 256 hexadecimal colors. However, it's not a bad idea to know the most common colors. The hexadecimal values for most common colors are listed in the following chart. If you need a more specific hue, here's a tip: Pick a color from the color picker in the **Color** panel in Flash. The corresponding RGB value will appear in the panel as soon as you choose the color. You can also sample a color from an existing color on the **Stage** using the **Eyedropper** tool.

Common Hexadecimal Colors

Color	Hexadecimal Value	RGB Value
Black	#000000	0, 0, 0
Red	#FF0000	255, 0, 0
Green	#00FF00	0, 255, 0
Blue	#00FF00	0, 0, 255
Yellow	#FFFF00	255, 255, 0
Purple	#FF00FF	255, 0, 255
Gray	#C0C0C0	192, 192, 192

11 Press **Ctrl+Enter** (Windows) or **Cmd+Return** (Mac) to test the movie.

Now the font is larger, 24 pixels to be exact, but the text is being cut off again.

Styling.swf

Here's some text in my t

12 Close the player window, and return to the **Actions** panel.

You could fix this problem in a couple of ways. You could increase the width of the text field again, but the most effective way would actually be to modify the `autosize` property of `TextField` so it will resize itself according to the length of the text it contains.

---

13 Select the code on Line 10, where you define the width of the text field, and press **Delete** to remove it. Now type the following:

`myText.autoSize = TextFieldAutoSize.LEFT;`

To those of you familiar with ActionScript 2.0, this might look a little foreign. In ActionScript 2.0, `autoSize` accepted a value of **true** or **false**. In 3.0, you define which side the field will grow from. Since text in most Western languages reads from the left to the right, you'll most often end up using **LEFT**.

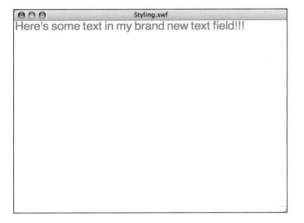

```
1   var myText:TextField = new TextField();
2   var myFormat:TextFormat = new TextFormat();
3
4   myFormat.font = "Helvetica";
5   myFormat.color = 0xFF0000;
6   myFormat.size = 24;
7
8   addChild(myText);
9   myText.text = "Here's some text in my brand new text field!!!";
10  myText.autoSize = TextFieldAutoSize.LEFT;
11
12  myText.setTextFormat(myFormat);
13
```

---

14 Press **Ctrl+Enter** (Windows) or **Cmd+Return** (Mac) to test the movie.

There you go. The text field has resized itself. Now you could add or delete as many characters as you want from the text string, and the field will adjust accordingly.

Here's some text in my brand new text field!!!

---

15 Close the player window, and close **Styling.fla**. You don't need to save your changes.

In the next exercise, you'll learn how to capture and reuse data typed in a text field.

---

3 | Capturing Data from a Text Field

In this exercise, you'll learn how to capture data from an input text field and display it somewhere else.

1 Choose **File > Open**, and open **Capturing.fla** from the **chap_08** folder on your desktop.

---

2 Choose **Window > Properties > Properties** to open the **Property inspector**. Select the **Selection** tool in the **Tools** panel, select the text field at the top of the **Stage**, and examine its properties in the **Property inspector**.

This text field is an input field, one of the three types of text fields in Flash also including static (which was the type you created in the previous exercise) and dynamic. An input text field doesn't display text, but it does allow to user to insert text. Notice the text field is named name_txt. The _txt suffice is similar to the _mc suffix you worked with in previous chapters. It tips Flash off to the object's class and enables code hinting for the object.

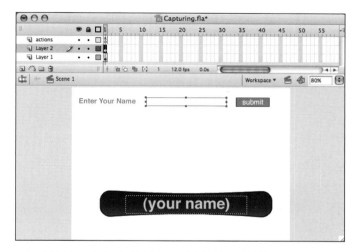

---

3 Select the rectangle labeled **submit** on the **Stage**, and examine its properties in the **Property inspector**.

This rectangle is actually a button named submit_btn. The _btn suffix does the same thing as _mc and _txt; it enables code hinting for the object.

---

4 Click to select the words **your name** in the snowboard on the bottom of the **Stage**, and examine its properties in the **Property inspector**.

This object is a dynamic text field.
Dynamic text fields, when used in combination with ActionScript, display text based on your instructions.

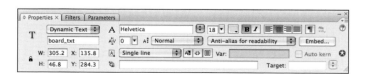

There are a lot of properties for this object, but notice that the field is named boarder_txt; that it's single line, meaning it will display only a single line of text; and that Selectable is not selected. This means the field will not be selectable once the movie is exported.

This application is designed so that when the user types their name in the input field and clicks submit, that data will automatically display in the snowboard below. Now you'll look at the ActionScript that will power this movie.

5 Select **Frame 1** on the **actions** layer, and press **F9** (Windows) or **Opt+F9** (Mac) to open the **Actions** panel, if it is not already open.

The first line of the code, as it stands so far, creates a new variable called **body_txt**, equal to a new **TextField** instance. This introduces a third text field into your movie. The x and y positions are already set up for you, and the **AutoSize** property is set to **LEFT**. Notice that one key component is still missing: body_txt has not been added to the display list of the document. Since there's no **addChild()** statement yet, the object will not be visible.

```
Actions - Frame ×
1   var body_txt:TextField = new TextField();
2
3   body_txt.x = 98;
4   body_txt.y = 66;
5   body_txt.autoSize = TextFieldAutoSize.LEFT;
6
7   submit_btn.addEventListener(MouseEvent.CLICK, onClick);
8
9
10  function onClick(event:MouseEvent):void
11  {
12
13  }
```
Line 13 of 13, Col 2

The second part of the code adds a **CLICK** event listener to the submit button. There's an event handler started at the bottom of the code, but it's still empty. Overall, it's a good start, but you still need to add the code to capture the data from that input field on the Stage. The first step is to create a variable to hold that data.

6 Position your cursor at the end of Line 1 after the first variable, press **Enter** (Windows) or **Return** (Mac), and type the following:

```
var yourName:String;
```

yourName will be the variable holding the user input. Because the user will be typing their name, you use the data type String. There's no need to assign a value since that will be passed in from the user.

7 Position your cursor on Line 13 in the event listener, and type the following:

```
addChild(body_txt);
```

By inserting this statement in the event listener, you'll make sure the body_txt field does not appear until after the button is clicked.

Now you need to add the value to the **yourName** variable. At this point in this chapter, you've added data to text field but you haven't retrieved data. It's actually a similar process.

```
Actions - Frame ×
1   var body_txt:TextField = new TextField();
2   var yourName:String;
3
4   body_txt.x = 98;
5   body_txt.y = 66;
6   body_txt.autoSize = TextFieldAutoSize.LEFT;
7
8   submit_btn.addEventListener(MouseEvent.CLICK, onClick);
9
10
11  function onClick(event:MouseEvent):void
12  {
13      addChild(body_txt);
14  }
```
Line 13 of 14, Col 21

8 Press **Enter** (Windows) or **Return** (Mac), and type the following:

`yourName = name_txt.text;`

Quite simply, this code means the **yourName** variable will be equal to whatever the user types in the name_txt field.

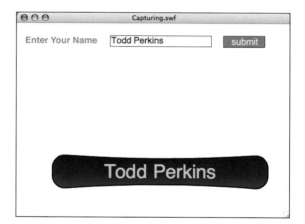

```
1   var body_txt:TextField = new TextField();
2   var yourName:String;
3
4   body_txt.x = 98;
5   body_txt.y = 66;
6   body_txt.autoSize = TextFieldAutoSize.LEFT;
7
8   submit_btn.addEventListener(MouseEvent.CLICK, onClick);
9
10
11  function onClick(event:MouseEvent):void
12  {
13      addChild(body_txt);
14      yourName = name_txt.text;
15  }
```

actions : 1
Line 14 of 15, Col 27

9 Press **Enter** (Windows) or **Return** (Mac), and type the following:

`board_txt.text = yourName;`

yourName is just a placeholder, but it becomes valuable because you can both assign a value to it, as you did in the previous line, and then assign its value to something else. Now you'll see how this runs in real time.

10 Press **Ctrl+Enter** (Windows) or **Cmd+Return** (Mac) to test the movie. When the player window opens, type your name in the field at the top of the screen, and click the **submit** button.

Your name automatically appears in the snowboard. Cool!

Capturing.swf

Enter Your Name   Todd Perkins   submit

Todd Perkins

11 Close the movie, and return to the **Actions** panel.

Now, you may have forgotten, but that third text field is still hanging around. Now that you know Flash is capturing and displaying the data from the input field properly, you can populate the body_txt field.

12 Position your cursor after the last line in the event handler, press **Enter** (Windows) or **Return** (Mac), and type the following:

```
body_txt.text = "Hi " + yourName
```

The plus sign works differently here than it does in math. When you use the plus sign with strings, it **concatenates**, or brings together, the two strings into one. So, body_txt will display a new string, Hi, plus the value of the **yourName** placeholder.

Make sure not to include **yourName** in the quotation marks of the string. Otherwise, the message would read "Hi yourName."

```
1   var body_txt:TextField = new TextField();
2   var yourName:String;
3
4   body_txt.x = 98;
5   body_txt.y = 66;
6   body_txt.autoSize = TextFieldAutoSize.LEFT;
7
8   submit_btn.addEventListener(MouseEvent.CLICK, onClick);
9
10
11  function onClick(event:MouseEvent):void
12  {
13      addChild(body_txt);
14      yourName = name_txt.text;
15      board_txt.text = yourName;
16      body_txt.text = "Hi " + yourName
17  }
```

Line 16 of 17, Col 34

---

13 After **yourName**, type a space, and type:

```
+ "! Here's your custom board.";
```

This adds another **literal expression**, just a fancy word for exactly what you typed, after the variable.

```
1   var body_txt:TextField = new TextField();
2   var yourName:String;
3
4   body_txt.x = 98;
5   body_txt.y = 66;
6   body_txt.autoSize = TextFieldAutoSize.LEFT;
7
8   submit_btn.addEventListener(MouseEvent.CLICK, onClick);
9
10
11  function onClick(event:MouseEvent):void
12  {
13      addChild(body_txt);
14      yourName = name_txt.text;
15      board_txt.text = yourName;
16      body_txt.text = "Hi " + yourName + "! Here's your custom board.";
17  }
```

Line 16 of 17, Col 67

---

14 Press **Ctrl+Enter** (Windows) or **Cmd+Return** (Mac) to test the movie. When the player window opens, type your name in the field at the top of the screen, and click the **submit** button.

Now your name appears on the snowboard and in the message in the center of the screen, "Hi, Todd! Here's your custom board." You've captured data from the input field and displayed it in two different locations. Congratulations!

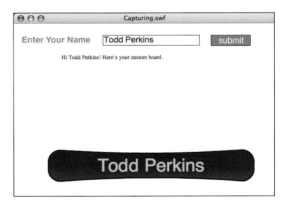

---

15 Close the player window, and close **Capturing.fla**. You don't need to save your changes.

In the next exercise, you'll load data from an external text file.

4 | Loading External Text

In this exercise, you'll learn how to fill a text field with text loaded from an external file. If you're a Flash designer, oftentimes you'll present a project to a client for review and then face a bevy of change requests. These requests often include changes to the text or copy on a page. Instead of hunting it down in Flash, it is a lot easier to make the changes to text using a word processing program and then just refresh the text field in Flash. Or even better, you can have the clients, who may not have the experience to edit a document in Flash, make the edits to the text file themselves. This is just one example, but you can see how using an external text file can make your workflow a lot more efficient.

1 Choose **File > Open**, and open **External.fla** from the **chap_08** folder on your desktop.

2 Select **Frame 1** on the **actions** layer, and press **F9** (Windows) or **Opt+F9** (Mac) to open the **Actions** panel, if it is not already open.

Here you have a variable called `external_txt` equal to a new instance of the `TextField` class. This is the same method you used in the previous exercise to create a text field dynamically. I've already set up a series of statements for you that will reposition and resize the new text field and add a border. The last line of code adds the text field to the document display list.

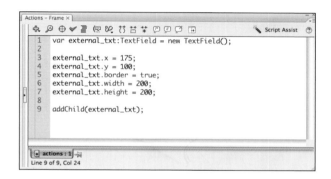

```
1   var external_txt:TextField = new TextField();
2
3   external_txt.x = 175;
4   external_txt.y = 100;
5   external_txt.border = true;
6   external_txt.width = 200;
7   external_txt.height = 200;
8
9   addChild(external_txt);
```

3 Press **Ctrl+Enter** (Windows) or **Cmd+Return** (Mac) to test the movie.

Ta-da! You have a text field at the center of the Stage. You could add text to the field by either assigning a string to the TextField's **text** property or loading it from an external file. A few more steps are involved to get external text, but as I explained, it can be really advantageous. The first step is to create a new object called `URLRequest`.

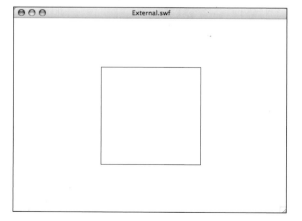

4 Close the player window, and return to the **Actions** panel. Position your cursor at the end of Line 1 after the variable statement, press **Enter** (Windows) or **Return** (Mac) to insert a new line, and type the following:

```
var externalReq
```

You might recall in the previous chapter you used **URLRequest** to link to an external Web site. You'll use the same keyword here. The

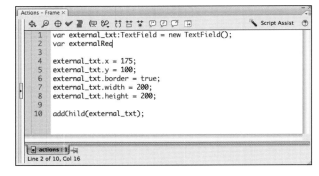

principle is basically the same: You're linking to a file external to Flash document, although in this case it will reside on your hard drive and not on a Web server.

---

5 After **externalReq**, type the following:

```
:URLRequest = new URLRequest(
```

If you were linking to a Web site, you would type the URL in the parentheses. Since you're linking to a local file, you just need to supply the file path. Like with class files, Flash will automatically look for the text file in the same folder where the Flash file has been saved, in this case, the chap_08 exercise folder. As it so happens, there is already a file named external.txt in this folder.

Also, remember that **URLRequest** accepts a string. The URL or file name must be in quotation marks.

---

6 After the open parenthesis, type the following:

```
"external.txt");
```

---

7 Press **Enter** (Windows) or **Return** (Mac) to insert a new line, and type the following:

```
var externalLoad:URLLoader = new
URLLoader();
```

externalLoad will be the name for the new instance of **URLLoader**. **URLLoader** is a companion to **URLRequest**. **URLRequest** links a Flash document to an external file or Web site, bringing the user to that file or site; **URLLoader** brings the data into the Flash document.

ActionScript 3.0 for Adobe Flash CS3 Professional : H·O·T

URLLoader can load data from text, binary data, or URL-encoded variable files. Most often, it's used for loading text or XML (eXtensible Markup Language) data into a Flash application.

Now you just need to build a relationship between the two objects; you need to instruct URLLoader to load the URLRequest object.

8 Press **Enter** (Windows) or **Return** (Mac) twice to insert two new lines, and type the following:

`externalLoad.load(externalReq);`

load() is a method of URLLoader that loads the URLRequest variable passed in the parentheses. URLLoader accepts only URLRequests.

So far, you have written the code to request and load data from an external text file located on your hard drive. But you haven't yet specified the destination for the data. One way to do this is to add an event listener to URLLoader. The event listener will trigger a function when the load is complete that will add the data to the text field.

```
Actions - Frame ×                                    Script Assist ⑦
1   var external_txt:TextField = new TextField();
2   var externalReq:URLRequest = new URLRequest("external.txt");
3   var externalLoad:URLLoader = new URLLoader();
4
5   externalLoad.load(externalReq);
6
7   external_txt.x = 175;
8   external_txt.y = 100;
9   external_txt.border = true;
10  external_txt.width = 200;
11  external_txt.height = 200;
12
13  addChild(external_txt);

  ● actions : 1
Line 5 of 13, Col 32
```

9 Press **Enter** (Windows) or **Return** (Mac) twice to insert two new lines, and type the following:

`externalLoad.addEventListener (Event.COMPLETE, textReady);`

COMPLETE is a type of event triggered when any methods or functions that are run on an object, such as the URLLoader here, are complete. Now you'll add an event handler to determine what function runs when the data has finished loading.

```
Actions - Frame ×                                    Script Assist ⑦
1   var external_txt:TextField = new TextField();
2   var externalReq:URLRequest = new URLRequest("external.txt");
3   var externalLoad:URLLoader = new URLLoader();
4
5   externalLoad.load(externalReq);
6
7   externalLoad.addEventListener(Event.COMPLETE, textReady);
8
9   external_txt.x = 175;
10  external_txt.y = 100;
11  external_txt.border = true;
12  external_txt.width = 200;
13  external_txt.height = 200;
14
15  addChild(external_txt);

  ● actions : 1
Line 7 of 15, Col 58
```

10 Position your cursor at the end of Line 15 after the **addChild** statement, and press **Enter** (Windows) or **Return** (Mac) twice to insert two new lines. Type the following:

```
function textReady(event:Event):void
{
  external_txt.text =
event.target.data;
}
```

This function will run once the **URLLoader** load is complete. It sets the **text** property of **external_txt** (the new text field) to include the data from the event target. The event target is the data retrieved by the **URLLoader**.

```
 8
 9    external_txt.x = 175;
10    external_txt.y = 100;
11    external_txt.border = true;
12    external_txt.width = 200;
13    external_txt.height = 200;
14
15    addChild(external_txt);
16
17    function textReady(event:Event):void
18    {
19        external_txt.text = event.target.data;
20    }
```

Line 20 of 20, Col 2

---

11 Press **Ctrl+Enter** (Windows) or **Cmd+Return** (Mac) to test the movie.

Sweet! The text from the external file appears in the text field. Imagine if you had a long document! Instead of typing it all or copying and pasting the text, making your code excessively long and hard to read, you could just load it right into your SWF at run time.

However, you still have to work out a few kinks. If you click and drag through the text, you'll notice that it scrolls to the right. In fact, every paragraph is on single line. It's not easy to read. Check out the video referenced next to learn some techniques for controlling the scrolling on text fields. Meanwhile, you can make the text wrap using the **wordWrap** property, so at least the paragraphs will be spaced over more than one line.

> Lorem ipsum dolor sit amet, consectetuer
> Vivamus eu neque. Ut lectus nibh, suscip
> Proin ac leo. Pellentesque vestibulum. Ph
> Mauris placerat quam non ligula. Vivamu
> Class aptent taciti sociosqu ad litora torqu

VIDEO: **scrollingtext.mov**

To learn more about controlling how the text in your text field displays, check out **scrollingtext.mov** in the **videos** folder of the **ActionScript HOT CD-ROM**.

12 Close the player window, and return to the **Actions** panel. Position your cursor at the end of Line 13 after the `external_txt.height` statement, and press **Enter** (Windows) or **Return** (Mac) to insert a new line. Type the following:

```
external_txt.wordWrap = true;
```

```
Actions - Frame ×
                                                          Script Assist

  8
  9    external_txt.x = 175;
 10    external_txt.y = 100;
 11    external_txt.border = true;
 12    external_txt.width = 200;
 13    external_txt.height = 200;
 14    external_txt.wordWrap = true;
 15
 16    addChild(external_txt);
 17
 18    function textReady(event:Event):void
 19    {
 20        external_txt.text = event.target.data;
 21    }

 actions : 1
Line 14 of 21, Col 30
```

13 Press **Ctrl+Enter** (Windows) or **Cmd+Return** (Mac) to test the movie again.

That's much better. Now each of the paragraphs wraps within the right and left borders of the text field. Instead of scrolling to the right, you'll find if you click and drag over the text, it now scrolls down toward the bottom of the player window.

To style the text, you can use the `TextFormat` class to change the font face, style, or color, as you did in the previous exercise.

Lorem ipsum dolor sit amet, consectetuer adipiscing elit. Curabitur faucibus erat et felis. Phasellus tempor. In eros lorem, mollis at, aliquam quis, sollicitudin hendrerit, pede. Nunc dignissim feugiat metus. Sed consequat tincidunt tortor. Quisque sagittis adipiscing dolor. Vestibulum quis eros vel ipsum scelerisque molestie. Mauris scelerisque. Phasellus porta nisi id odio. Ut felis odio, bibendum non, commodo nec, convallis et, odio. Vestibulum metus. Nunc vitae dolor.

Vivamus eu neque. Ut lectus nibh, suscipit a, auctor ac, tincidunt at, nisi.

14 Close the player window, and close **External.fla**. You don't need to save your changes.

So, that's how to load data from an external file. Create a `URLRequest` variable to hold the information about where the file is located, create a `URLLoader`, load the data using the `load()` method, add a `COMPLETE` event listener to the loader, and then create an event handler that makes the **text** property of the text field equal to the data of the event target. Whew!

The thing about text fields is that they are designed to hold only a single string of text. A situation might arise where you need a field to hold multiple values. In the next exercise, you'll learn all about arrays, a type of variable that can hold more than one variable, including multiple strings.

EXERCISE

5 | Understanding Arrays

In this exercise, you'll learn what arrays are, what they do, and how to code your own arrays. An **array** is a special type of variable that can hold multiple variables.

---

1 Choose **File > Open**, and open **Array.fla** from the **chap_08** folder on your desktop.

To better explain exactly what an array is, I've created this example file. Let's say you have a Web site with some basic security applied to it. Every user of the site has a user name and password to access the site. When the user types their user name in the text field and clicks the enter button, you want to check the input against a list of registered users. You can use an array to hold the list of the user names for all the registered users of your Web site.

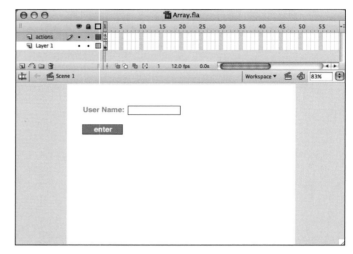

Of course, you may want to use something more robust than Flash to manage your Web site's security, but by following along with this exercise, you'll learn how you can use the same principle to manage other types of lists that might best be captured in an array.

Note that an array can contain objects other than strings. In fact, it can contain a set of variables that aren't even of the same class. Think of an array simply as a container for whatever you want to throw in there!

---

2 Select **Frame 1** on the **actions** layer, and press **F9** (Windows) or **Opt+F9** (Mac) to open the **Actions** panel, if it is not already open.

As you can see, there's already an event listener and event handler set up for you, both attached to the enter button. However, it's just a skeleton; you'll add all the meat to this code.

```
enter_btn.addEventListener(MouseEvent.CLICK, onClick);

function onClick(event:MouseEvent):void
{

}
```

---

3 Position your cursor at the beginning of Line 1, and press **Enter** (Windows) or **Return** (Mac) five times to insert five new lines. Return to Line 1, and type the following:

```
var users:Array = new Array();
```

users will be the name of your new array. This statement doesn't represent the only way to create a new array, but since you're already familiar with the syntax, it's by far the easiest. Now you add values to the array.

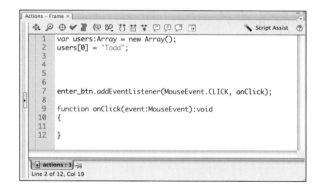

---

4 Press **Enter** (Windows) or **Return** (Mac) to go to the next line, and type the following:

```
users[0]
```

The closed brackets are something new. An array holds its data in an index, similar to the index used in a loop. In an array, every element corresponds to a number in the index. The first number in an index is 0.

---

5 After the closed bracket, type a space, and then type the following:

```
= "Todd";
```

Todd is a value in the array representing one of the users who will be logging in to this Web site…me!

---

6 Press **Enter** (Windows) or **Return** (Mac) to go to the next line, and type the following:

```
users[1] = "Jimmy";
```

You can use any name you want, even your own. Next, you'll add a trace statement to confirm the array is written properly.

---

7 Press **Enter** (Windows) or **Return** (Mac) to go to the next line, and type the following:

`trace(users);`

```
1   var users:Array = new Array();
2   users[0] = "Todd";
3   users[1] = "Jimmy";
4   trace(users);
5
6
7
8
9   enter_btn.addEventListener(MouseEvent.CLICK, onClick);
10
11  function onClick(event:MouseEvent):void
12  {
13
```

8 Press **Ctrl+Enter** (Windows) or **Cmd+Return** (Mac) to test the movie.

Both the player window and the Output panel should open. The Output panel should read "Todd,Jimmy." Values in an array are separated by commas, so you know the array is working. Onward and upward!

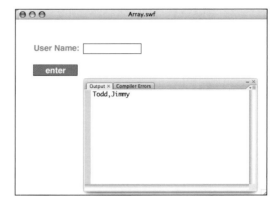

9 Close the player window and the **Output** pane. Return to the **Actions** panel.

10 Select Lines 2–3 that describe the values in the array, and press **Delete**. Leave the array variable statement as is for now.

I mentioned previously that there was more than one way to create an array. There's actually a shortcut.

11 Position your cursor at the end of Line 1, and delete the last half of the statement, up to the equals sign. It should read simply **var users:Array =**. Now press the **spacebar**, and type **[ ];**.

Now between the square brackets, you can type the values in the array.

```
1   var users:Array = [ ];
2   trace(users);
3
4
5
6
7   enter_btn.addEventListener(MouseEvent.CLICK, onClick);
8
9   function onClick(event:MouseEvent):void
10  {
11
12  }
```

12 Position your cursor between the square brackets in Line 1, and type the following:

"Todd", "Jimmy", "Mary"

Now you'll test the new array statement to make sure it's still working.

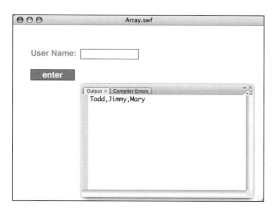

13 Press **Ctrl+Enter** (Windows) or **Cmd+Return** (Mac) to test the movie.

Both the player window and the Output panel should open. The Output panel should read "Todd,Jimmy,Mary." The array is still working, even though you shortened it a bit.

Now how would you check input from the text field against this array? One way to do that is to create a conditional loop that checks every value in the array and runs a function if it finds a match. Remember that like an array, a **for** statement also contains an index. You can use this fact to your advantage so that instead of looking for matching strings, you look for matching index numbers.

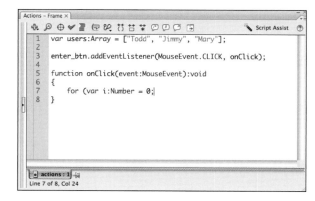

14 Close the player window and the **Output** panel. Return to the **Actions** panel. Select the trace statement on Line 2, and press **Delete**. Also, delete all but one of extra lines between Line 1 and Line 6.

15 Position your cursor in the curly brackets of the **onClick** event handler, and type the following:

for (var i:Number = 0;

If this **for** statement doesn't look familiar to you, review the information on loops in Chapter 6, *"Decision Making and Repetition."*

The next thing the **for** statement calls for is an **interval**, or how many times the statement will run. In Chapter 6, you used a less than expression, such as **i < 6**, to establish a finite number of times it would run. Since you're working with an array, you can actually use the array's **length** property instead (**length** being equal to the number of values in the array).

16 After the semicolon, type a space, and type the following:

`i < users.length; i++)`

Since you have only three names, you could have used 3 instead of **users.length**. However, should the length of your list change, if you add or remove users, 3 would be incorrect. You'd have to remember to change it every time you changed the array.

Now you'll write the conditional statement that will run every time the loop runs.

```
Actions - Frame
1  var users:Array = ["Todd", "Jimmy", "Mary"];
2
3  enter_btn.addEventListener(MouseEvent.CLICK, onClick);
4
5  function onClick(event:MouseEvent):void
6  {
7      for (var i:Number = 0; i < users.length; i++)
8  }
```
Line 8 of 8, Col 2

17 Press **Enter** (Windows) or **Return** (Mac) to go to the next line, and type the following:

```
{
    if(users[i] == user_txt.text)
```

The loop will run over and over again, increasing the value of **i** by one every time, until **i** is less than the length of the array.

So this **if** statement says that if at any point **i** is equal to the index number corresponding to the text string that was typed in user_txt, the input text field on the Stage, something will happen. You'll write that "something" now.

18 Press **Enter** (Windows) or **Return** (Mac) to go to the next line, and type the following:

```
    {
        trace("Access granted");
    }
}
```

Of course, you're not granting actual access to anything. This code isn't tied to Flash permissions. But the trace statement will allow you to see whether the loop ran properly.

```
Actions - Frame
1   var users:Array = ["Todd", "Jimmy", "Mary"];
2
3   enter_btn.addEventListener(MouseEvent.CLICK, onClick);
4
5   function onClick(event:MouseEvent):void
6   {
7       for (var i:Number = 0;i < users.length; i++)
8       {
9           if(users[i] == user_txt.text)
10          {
11              trace("Access granted");
12          }
13      }
14  }
```
Line 11 of 14, Col 28

19 Press **Ctrl+Enter** (Windows) or **Cmd+Return** (Mac) to test the movie. When the player window opens, type **Todd** in the text field, and click the **enter** button.

The Output panel should open and read "Access granted." Awesome.

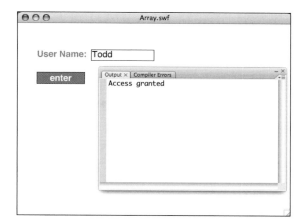

20 Close the **Output** panel. Type another name in the text field in the player window that does not match any of the three values in your array, such as Mike or Steve.

Now, nothing happens. The loop never found a match, so the condition wasn't true, and the trace statement couldn't run.

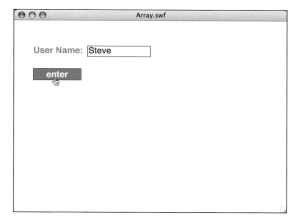

21 Close the player window, and close **Array.fla**. You don't need to save your changes.

In this exercise, you learned how to write an array. By using a loop, you can check the data against all the values in the array and build in functions to run if it finds a match.

In the next exercise, you'll combine arrays and loops to create a game.

6 | Using Text and Arrays to Create a Game

In this exercise, you'll learn a little bit more about text and arrays.

1 Choose **File > Open**, and open **Text_Game.fla** from the **chap_08** folder on your desktop. Choose **Window > Properties > Properties** to open the **Property inspector**, and select the **Selection** tool in the **Tools** panel so you can review some of the properties of the objects on the **Stage**.

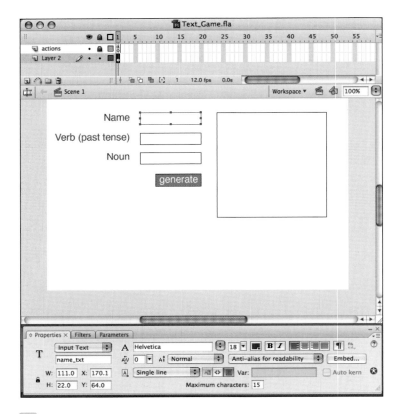

2 Select the text field next to **Name**.

This object is an input text field named name_txt. Remember the _txt enables code hinting for text objects in the Actions panel. The two fields below name_txt are also input text fields, named verb_txt and noun_txt, respectively.

3 Select the rectangle labeled **generate**.

This rectangle is actually a movie clip called generate_mc.

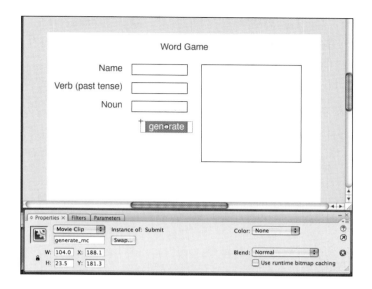

4 Now select the text field on the right side of the **Stage**.

Here you have a fourth input text field, named game_txt. If you haven't guessed already, this is an interactive word game. Once the user types their name, a verb, and a noun and clicks generate, Flash will generate a sentence using those terms. It's kind of like Mad Libs! Now the objects are all there. It's going to be up to you to animate them using ActionScript.

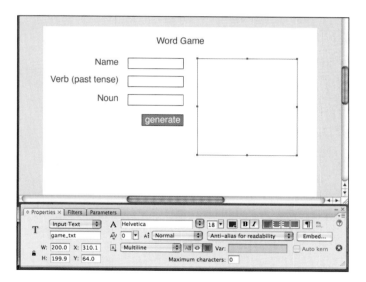

```
Actions - Frame ×
                                                                    Script Assist  ?
1   var yourName:String;
2
3   generate_mc.addEventListener(MouseEvent.CLICK, onClick);
4
5   function onClick(event:MouseEvent):void
6   {
7       game_txt.text = "Jerry flew down the mountain on his snowboard, hoping to escape the giant snowball." ;
8   }

actions : 1
Line 8 of 8, Col 2
```

5 Select **Frame 1** on the **actions** layer, and press **F9** (Windows) or **Opt+F9** (Mac) to open the **Actions** panel, if it is not already open.

The first line of the existing code generates a variable called `yourName`, which is the data type String. The variable does not yet have a value assigned to it.

The next line of code attaches an event listener to the generate_mc button. The listener is looking for a `CLICK` event.

The event listener triggers the third part of the code, the `onClick()` event handler. The handler runs a statement that fills the game_txt text field with a text string, defined in the quotation marks in the open parentheses: "Jerry flew down the mountain...", and so on. Let's test the movie to see what it does so far.

6 Press **Ctrl+Enter** (Windows) or **Cmd+Return** (Mac) to test the movie. When the player window opens, click the **generate** button.

The text string appears in the game_txt window. You'll personalize this a bit and make the game more interesting. You'll first replace the name Jerry with the name the user types in the name_txt field. Remember there's already a variable, `yourName`, that has been created for just this purpose.

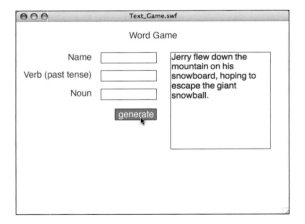

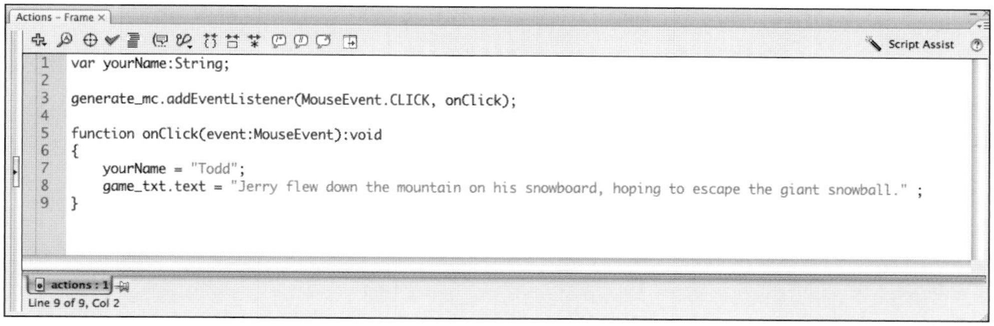
Actions - Frame
Script Assist
1 var yourName:String;
2
3 generate_mc.addEventListener(MouseEvent.CLICK, onClick);
4
5 function onClick(event:MouseEvent):void
6 {
7 yourName = "Todd";
8 game_txt.text = "Jerry flew down the mountain on his snowboard, hoping to escape the giant snowball." ;
9 }
actions : 1
Line 9 of 9, Col 2

7 Close the player window. Return to the **Actions** panel. Position your cursor at the beginning of Line 7 before the event handler, press **Enter** (Windows) or **Return** (Mac) to insert a new line, and type the following:

```
yourName = "Todd";
```

Instead of Todd, go ahead and use your own name.

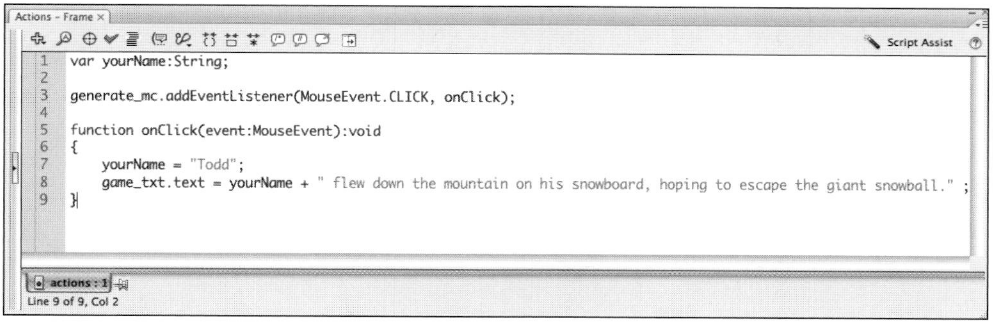
Actions - Frame
Script Assist
1 var yourName:String;
2
3 generate_mc.addEventListener(MouseEvent.CLICK, onClick);
4
5 function onClick(event:MouseEvent):void
6 {
7 yourName = "Todd";
8 game_txt.text = yourName + " flew down the mountain on his snowboard, hoping to escape the giant snowball." ;
9 }
actions : 1
Line 9 of 9, Col 2

8 Select the word **Jerry** in the text string on Line 8, and press **Delete** to remove it. Then position your cursor before the left quotation mark, and type **yourName** + . Make sure to include a space between the plus sign and the left quotation mark that starts the text string, as well as a space between the left quotation mark and the word **flew**.

`yourName` is the variable you assigned your own name to in the previous step. Remember that when you're building an expression with strings, + does not add the terms mathematically; it concatenates them.

---

9 Press **Ctrl+Enter** (Windows) or **Cmd+Return** (Mac) to test the movie. When the player window opens, click the **generate** button.

The text string that appears in the game_txt window now uses your name instead of Jerry. Now, this game should be able to be used by more than one person. Let's replace your name with the name_txt.data property, whatever the user types in the Name field.

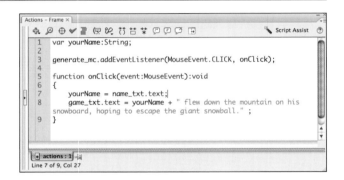

10 Close the player window. Return to the **Actions** panel. Click the **Actions** panel menu button in the upper-right corner of the panel, and choose **Word Wrap** in the contextual menu.

The Word Wrap feature makes sure your code wraps within the confines of your Actions panel. This lets you view long lines of code, like Line 8, all at once.

11 Now select the phrase **"Todd"** (or your name) on Line 7, and replace it with **name_txt.text**.

```
1  var yourName:String;
2
3  generate_mc.addEventListener(MouseEvent.CLICK, onClick);
4
5  function onClick(event:MouseEvent):void
6  {
7      yourName = name_txt.text;
8      game_txt.text = yourName + " flew down the mountain on his
   snowboard, hoping to escape the giant snowball." ;
9  }
```

12 Press **Ctrl+Enter** (Windows) or **Cmd+Return** (Mac) to test the movie. When the player window opens, type **Jeff** in the **Name** field, and click the **generate** button.

The text string that appears in the game_txt field now uses Jeff. You could do the same thing with the Verb and Noun fields, but instead of the user simply plugging in values, let's use an array of values that automatically pop in the sentence when the event handler runs.

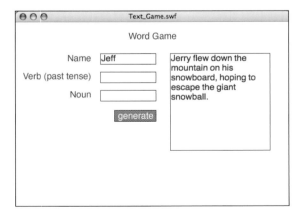

13 Close the player window. Return to the **Actions** panel. Position your cursor at the end of Line 1, press **Enter** (Windows) or **Return** (Mac) to go to the next line, and type the following:

```
var verbs:Array = ["jumped","ran"];
```

```
Actions - Frame ×
                                                    Script Assist  ?
1   var yourName:String;
2   var verbs:Array = ["jumped","ran"];
3
4   generate_mc.addEventListener(MouseEvent.CLICK, onClick);
5
6   function onClick(event:MouseEvent):void
7   {
8       yourName = name_txt.text;
9       game_txt.text = yourName + " flew down the mountain on his
    snowboard, hoping to escape the giant snowball." ;
10  }

 actions : 1
Line 2 of 10, Col 34
```

14 Press **Enter** (Windows) or **Return** (Mac) to go to the next line, and type the following:

```
var nouns:Array = ["bear","tree"];
```

Now you need to replace the verbs and nouns in the text string in the event handler with these two arrays.

15 Select the word **flew** in Line 10, and press **Delete** to remove it from the string. Do not delete the leading space. Type a right quotation mark (this will break up the text string.)

16 After the right quotation mark, type a space, and type the following:

```
+ verbs[0] + "
```

This new syntax will concatenate the following items to create a sentence in the game_txt field using:

```
Actions - Frame ×
                                                    Script Assist  ?
1   var yourName:String;
2   var verbs:Array = ["jumped","ran"];
3   var nouns:Array = ["bear","tree"];
4
5   generate_mc.addEventListener(MouseEvent.CLICK, onClick);
6
7   function onClick(event:MouseEvent):void
8   {
9       yourName = name_txt.text;
10      game_txt.text = yourName + " " + verbs[0] + " down the mountain on his
    snowboard, hoping to escape the giant snowball.";
11  }

 actions : 1
Line 10 of 11, Col 46
```

- The name that was typed in the Name field.

- A space (using the space you left in the first set of quotation marks).

- The word *jumped*, which is the first value from the **verbs** array. Remember that the index of an array starts with zero.

- The last text string.

Now you'll swap out the nouns in the text string.

17 Select the word **mountain** in Line 10, and press **Delete** to remove it from the string. Leave a single space after the word **the**, and then type a right quotation mark (this will break up the text string).

---

18 After the right quotation mark, type a space, and type the following:

+ nouns[0] + "

The word *bear*, the first value in the **nouns** array, will replace the word *mountain* in the sentence.

```
Actions - Frame ×
                                                              Script Assist
1   var yourName:String;
2   var verbs:Array = ["jumped","ran"];
3   var nouns:Array = ["bear","tree"];
4
5   generate_mc.addEventListener(MouseEvent.CLICK, onClick);
6
7   function onClick(event:MouseEvent):void
8   {
9       yourName = name_txt.text;
10      game_txt.text = yourName + " " + verbs[0] + " down the " + nouns[0] + " on
    his snowboard, hoping to escape the giant snowball.";
11  }

 actions : 1
Line 10 of 11, Col 130
```

---

19 Select the following in Line 10: **" + nouns[0] + "**. Press **Ctrl+C** (Windows) or **Cmd+C** (Mac) to copy this section of the code.

---

20 Select the word **snowboard** on Line 10, and press **Ctrl+V** (Windows) or **Cmd+V** (Mac) to replace it with the code you copied in Step 19.

---

21 Select the word **snowball** on Line 10, and press **Ctrl+V** (Windows) or **Cmd+V** (Mac) to replace it with the code you copied in Step 19.

```
Actions - Frame ×
                                                              Script Assist
1   var yourName:String;
2   var verbs:Array = ["jumped","ran"];
3   var nouns:Array = ["bear","tree"];
4
5   generate_mc.addEventListener(MouseEvent.CLICK, onClick);
6
7   function onClick(event:MouseEvent):void
8   {
9       yourName = name_txt.text;
10      game_txt.text = yourName + " " + verbs[0] + " down the " + nouns[0] + " on
    his " + nouns[0] + ", hoping to escape the giant " + nouns[0] + ".";
11  }

 actions : 1
Line 10 of 11, Col 145
```

---

22 Press **Ctrl+Enter** (Windows) or **Cmd+Return** (Mac) to test the movie. When the player window opens, type your name in the **Name** field, and click the **generate** button.

The new string reads, "Todd (or your name) jumped down the bear on his bear, hoping to escape the giant bear." OK, it's kind of silly, but pat yourself on the back. You just created a simple word game.

In the next exercise, you'll refine this game by adding values from the Verb and Noun input fields to the array and grabbing a random value from each array to display in the game_txt window at run time.

23 Close the player window. Save your changes, and leave **Text_Game.fla** open for the next exercise.

7 | Finishing the Text Game

In this exercise, you'll learn how to dynamically add to the **verb** and **noun** arrays you created in the previous exercise. Then you'll write code that will grab a random value from the arrays to replace the variables in the text string.

---

1 If you just complete Exercise 6, **Text_Game.fla** should be open. If not, complete Exercise 6, and then return to this exercise.

---

2 Select **Frame 1** on the **actions** layer, and press **F9** (Windows) or **Opt+F9** (Mac) to open the **Actions** panel, if it is not already open.

```
1  var yourName:String;
2  var verbs:Array = ["jumped","ran"];
3  var nouns:Array = ["bear","tree"];
4
5  generate_mc.addEventListener(MouseEvent.CLICK, onClick);
6
7  function onClick(event:MouseEvent):void
8  {
9      yourName = name_txt.text;
10     game_txt.text = yourName + " " + verbs[0] + " down the " + nouns[0] + " on
his " + nouns[0] + ", hoping to escape the giant " + nouns[0] + ".";
11 }
```

Your Actions panel should look like the one in the illustration shown here. Please review Exercise 6 if you need to brush up on what you've written so far.

The event handler currently publishes a combination of values from the **verb** and **noun** arrays and literal text strings. The array values that it uses are specifically called out in the code, such as index value 0. You'll change this up a bit by grabbing a random value instead.

---

3 Select the zero in the brackets of the first **verbs[0]** expression on Line 10.

You'll replace the zero with some math that will generate a random number in the index of this array. If you followed along with the previous chapter, Chapter 7, *"Using Math—and Loving It,"* you probably already have a pretty good idea of how this will work.

---

4 With 0 still selected, type the following:

Math.floor

```
1  var yourName:String;
2  var verbs:Array = ["jumped","ran"];
3  var nouns:Array = ["bear","tree"];
4
5  generate_mc.addEventListener(MouseEvent.CLICK, onClick);
6
7  function onClick(event:MouseEvent):void
8  {
9      yourName = name_txt.text;
10     game_txt.text = yourName + " " + verbs[Math.floor] + " down the " + nouns[0]
+ " on his " + nouns[0] + ", hoping to escape the giant " + nouns[0] + ".";
11 }
```

floor is a rounding method of the **Math** class that's reviewed in detail in Exercise 3 of Chapter 7. **floor** rounds any number down to the next whole number.

5 After **Math.floor**, type the following:

```
(Math.random()
```

Math.random generates a random number between 0 and 1, not including 1. These are usually long numbers with a large number of decimal places, so using a rounding method with this method makes them more useful.

---

6 Next type the following:

```
* verbs.length)
```

Since we are dealing with math, * becomes a multiplier. The random number will be multiplied by the **length** property of the **verbs** array object. The **length** property will return a value equal to the number of items in an array, and there happens to be two items in each array right now. So basically, you're multiplying the random number by 2.

```
1  var yourName:String;
2  var verbs:Array = ["jumped","ran"];
3  var nouns:Array = ["bear","tree"];
4
5  generate_mc.addEventListener(MouseEvent.CLICK, onClick);
6
7  function onClick(event:MouseEvent):void
8  {
9      yourName = name_txt.text;
10     game_txt.text = yourName + " " + verbs[Math.floor(Math.random() * verbs.length)]
   + " down the " + nouns[0] + " on his " + nouns[0] + ", hoping to escape the giant " +
   nouns[0] + ".";
11 }
```

Line 10 of 11, Col 81

---

7 Select the code you wrote in Steps 5–7, which is everything in the square brackets, and press **Ctrl+C** (Windows) or **Cmd+C** (Mac) to copy it.

---

8 Select **0** in the first instance of **nouns[0]** on Line 10, and press **Ctrl+V** (Windows) or **Cmd+V** (Mac) to replace it with the code you copied in Step 8. Repeat this step for the second and third instance on **nouns[0]** on Line 10.

```
1  var yourName:String;
2  var verbs:Array = ["jumped","ran"];
3  var nouns:Array = ["bear","tree"];
4
5  generate_mc.addEventListener(MouseEvent.CLICK, onClick);
6
7  function onClick(event:MouseEvent):void
8  {
9      yourName = name_txt.text;
10     game_txt.text = yourName + " " + verbs[Math.floor(Math.random() * verbs.length)]
   + " down the " + nouns[Math.floor(Math.random() * verbs.length)] + " on his " + nouns
   [Math.floor(Math.random() * verbs.length)] + ", hoping to escape the giant " + nouns[
   Math.floor(Math.random() * verbs.length)] + ".";
11 }
```

Line 10 of 11, Col 138

9 Replace **verbs.length** in the code you just pasted in each instance of **nouns[…]** with **nouns.length**.

Now it's time to test the movie!

```
1   var yourName:String;
2   var verbs:Array = ["jumped","ran"];
3   var nouns:Array = ["bear","tree"];
4
5   generate_mc.addEventListener(MouseEvent.CLICK, onClick);
6
7   function onClick(event:MouseEvent):void
8   {
9       yourName = name_txt.text;
10      game_txt.text = yourName + " " + verbs[Math.floor(Math.random() * verbs.length)]
    + " down the " + nouns[Math.floor(Math.random() * nouns.length)] + " on his " + nouns
    [Math.floor(Math.random() * nouns.length)] + ", hoping to escape the giant " + nouns[
    Math.floor(Math.random() * nouns.length)] + ".";
11  }
```

10 Press **Ctrl+Enter** (Windows) or **Cmd+Return** (Mac) to test the movie. When the player window opens, type your name in the **Name** field, and click the **generate** button.

Now, instead of "Todd jumped down the bear on his bear, hoping to escape the giant bear." you get random instances of the two verbs and two nouns. Click generate again to generate a different sentence with different values from the arrays. Excellent! Now let's add to the arrays.

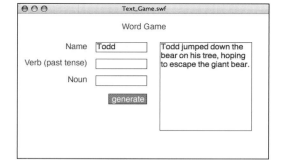

11 Close the player window. Return to the **Actions** panel. Position your cursor at the end of Line 8 after the open curly brace of the event handler, press **Enter** (Windows) or **Return** (Mac) to go insert a new line, and type the following:

verbs.push

push adds a new value to the array at the beginning of the index. Currently, **jumped** is the first value, and **ran** is the second.

12 After the word **push**, type the following:

(verb_txt.text);

This code tells **push** to add a value to the array using whatever was typed in the Verb text field. You'll duplicate this for the Noun text field and array.

```
1   var yourName:String;
2   var verbs:Array = ["jumped","ran"];
3   var nouns:Array = ["bear","tree"];
4
5   generate_mc.addEventListener(MouseEvent.CLICK, onClick);
6
7   function onClick(event:MouseEvent):void
8   {
9       verbs.push(verb_txt.text);
10      yourName = name_txt.text;
11      game_txt.text = yourName + " " + verbs[Math.floor(Math.random() * verbs.length
    )] + " down the " + nouns[Math.floor(Math.random() * nouns.length)] + " on his " +
    nouns[Math.floor(Math.random() * nouns.length)] + ", hoping to escape the giant " +
    nouns[Math.floor(Math.random() * nouns.length)] + ".";
12  }
```

13 Press **Enter** (Windows) or **Return** (Mac) to go insert a new line, and type the following:

```
nouns.push(noun_txt.text);
```

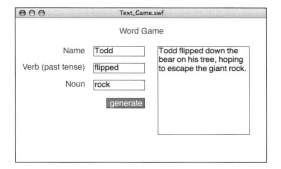

14 Press **Ctrl+Enter** (Windows) or **Cmd+Return** (Mac) to test the movie. When the player window opens, type your name in the **Name** field, type a new verb in the **Verb** field, type a new noun in the **Noun** field, and click the **generate** button.

I used *flipped* and *rock*. And my name, of course. When I clicked generate, the following sentence appeared: "Todd flipped down the bear on his tree, hoping to escape the giant rock." The new verb and noun you typed may not appear on the first try since the event handler is grabbing random words from the arrays.

15 Close the player window. Save your **Text_Game.fla** file by choosing **File > Save**. Close the file.

Congratulations on finishing this chapter! These exercises were very complex. I hope you've learned the benefit of powering your text fields with ActionScript. You don't have to use them just for games; you can also use them to create easy-to-update and versatile Web sites for clients, Web forms, and even for data verification. In the next chapter, you'll review key concepts from the previous eight chapters, using different principles from each of the chapters to build a more complex game.

Creating a Memory Game

In this chapter, you'll take everything you've learned so far and use it to create a more advanced application. In fact, you'll create a game. Adobe Flash games are more popular than ever. You can find and play Flash games on the Internet, and some have even been adapted for desktop gaming and certain game consoles.

In addition to being popular, Flash games are excellent practice for learning and applying ActionScript. Since most games require complex interactivity, creating them prepares you for creating all types of Flash applications. Games also help you understand how ActionScript elements (variables, functions, classes, events, loops, and so on) work together. Plus, games are fun!

In this exercise, you'll learn how to plan your Flash project effectively, whether it's a game like this one or a different kind of application.

1 Copy the **chap_09** folder from the **ActionScript HOT CD-ROM** to your desktop. Open **Memory.fla** from the **chap_09/9-1** folder.

The goal with this project is to create a memory game, similar to the game you play with a card deck in real life. The first step when you're creating an application is to imagine the finished product. Think about how the card game actually works. Cards start out face down; you flip two cards over and see whether they match. If they match, they are left face up, and you turn over another two cards and look for a match. If the first pair doesn't match, you turn them back over and look for another match, based on what you know about the cards you've turned over previously. This Flash game needs to re-create that interactivity.

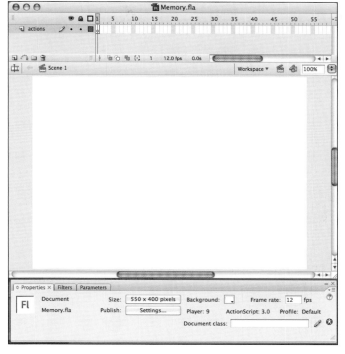

Another stage in planning your application is to think about what assets or objects in the file you need and which ones you will be able to recycle. With a memory card game, all the cards start face down. They flip up and flip down. So, they all have the same basic functionality. The cards can be recycled; you just need to be able to apply different graphics to the cards so they appear different to the person playing the game. For example, look at the Card symbol that already exists in the Library panel of this file.

2 Choose **Window > Library** to open the **Library** panel, if it is not already open. Double-click the **Card** movie clip symbol to open its **Timeline**. Scrub the playhead on the **Timeline** to preview the animations that have been embedded in this movie clip.

The card, a basic black rectangle, appears to flip over once to reveal a white "side" and then flips back over. The shape tweens used to accomplish this are located in the card layer on the Timeline.

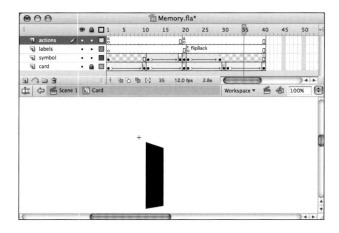

3 Select the **symbol** layer on the **Card** symbol's **Timeline**. The contents of the layer should automatically be selected on the **Stage**. Choose **Window > Properties > Properties** to open the **Property inspector**, if it is not already open, and examine the properties of the object on this layer.

The symbol layer contains another movie clip, labeled loader_mc, whose Alpha value has been set to zero. This movie clip will contain the graphics that makes each set of cards appear different. You will load this content in a later exercise using ActionScript.

Notice that the symbol layer also contains tweens. This will make it appear that the contents of the card are moving and skewing along with the card shape.

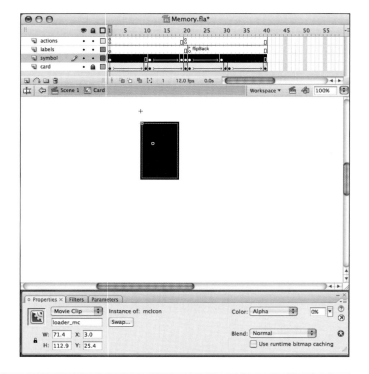

4 Review the **labels** layer on the **Timeline**.

The labels layer contains only one thing: a label called flipBack. This label will be used to call ActionScript to play the rest of the animation, where the card flips back over, if the match is incorrect.

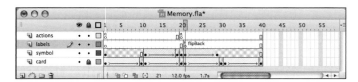

5 Select **Frame 1** on the **actions** layer, and press **F9** (Windows) or **Opt+F9** (Mac) to open the **Actions** panel.

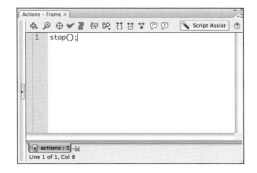

The Actions panel contains a simple **stop()** action that will prevent the movie clip from playing automatically at run time.

---

6 With the **Actions** panel still open, click **Frame 20** on the **actions** layer.

Frame 20 contains another **stop()** action, which will stop the movie at Frame 20, after it is started.

---

7 Close the **Actions** panel, and click the **Scene 1** button in the **edit bar** to return to the main **Timeline**.

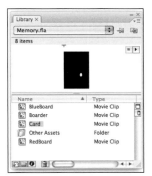

The Library panel of this file also contains graphics for the cards. These are the symbols BlueBoard, Boarder, and RedBoard. These assets are recyclable, meaning they can be shared by more than one card. So as you can see, a lot of the groundwork has already been done for you. What you should take away from this exercise is that when you are planning an application, if you can identify assets that can be recycled, you'll make the application more efficient in terms of both file size and load times, and you can save yourself a lot of work duplicating assets. Thinking of the application as a real-world event can also be tremendous help when you are trying to identify common functionality and properties.

---

8 Close **Memory.fla**.

In the next exercise, you'll dive into building the game itself.

---

2 | Writing a Memory Card Class

In this exercise, you'll create a memory card class that you'll use in later exercises to build the functionality into the many cards needed to play the game.

---

1 Open **Memory.fla** from the **9-2** folder in the **chap_09** exercise folder. Choose **File > New**, click **ActionScript File** in the **New Document** window, and click **OK**.

Remember that when you build a class file, you create an external ActionScript (.as) file.

---

2 Choose **File > Save** to save the new ActionScript file. Name the file **Card.as**, and save it in the **9-2** folder where **Memory.fla** is located.

Class files must start with a capital letter and be the same name as the class you intend to create. Notice this is the same name as the Card movie clip symbol in the Library panel. In a later exercise, you'll use the Linkage properties to reassign Card to the **Card** class.

---

3 In the first line of **Card.as**, type the following:

```
package
{
    public class Card extends MovieClip
}
```

All external Flash files must be contained in a package. You are declaring the **Card** class to be public so you can reference it outside the ActionScript file.

The **Card** class will inherit and extend the methods and properties of the **MovieClip** class. Now that you've referenced a class in an external ActionScript file, you must import the class.

---

4 Position your cursor at the end of Line 2 after the right curly brace, and press **Enter** (Windows) or **Return** (Mac) twice to insert two new lines. Press the **up arrow** key to return to Line 3. Type the following:

```
import flash.display.MovieClip;
```

5 Position your cursor after the class declaration on Line 5, and press **Enter** (Windows) or **Return** (Mac) to go to the next line. Type the following:

```
{
   public function Card()
```

This code establishes the constructor function for the class. A constructor function runs automatically as soon as a new instance of the class is created. The constructor function must use the same name as the class and the ActionScript file.

Now if the card were a button, as soon as you rolled over it your cursor would automatically change to the hand icon. That doesn't happen automatically with movie clips. To force the cursor to change, you have to set the button mode to **true** so the movie clip responds like a button.

---

6 Press **Enter** (Windows) or **Return** (Mac) to go to the next line, and type the following:

```
{
   this.buttonMode = true;
```

this refers to the root of the document, the **Card** class.

---

7 Save the file by choosing **File > Save**. Position your cursor after Line 10 where you specified the button mode, and press **Enter** (Windows) or **Return** (Mac). Type the following:

```
   this.addEventListener(MouseEvent.CLICK,
   onClick);
   }
}
```

The cards are designed to be clickable. Once a user clicks a card, an event should happen. You trigger the event using an event listener like the one you just wrote. The name of the event handler will be **onClick**. But before you get to that, you need to import **MouseEvent**, just like you imported **MovieClip**.

---

8 Position your cursor at the end of Line 3, press **Enter** (Windows) or **Return**, and type the following:

```
import flash.events.MouseEvent;
```

9 Position your cursor after the right curly brace of the constructor function on Line 12, and press **Enter** (Windows) or **Return** (Mac) twice to insert two new lines. Type the following:

```
private function
onClick(event:MouseEvent):void
```

Here's the beginning of the event handler. Now whenever the card is clicked, this function will be triggered, which should turn the card over. Since the Card movie clip already contains this animation, all you need to do is play it.

```
package
{
    import flash.display.MovieClip;
    import flash.events.MouseEvent;

    public class Card extends MovieClip
    {
        public function Card()
        {
            this.buttonMode = true;
            this.addEventListener(MouseEvent.CLICK, onClick);
        }

        private function onClick(event:MouseEvent):void
    }
```

10 Press **Enter** (Windows) or **Return** (Mac) to go to the next line. Type the following:

```
{
  this.play();
}
```

```
package
{
    import flash.display.MovieClip;
    import flash.events.MouseEvent;

    public class Card extends MovieClip
    {
        public function Card()
        {
            this.buttonMode = true;
            this.addEventListener(MouseEvent.CLICK, onClick);
        }

        private function onClick(event:MouseEvent):void
        {
            this.play();
        }
    }
}
```

11 Save **Card.as** by choosing **File > Save**. Click the **Memory.fla** tab to return to the Flash file.

Now to associate the Card movie clip symbol with the **Card** class, you need to modify the object's Linkage properties.

12 **Right-click** (Windows) or **Ctrl-click** (Mac) the **Card** symbol in the **Library** panel. Choose **Linkage** in the contextual menu.

13 In the **Linkage Properties** dialog box, select **Export for ActionScript**, and confirm that the **Class** is set to **Card**. Click **OK** to close the dialog box.

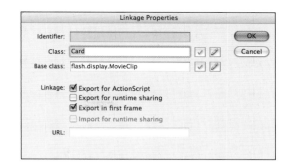

14 Drag three instances of the **Card** symbol from the **Library** panel to the **Stage**.

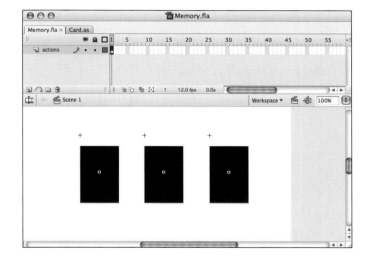

15 Press **Ctrl+Enter** (Windows) or **Cmd+Return** (Mac) to test the movie. Click each of the cards once.

The cards flip over as you click them. Click them again, and they flip back. This is the basic animation behind your game! In the next exercise, you'll add the cards to the Stage using ActionScript and add some artwork to them.

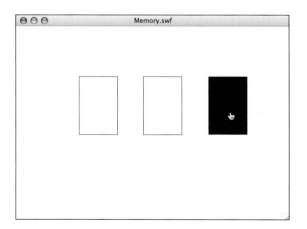

16 Close the player window, and close **Memory.fla**. You don't need to save your changes.

3 | Writing a Memory Game Class

In this exercise, you'll write a document class that will hold the entire memory game. Through this class, you will bring instances of the **Card** class from the **Library** panel and then add images to the instances.

---

1 Choose **File > Open**, and open **Memory.fla** and **Card.as** from the **9-3** folder of the **chap_09** folder on your desktop.

These files contain the same code you wrote in the previous exercise. If you are working with the files from the previous exercise, that's fine.

---

2 Choose **File > New**, click **ActionScript File** in the **New Document** dialog box, and click **OK** to open a new ActionScript document.

---

3 Choose **File > Save**. Name the file **MemoryGame.as**, and save the file in the same folder as the two open files you are working with (either **9-2** or **9-3**).

---

4 In the first line of **MemoryGame.as**, type the following:

```
package
{
    public class MemoryGame extends MovieClip
```

As with the **Card** class, you want to define the document class as public so that it can be referenced outside this ActionScript file.

Now you'll create the constructor function.

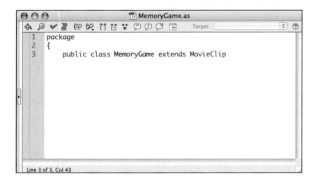

---

5 Press **Enter** (Windows) or **Return** (Mac) to insert a new line, and type the following:

```
{
    public function MemoryGame()
```

Because you extended the **MovieClip** class in Step 4, you need to import that class. If you want to add instances of the **Card** class within this document class, you'll need to import **Card** as well.

6 Position your cursor at the end of Line 2 after the first left curly brace, and press **Enter** (Windows) or **Return** (Mac) twice to insert two new lines. Press the **up arrow** key to go to Line 3, and type the following:

```
import flash.display.MovieClip;
import Card;
```

7 Position your cursor on Line 7 inside the constructor function, and press **Enter** (Windows) or **Return** (Mac) twice to insert two new lines. Press the **up arrow** key to go to Line 8, and type the following:

```
private var _card:Card;
```

This variable will hold the temporary instance name for each of the cards.

8 Position your cursor after the constructor function on Line 10, press **Enter** (Windows) or **Return** (Mac), and type the following:

```
    {
        _card = new Card();
        addChild(_card);
    }
  }
}
```

This code assigns a new instance of **Card** to the variable you created in the previous step, **_card**. The **addChild()** method adds the card to the document's display list. The two extra right curly braces close the class and then the package.

9 Close **MemoryGame.as**, **Card.as**, and **Memory.fla**. You don't need to save your changes.

Congratulations, you just created another class! In the next exercise, you'll place a graphic inside the Card instances.

4 | Adding Graphics to Cards

In this exercise, you'll take the graphic contained in the symbols in the Flash document's **Library** panel and place them onto the instances of the cards or, rather, inside the cards.

---

1 Choose **File > Open**, and open **Memory.fla**, **Card.as**, and **MemoryGame.as** from the **9-4** folder in the **chap_09** folder on your desktop.

I've added some additional code to these files. If you still have the files from the previous exercise open, close them and then open the files from the 9-4 folder instead.

---

2 Select **Memory.fla**. Choose **Window > Library** to open the file's **Library** panel, if it is not already open. **Right-click** (Windows) **or Ctrl-click** (Mac) the **Boarder** symbol, and choose **Linkage** in the contextual menu.

If you recall from previous exercises, to make this symbol usable in external ActionScript files, you need to select Export for ActionScript. This option exports the class definition, including the methods and properties, at run time.

---

3 Select **Export for ActionScript**, and click **OK**.

A message will appear saying that a class definition could not be found for Boarder, so one will be exported at run time. That's OK; there's no predefined class called Boarder in Flash, and you haven't created one either. You'll leave this to Flash. Flash will write the class so that Boarder extends MovieClip, and because you're not adding any special instructions, Boarder will behave exactly like a regular movie clip.

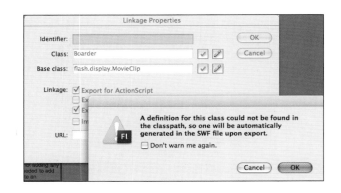

The other graphic you're going to use for the cards is BlueBoard.

---

4 Click **OK** to close the message dialog box.

---

5 **Right-click** (Windows) or **Ctrl-click** (Mac) the **BlueBoard** symbol, and choose **Linkage** in the contextual menu. In the **Linkage Properties** dialog box, select **Export for ActionScript**, and click **OK**. Click **OK** again to dismiss the warning message from Flash.

---

6 Select **MemoryGame.as**.

Notice that I've renamed the function you wrote in the previous exercise, `createCards()`, and embedded it in the constructor function so it runs automatically. `createCards()` still creates new instances of the `Card` class and adds them to the document's display list.

Now you need to pass the card images into the `createCards()` function. The first step is to import the classes for those graphics, which you exported specifically for this purpose in the first few steps of this exercise.

```
1  package
2  {
3      import flash.display.MovieClip;
4      import Card;
5
6      public class MemoryGame extends MovieClip
7      {
8          private var _card:Card;
9
10         public function MemoryGame()
11         {
12             createCards();
13         }
14
15         private function createCards():void
16         {
17             _card = new Card();
18             addChild(_card);
19         }
20     }
21 }
```
Line 1 of 21, Col 1

7 Position your cursor at the end of Line 4, press **Enter** (Windows) or **Return** (Mac) to insert a new line, and type the following:

```
import Boarder;
import BlueBoard;
```

```
1  package
2  {
3      import flash.display.MovieClip;
4      import Card;
5      import Boarder;
6      import BlueBoard;
7
8      public class MemoryGame extends MovieClip
9      {
10         private var _card:Card;
11
12         public function MemoryGame()
13         {
14             createCards();
```
Line 6 of 23, Col 19

8 Position your cursor at the end of Line 10 after the **_card** variable statement, press **Enter** (Windows) or **Return** (Mac), and type the following:

```
private var _boarder:Boarder;
private var _blueBoard:BlueBoard;
```

_boarder and **_blueBoard** will be the placeholder names for the instances of the snowboarder and the blue snowboard graphics you will create.

```
1  package
2  {
3      import flash.display.MovieClip;
4      import Card;
5      import Boarder;
6      import BlueBoard;
7
8      public class MemoryGame extends MovieClip
9      {
10         private var _card:Card;
11         private var _boarder:Boarder;
12         private var _blueBoard:BlueBoard;
13
14         public function MemoryGame()
```
Line 12 of 25, Col 3

You can add these graphics in the card instances in a couple of ways. In this exercise, you'll create a function in the Card.as file to accept the graphics.

9 Save **MemoryGame.as** by choosing **File > Save**, and select **Card.as**.

Card.as has also changed since the previous exercise. I've added an event listener to listen for a `CLICK` event, which triggers an event handler that plays the Card movie clip. I've also set the button mode for the class to **true** so the user's cursor turns into the hand icon when they move the cursor over an instance of Card.

---

10 Position your cursor at the end of Line 17 after the event handler, and press **Enter** (Windows) or **Return** (Mac) twice insert two new lines. Type the following:

```
public function setType(type:*):void
```

You're defining **setType** as a public function so you can call it from MemoryGame.as—or anywhere else outside of Card.as, for that matter. When you create a new instance of the **Card** class in MemoryGame.as, **setType** will receive and set the type of graphic, the snowboarder or the blue snowboard, that should be on the card.

```
                                    Card.as*
Card.as* ×  Memory.fla*  MemoryGame.as                         Target: Memory.fla
 1  package
 2  {
 3      import flash.display.MovieClip;
 4      import flash.events.MouseEvent;
 5
 6      public class Card extends MovieClip
 7      {
 8          public function Card()
 9          {
10              this.buttonMode = true;
11              this.addEventListener(MouseEvent.CLICK, onClick);
12          }
13
14          private function onClick(event:MouseEvent):void
15          {
16              this.play();
17          }
18
19          public function setType(type:*):void
20      }
21  }

Line 19 of 21, Col 3
```

In the parentheses, you are defining the data type as *. An asterisk is not a multiplier in this statement but a wildcard. You want to make sure this function accepts different types of data because at some points, you might be sending Boarder in or BlueBoard in, or you could use an entirely new class.

Next you'll add a variable to hold the card's graphic type and use the **setType** function.

---

11 Position your cursor at the end of Line 7, after the left curly brace, press **Enter** (Windows) or **Return** (Mac) twice to insert two new lines, and press the **up arrow** key once. Type the following:

```
private var _type:*;
```

This variable, **_type**, will hold the card type.

---

12 Position your cursor at the end of Line 21 after the **setType** function, press **Enter** (Windows) or **Return** (Mac) to insert a new line, and type the following:

```
{
    _type = type;
}
```

This might seem a little confusing right now. **type**, without an underscore, is each card instance's data type as defined when **setType()** runs. In order to capture that data and reuse it in Card.as, the workaround is to set **type** to a variable that can be used anywhere in the code, ergo **_type** = **type**.

But you still have to set the graphic types in MemoryGame.as. On to the next step!

```
package
{
    import flash.display.MovieClip;
    import flash.events.MouseEvent;

    public class Card extends MovieClip
    {
        private var _type:*;

        public function Card()
        {
            this.buttonMode = true;
            this.addEventListener(MouseEvent.CLICK, onClick);
        }

        private function onClick(event:MouseEvent):void
        {
            this.play();
        }

        public function setType(type:*):void
        {
            _type = type;
        }
    }
}
```

---

13 Choose **File > Save** to save your changes to **Card.as**. Select **MemoryGame.as**. Position your cursor at the end of Line 22 after the **addChild** function, and press **Enter** (Windows) or **Return** (Mac) to insert a new line. Type the following:

```
_boarder = new Boarder();
```

This just creates a new instance of the **Boarder** class, which you'll send inside the card.

---

14 Press **Enter** (Windows) or **Return** (Mac) to insert a new line. Type the following:

```
_card.setType(_boarder);
```

Although **setType** resides in Card.as, you can call it outside the file because it's set to **public**.

This code runs the **setType** function inside **_card**, those new instances of the **Card** class, using **_boarder** as the data type. Basically, this function makes the boarder display on the card.

```
        private var _blueBoard:BlueBoard;

        public function MemoryGame()
        {
            createCards();
        }

        private function createCards():void
        {
            _card = new Card();
            addChild(_card);
            _boarder = new Boarder();
            _card.setType(_boarder);
        }
    }
}
```

15 Select **Card.as**. Position your cursor at the end of Line 23 after **_type = type**, and press **Enter** (Windows) or **Return** (Mac) to insert a new line. Type the following:

```
loader_mc.addChild(_type);
```

loader_mc is the movie clip symbol in the Card symbol that you'll use as the destination for the graphics.

Things are getting pretty complicated, so let's review what the code looks like so far.

```
12              this.buttonMode = true;
13              this.addEventListener(MouseEvent.CLICK, onClick);
14          }
15
16          private function onClick(event:MouseEvent):void
17          {
18              this.play();
19          }
20
21          public function setType(type:*):void
22          {
23              _type = type;
24              loader_mc.addChild(_type);
25          }
26      }
27  }
```

Line 24 of 27, Col 30

16 Select **MemoryGame.as**.

The critical lines of code in this file are Lines 19–25. The **createCards()** function does the following:

- **Line 21:** Creates a new instance of the **Card** class, named _card

- **Line 22:** Adds the Card instance to the display list

- **Line 23:** Creates a new instance of the **Boarder** class, named _boarder

- **Line 24:** Sets the Card instance created on Line 21 to the data type _boarder created on Line 23

Now you'll examine Card.as.

```
1  package
2  {
3      import flash.display.MovieClip;
4      import Card;
5      import Boarder;
6      import BlueBoard;
7
8      public class MemoryGame extends MovieClip
9      {
10          private var _card:Card;
11          private var _boarder:Boarder;
12          private var _blueBoard:BlueBoard;
13
14          public function MemoryGame()
15          {
16              createCards();
17          }
18
19          private function createCards():void
20          {
21              _card = new Card();
22              addChild(_card);
23              _boarder = new Boarder();
24              _card.setType(_boarder);
25          }
26      }
27  }
```

Line 24 of 27, Col 28

17 Select **Card.as**.

The critical lines of code in this file are Lines 21–25. The **createCards** function does the following:

- **Line 21:** The **setType** function that runs in MemoryGame.as is defined here.

- **Line 23:** The **_type** variable is assigned the type received from **setType** (that is, _boarder).

- **Line 24:** The **loader** movie clip, already embedded in the Card movie clip, will add the **_type** variable, a placeholder for **_boarder** at this point, to the Stage via the **addChild** method.

I think it's time to test the movie to see all your hard work in action.

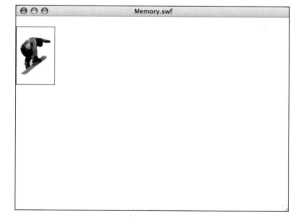

```
package
{
    import flash.display.MovieClip;
    import flash.events.MouseEvent;

    public class Card extends MovieClip
    {
        private var _type:*;

        public function Card()
        {
            this.buttonMode = true;
            this.addEventListener(MouseEvent.CLICK, onClick);
        }

        private function onClick(event:MouseEvent):void
        {
            this.play();
        }

        public function setType(type:*):void
        {
            _type = type;
            loader_mc.addChild(_type);
        }
    }
}
```

Line 24 of 27, Col 30

18 Save your changes to all three files by choosing **File > Save All**. Press **Ctrl+Enter** (Windows) or **Cmd+Return** (Mac) to test the movie.

When the movie loads, click the card that appears on Stage. It will flip over and contain the snowboarder graphic. Woo-hoo! You've successfully added a movie clip to another movie clip using ActionScript. In the next exercise, you'll add more images and place the cards on the Stage.

5 | Placing Cards

In this exercise, you'll create a few more cards with different images and place the cards on the **Stage**.

---

1 Choose **File > Open**, and open **Memory.fla**, **Card.as**, and **MemoryGame.as** from the **9-5** folder in the **chap_09** folder on your desktop.

---

2 Select **MemoryGame.as**. Scroll down to Line 19, the start of `createCards()`.

To create more than one card, you'll need to create loops to create multiple instances of the **Card** class. You'll also add X and Y property statements to the loop in order to position the cards uniformly.

---

3 Position your cursor at the end of Line 20, and press **Enter** (Windows) or **Return** (Mac) to insert a new line. Type the following:

```
for(var i:Number = 0; i < 2; i++)
```

This loop will run twice, creating two snowboarder cards.

```
package
{
    import flash.display.MovieClip;
    import Card;
    import Boarder;
    import BlueBoard;

    public class MemoryGame extends MovieClip
    {
        private var _card:Card;
        private var _boarder:Boarder;
        private var _blueBoard:BlueBoard;

        public function MemoryGame()
        {
            createCards();
        }

        private function createCards():void
        {
            for(var i:Number = 0; i < 2; i++)
            _card = new Card();
            addChild(_card);
            _boarder = new Boarder();
            _card.setType(_boarder);
        }
    }
}
```

---

4 Press **Enter** (Windows) or **Return** (Mac) to go to the next line, and type the following:

```
{
```

---

5 Position your cursor at the end of Line 26 after the **setType** function, press **Enter** (Windows) or **Return** (Mac) to go to the next line, and type the following:

```
}
```

The curly braces enclose what was formerly just in the **createCards** function into a **for** statement in that function.

If you were to test the code now, the four cards that this loop creates would stack on top of each other. You need to change the X and Y properties so that the placement of the cards increments every time the loop runs. First you have to create variables to hold the X and Y values.

---

6 Scroll to the top of the code, and position your cursor after Line 12, the last variable statement. Press **Enter** (Windows) or **Return** (Mac) to go to the next line, and type the following:

```
private var _cardX:Number;
private var _cardY:Number;
```

Now before you return to the loop, you want to set initial values for the X and Y properties, represented by these two new variables, *outside* the loop.

```
1    package
2    {
3        import flash.display.MovieClip;
4        import Card;
5        import Boarder;
6        import BlueBoard;
7
8        public class MemoryGame extends MovieClip
9        {
10           private var _card:Card;
11           private var _boarder:Boarder;
12           private var _blueBoard:BlueBoard;
13           private var _cardX:Number;
14           private var _cardY:Number;
15
16           public function MemoryGame()
17           {
18               createCards();
19           }
20
```

---

7 Position your cursor on Line 22 after the left curly brace of the **createCards()** function. Press **Enter** (Windows) or **Return** (Mac) twice to insert two new lines, press the **up arrow** key once, and type the following:

```
_cardX = 45;
_cardY = 31;
```

This code assigns numbers to the X and Y position placeholder variables, which you'll use in the next step to place the first card 45 pixels from the left side of the Stage and 31 pixels from the top.

```
18               createCards();
19           }
20
21           private function createCards():void
22           {
23               _cardX = 45;
24               _cardY = 31;
25
26               for(var i:Number = 0; i < 2; i++)
27               {
28                   _card = new Card();
29                   addChild(_card);
30                   _boarder = new Boarder();
31                   _card.setType(_boarder);
32               }
33           }
34       }
35   }
```

8 Position your cursor at the end of Line 31 after the last line of the loop. Press **Enter** (Windows) or **Return** (Mac), and type the following:

```
_card.x = _cardX;
_card.y = _cardY;
```

This sets the card instance's X and Y properties to the values that the _cardX and _cardY variables represent, in this case 45 and 31. Now you need to add pixels to the X and Y values so that every time the loop runs, the next card is shifted over and down.

```
 20
 21        private function createCards():void
 22        {
 23            _cardX = 45;
 24            _cardY = 31;
 25
 26            for(var i:Number = 0; i < 2; i++)
 27            {
 28                _card = new Card();
 29                addChild(_card);
 30                _boarder = new Boarder();
 31                _card.setType(_boarder);
 32                _card.x = _cardX;
 33                _card.y = _cardY;
 34            }
 35        }
 36    }
 37 }
```

Line 33 of 37, Col 22

9 Press **Enter** (Windows) or **Return** (Mac), and type the following:

```
_cardX += _card.width + 50;
```

This line of code takes the current card X value and adds the width of the card. Since you don't want them to touch, you add 50 pixels so that the cards will be 50 pixels apart.

```
 20
 21        private function createCards():void
 22        {
 23            _cardX = 45;
 24            _cardY = 31;
 25
 26            for(var i:Number = 0; i < 2; i++)
 27            {
 28                _card = new Card();
 29                addChild(_card);
 30                _boarder = new Boarder();
 31                _card.setType(_boarder);
 32                _card.x = _cardX;
 33                _card.y = _cardY;
 34                _cardX += _card.width + 50;
 35            }
 36        }
 37    }
 38 }
```

Line 33 of 38, Col 12

10 Save **MemoryGame.as** by choosing **File >
Save**. Press **Ctrl+Enter** (Windows) or
Cmd+Return (Mac) to test the movie.

Two cards appear on the Stage, both 31 pixels
from the top, but they're spaced 50 pixels apart
on the X axis. Only two cards appear. Luckily, a
lot of the work you've done for the _boarder
card type can be recycled.

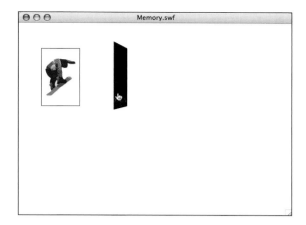

11 Close the player window, and return to **MemoryGame.as**. Select the entire **for** statement, which is
on Lines 26–35, and press **Ctrl+C** (Windows) or **Cmd+C** (Mac) to copy it.

12 Position your cursor after the right curly brace on Line 35, press **Enter** (Windows) or **Return** (Mac)
twice to insert two lines, and then press **Ctrl+V** (Windows) or **Cmd+V** (Mac) to paste the code.

13 Select all three instances of the letter
i on Line 37, and change them to **j**.

The variable representing the index in a
for statement must be unique within the
.as file.

```
25
26              for(var i:Number = 0; i < 2; i++)
27              {
28                  _card = new Card();
29                  addChild(_card);
30                  _boarder = new Boarder();
31                  _card.setType(_boarder);
32                  _card.x = _cardX;
33                  _card.y = _cardY;
34                  _cardX += _card.width + 50;
35              }
36
37              for(var j:Number = 0; j < 2; j++)
38              {
39                  _card = new Card();
40                  addChild(_card);
41                  _boarder = new Boarder();
42                  _card.setType(_boarder);
43                  _card.x = _cardX;
44                  _card.y = _cardY;
45                  _cardX += _card.width + 50;
46              }
47          }
```

Line 37 of 49, Col 34

14 Select all instances of **_boarder** on Lines 41 and 42, and change them to **_blueBoard**.

15 Select **Boarder** on Line 41, and change it to **BlueBoard**.

So, this block of code, similar to the block before it, will generate instances of the **Card** class and set the card type to **_blueboard**. Card.as will perform the work of loading the **BlueBoard** movie clip into the **loader_mc** part of the cards. The cards will also be evenly spaced, exactly like the snowboarder cards.

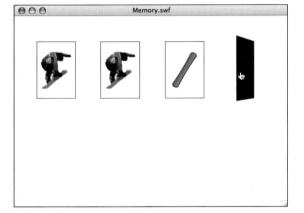

```
36
37              for(var j:Number = 0; j < 2; j++)
38              {
39                  _card = new Card();
40                  addChild(_card);
41                  _blueBoard = new BlueBoard();
42                  _card.setType(_blueBoard);
43                  _card.x = _cardX;
44                  _card.y = _cardY;
45                  _cardX += _card.width + 50;
46              }
47          }
48      }
49  }
```

Line 41 of 49, Col 31

---

16 Save the three open files by choosing **File > Save All**, and then press **Ctrl+Enter** (Windows) or **Cmd+Return** (Mac) to test the movie.

Now there are four cards. Click the two cards on the right, and they turn over and reveal snowboards. Click the cards of the left, and they turn over and reveal boarders.

In the next movie, you'll write the code to check whether the cards match.

---

17 Close the preview window, and then close **Memory.fla**, **Card.as**, and **MemoryGame.as**.

EXERCISE

6 | Detecting Matches

In this exercise, you'll learn how to write code to determine whether two cards are matching.

---

1 Choose **File > Open**, and open **Memory.fla**, **Card.as**, and **MemoryGame.as** from the **9-6** folder in the **chap_09** folder on your desktop.

---

2 Select **MemoryGame.as**.

To check whether cards are matching, you'll need to add an event listener to every instance you create. Since the user won't know whether they match until the cards are turned over, you'll need to add a mouse event to listen for a mouse click. The first step is to import `MouseEvent`.

---

3 Position your cursor at the end of Line 6, and press **Enter** (Windows) or **Return** (Mac). Type the following:

`import flash.events.MouseEvent;`

The next step is create a variable for each card instance to which you can add the event listener. Right now, they're all **_card**. But you need to be able to compare two instances at once. How do you do that? Well, if you assign a variable name to the first card instance the user chooses, you don't need to worry about the others. No matter what the second card the user chooses is, its name **_card** will be

different from the first card's, so you will be able to make a comparison.

---

4 Position your cursor at the end of Line 15 after the block of variables, and press **Enter** (Windows) or **Return** (Mac). Type the following:

`private var _firstCard:*;`

You're setting the data type of this first card to a wildcard, since you can't determine beforehand which type of card the user may choose first.

The next step is to add the event listeners.

5 Position your cursor at the end of Line 36 after the last line of the first **for** loop, and press **Enter** (Windows) or **Return** (Mac). Type the following:

```
_card.addEventListener
(MouseEvent.CLICK,
checkCards);
```

```
 22
 23        private function createCards():void
 24        {
 25            _cardX = 45;
 26            _cardY = 31;
 27
 28            for(var i:Number = 0; i < 2; i++)
 29            {
 30                _card = new Card();
 31                addChild(_card);
 32                _boarder = new Boarder();
 33                _card.setType(_boarder);
 34                _card.x = _cardX;
 35                _card.y = _cardY;
 36                _cardX += _card.width + 50;
 37                _card.addEventListener(MouseEvent.CLICK, checkCards);
 38            }
 39
 40            for(var j:Number = 0; j < 2; j++)
```
Line 64 of 69, Col 5

6 Select Line 37, the line of code you just typed, and press **Ctrl+C** (Windows) or **Cmd+C** (Mac) to copy it.

7 Position your cursor at the end of Line 48 after the last line of the second for loop, and press **Enter** (Windows) or **Return** (Mac). Press **Ctrl+V** (Windows) or **Cmd+V** (Mac) to paste the code.

Because both loops use the **_card** variable, there's no need to make any changes to this statement! Now you'll build the **checkCards()** event handler.

8 Position your cursor at the end of Line 51 after the right curly brace of the **createCards()** function, and press **Enter** (Windows) or **Return** (Mac) twice. Type the following:

```
private function checkCards
(event:MouseEvent):void
```

Make sure not to write this code in the **createCards()** function.

Now this event handler is going to check *if* one card matches the other. So why not use an **if** conditional statement?

```
 41            {
 42                _card = new Card();
 43                addChild(_card);
 44                _blueBoard = new BlueBoard();
 45                _card.setType(_blueBoard);
 46                _card.x = _cardX;
 47                _card.y = _cardY;
 48                _cardX += _card.width + 50;
 49                _card.addEventListener(MouseEvent.CLICK, checkCards);
 50            }
 51        }
 52
 53        private function checkCards(event:MouseEvent):void
 54    }
 55 }
```
Line 53 of 55, Col 53

9 Press **Enter** (Windows) or **Return** (Mac), and type the following:

```
{
   if(_firstCard == undefined)
```

The code checks whether the variable **_firstCard** you defined in Step 4 is undefined, meaning whether it has a data type yet. And you know this condition is true; **_firstCard** is undefined. You set it to be a wild-card on Line 16.

---

10 Press **Enter** (Windows) or **Return** (Mac), and type the following:

```
{
   _firstCard = event.currentTarget;
}
```

So, now **_firstCard** is defined as the tar-get of the event listener, which is what-ever card the user is clicking. If you just used the **target** keyword here, you might be capturing the data of the graphic on the target. Using **currentTarget** ensures you're capturing the event from **_card**, the card itself.

Once this statement runs, **_firstCard** will no longer be undefined. The original condition will be false. You can take advantage of this by following it with an **else if** statement.

---

11 Press **Enter** (Windows) or **Return** (Mac), and type the following:

```
else if(String(_firstCard._type)
```

This condition contains something you haven't worked with before. **String()** converts anything contained within the parentheses to a string. In this case, the type of **_firstCard** could be **_boarder** or **_blueBoard**. If you didn't use String and just typed **_firstCard._type**, it would produce an instance name. But you don't want an instance name. **String()** is what will make this code work.

---

12 After the right parenthesis, type a space, and then type the following:

```
== String(event.currentTarget._type))
```

This part of the code checks to see whether the string value of the first card's data type (now defined) is equal to the second card's, the next event target.

```
47            _card.y = _cardY;
48            _cardX += _card.width + 50;
49            _card.addEventListener(MouseEvent.CLICK, checkCards);
50        }
51    }
52
53    private function checkCards(event:MouseEvent):void
54    {
55        if(_firstCard == undefined)
56        {
57            _firstCard = event.currentTarget;
58        }
59        else if(String(_firstCard._type) == String(event.currentTarget._type))
60    }
61 }
```

Line 59 of 61, Col 36

---

13 Press **Enter** (Windows) or **Return** (Mac) to go to the next line, and type the following:

```
{
    trace("Match!");
}
```

If the **else if** condition is true, meaning if the first card's data type is the same as the second card that the user flips over, Flash will trace the string "Match!" But if it's not the same, Flash should do something else.

---

14 Press **Enter** (Windows) or **Return** (Mac) to go to the next line, and type the following:

```
else
{
    trace("Wrong.");
}
}
```

So if the cards don't match, Flash will trace "Wrong."

```
52
53    private function checkCards(event:MouseEvent):void
54    {
55        if(_firstCard == undefined)
56        {
57            _firstCard = event.currentTarget;
58        }
59        else if(String(_firstCard._type) == String(event.currentTarget._type))
60        {
61            trace("Match!");
62        }
63        else
64        {
65            trace ("Wrong.");
66        }
67    }
68  }
69 }
```

Line 64 of 69, Col 5

---

15 Save **MemoryGame.as** by choosing **File > Save**.

---

16 Press **Ctrl+Enter** (Windows) or **Cmd+Return** (Mac) to test the movie. When the player window opens, click the two left cards.

The cards should flip over and reveal snowboarders. The Output panel should open with the message "Match!" Very good.

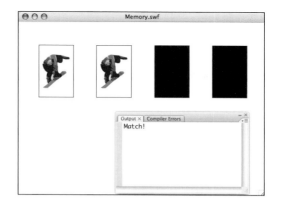

17 Close the player window and the **Output** panel. Press **Ctrl+Enter** (Windows) or **Cmd+Return** (Mac) to test the movie again. When the player window reopens, click the two outside cards.

Both cards should flip over. The left card should reveal a snowboarder, and the second card should show a blue board. The Output panel should open with the message "Wrong." Now you know the code is definitely working.

If you do not get this result, review Steps 2–15. This is a complex exercise, and it's easy to get lost.

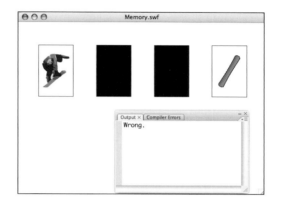

18 Before you close any windows, click the card that matches the first you clicked, and examine the **Output** panel.

Oops. The Output panel says "Match!" again. It looks like there's still some work to do refining the game. The reason why it says "Match!" again is because you never reset the _firstCard variable. You'll take care of this in the next exercise.

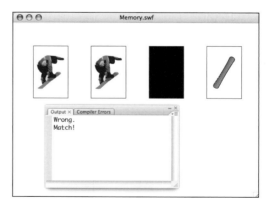

19 Close the player window and the **Output** panel. Close **MemoryGame.as**, **Card.as**, and **Memory.fla**.

Resetting Cards

In this exercise, you'll reset the **_firstCard** variable and learn how to turn off interactivity when the cards are face up.

---

1 Choose **File > Open**, and open **Memory.fla**, **Card.as**, and **MemoryGame.as** from the **9-7** folder in the **chap_09** folder on your desktop.

First you'll test the movie to review the problems with the code as it is written so far.

---

2 Press **Ctrl+Enter** (Windows) or **Cmd+Return** (Mac) to test the movie. When the player window opens, click the two left cards.

The cards flip over and reveal snowboarders. The Output panel should open with the message "Match!"

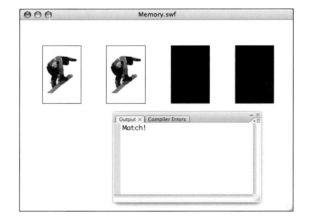

---

3 Without closing any windows, click a third unflipped card.

The card flips over and reveals a blue snowboard. The Output panel now says "Wrong," but you haven't chosen a second card. This is because the **_firstCard** variable is still set to the initial card you clicked. It needs to be reset.

---

4 Click one of the cards that is flipped over.

The card flips face down again. Now you don't really want the cards to flip back over once they are face up. It kind of defeats the purpose of the game. You'll have to make the cards unclickable once they are face up.

---

5 Close the player window and the **Output** panel. Select **MemoryGame.as**.

---

6 Position your cursor at the end of Line 61 after the "Match!" trace statement, and press **Enter** (Windows) or **Return** (Mac) to go to the next line. Type the following:

`_firstCard = undefined;`

You're intentionally setting the value of **_firstCard** back to **undefined**, because if this statement runs, that means you've already found a match.

```
                          MemoryGame.as*
Card.as   MemoryGame.as* ×   Memory.fla
                                                    Target:  Memory.fla
55              if(_firstCard == undefined)
56              {
57                  _firstCard = event.currentTarget;
58              }
59              else if(String(_firstCard._type) == String(event.currentTarget._type))
60              {
61                  trace("Match!");
62                  _firstCard = undefined;
63              }
64              else
65              {
66                  trace("Wrong.");
67              }
68          }
69      }
70  }
Line 66 of 70, Col 21
```

---

7 Select the code on Line 62 you just wrote, and press **Ctrl+C** (Windows) or **Cmd+C** (Mac) to copy it.

---

8 Position your cursor at the end of Line 66 after the "Wrong" trace statement, and press **Enter** (Windows) or **Return** (Mac) to go to the next line. Press **Ctrl+V** (Windows) or **Cmd+V** (Mac) to paste the code.

```
                          MemoryGame.as*
Card.as   MemoryGame.as* ×   Memory.fla
                                                    Target:  Memory.fla
55              if(_firstCard == undefined)
56              {
57                  _firstCard = event.currentTarget;
58              }
59              else if(String(_firstCard._type) == String(event.currentTarget._type))
60              {
61                  trace("Match!");
62                  _firstCard = undefined;
63              }
64              else
65              {
66                  trace("Wrong.");
67                  _firstCard = undefined;
68              }
69          }
70      }
71  }
Line 67 of 71, Col 28
```

---

9 Save **MemoryGame.as** by choosing **File > Save**, and then press **Ctrl+Enter** (Windows) or **Cmd+Return** (Mac) to test the movie. When the player window opens, click the two left cards.

You get a match.

---

10 Now click a third card.

No message appears in the Output panel. So far, so good!

11 Click the last card.

Now, since the last two cards you chose match, you get another "Match!" message in the Output panel. Perfect!

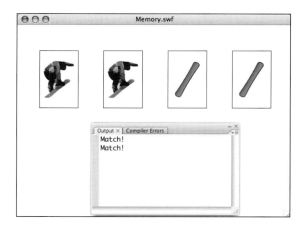

12 Close the player window and the **Output** panel.

Now you'll disable any card that is face up.

13 Position your cursor after the open curly brace on Line 54 of **MemoryGame.as**, and press **Enter** (Windows) or **Return** (Mac) twice. Press the **up arrow** key once, and type the following:

```
event.currentTarget
.removeEventListener
(MouseEvent.CLICK,
checkCards);
```

```
52
53          private function checkCards(event:MouseEvent):void
54          {
55              event.currentTarget.removeEventListener(MouseEvent.CLICK, checkCards);
56
57              if(_firstCard == undefined)
58              {
59                  _firstCard = event.currentTarget;
60              }
61              else if(String(_firstCard._type) == String(event.currentTarget._type))
62              {
63                  trace("Match!");
64                  _firstCard = undefined;
65              }
```

Line 55 of 73, Col 74

This code tells Flash to remove the **CLICK** event listener on the card the event handler is triggered on.

14 Save **MemoryGame.as** by choosing **File > Save**.

15 Press **Ctrl+Enter** (Windows) or **Cmd+Return** (Mac) to test the movie. Click any card, and then click it again.

Hmmm. It flips face down again. Why? Because it was told to in Card.as. You need to make changes there as well.

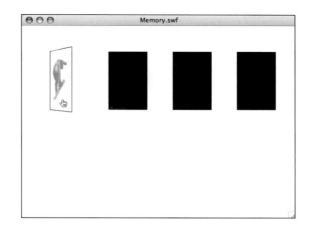

16 Close the player window. Select **Card.as**. Scroll down to Line 16 to examine the **onClick** event handler.

The **onClick** event handler says that whenever you click a card, the Card movie clip's Timeline, which manages the flipping, will play. A way to control this is to tell it to play only when the card is starting from Frame 1. That way cards that are face up, on Frame 20 of their animation, won't play any further.

```
     package
     {
         import flash.display.MovieClip;
         import flash.events.MouseEvent;

         public class Card extends MovieClip
         {
             public var _type:*;

             public function Card()
             {
                 this.buttonMode = true;
                 this.addEventListener(MouseEvent.CLICK, onClick);
             }

             private function onClick(event:MouseEvent):void
             {
                 this.play();
             }
```

17 Position your cursor after the left curly brace on Line 17, and press **Enter** (Windows) or **Return** (Mac). Type the following:

```
if(this.currentFrame == 1)
{
```

By creating a conditional statement around **this.play()**, you ensure the movie clip will not play unless the current frame of the card is equal to 1.

```
         public var _type:*;

         public function Card()
         {
             this.buttonMode = true;
             this.addEventListener(MouseEvent.CLICK, onClick);
         }

         private function onClick(event:MouseEvent):void
         {
             if(this.currentFrame == 1)
             {
                 this.play();
             }
```

18 Position your cursor after **this.play();** on Line 20, press **Enter** (Windows) or **Return** (Mac), and type the right curly brace for the **if** statement.

19 Save **Card.as** by choosing **File > Save**.

20 Press **Ctrl+Enter** (Windows) or **Cmd+Return** (Mac) to test the movie. Click any card, and then click it again.

There you go. The first time you click, the card turns over. Click it again (and again and again), and nothing happens. The movie clip is stopped on Frame 19.

I hate to be the bearer of bad news, but there's still one more problem.

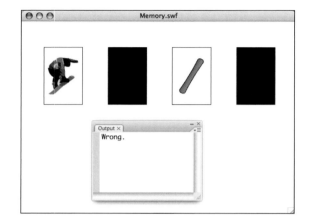

21 Without closing any windows, click a card you know is not a match with the first card.

The card flips over, the Output panel opens, and you know you don't have a match. So, is the game over? Try to click either of the nonmatching cards, and they stay put. In a traditional memory card game, when you don't get a match, you're supposed to turn the cards back over and try again. Let's see whether you can replicate this in the Flash game in the next exercise.

22 Close the player window and the **Output** panel. Close **MemoryGame.as**, **Card.as**, and **Memory.fla**.

8 | Handling Incorrect Matches

In this exercise, you'll solve the problem of not being able to flip incorrect matches back over.

---

1 Choose **File > Open**, and open **Memory.fla**, **Card.as**, and **MemoryGame.as** from the **9-8** folder in the **chap_09** folder on your desktop.

---

2 Select **Memory.fla**. Choose **Window > Library** to open the **Library** panel, if it is not open already. Double-click the **Card** symbol to open its **Timeline**.

Halfway through the animation of this symbol, there's a frame label called flipBack. If you scrub the animation from this point, Frame 21 to be precise, you'll see the card flips back over. So, all you have to do is play this section of the animation if there's a wrong match.

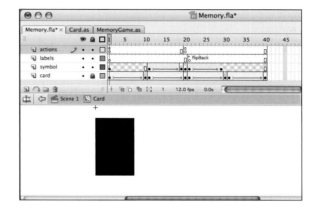

---

3 Click the **Scene 1** button in the **edit bar** to return to the main **Timeline**.

---

4 Select **MemoryGame.as**. Scroll down to Lines 66–70 of the **checkCards()** event handler.

---

5 Position your cursor at the end of Line 68 after the trace statement, and press **Enter** (Windows) or **Return** (Mac) to go to the next line. Type the following:

```
_firstCard.gotoAndPlay
("flipBack");
```

```
61          else if(String(_firstCard._type) == String(event.currentTarget._type))
62          {
63              trace("Match!");
64              _firstCard = undefined;
65          }
66          else
67          {
68              trace("Wrong.");
69              _firstCard.gotoAndPlay("flipBack");
70              _firstCard = undefined;
71          }
72      }
73  }
74 }
```

Line 69 of 74, Col 40

6 Save **MemoryGame.as** by choosing **File > Save**. Press **Ctrl+Enter** (Windows) or **Cmd+Return** (Mac) to test the movie. When the player window opens, click the two outside cards.

The two outside cards are not a match. The Output panel even says so: "Wrong." But notice that only the first card you chose flips back over. Click the second card again, and it still won't flip over. But you can fix that.

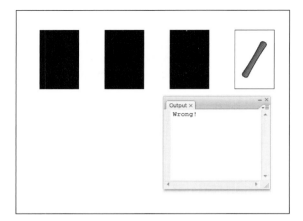

---

7 Close the player window and the **Output** panel. Select **MemoryGame.as**.

---

8 Position your cursor at the end of Line 69 after the code you just wrote, and press **Enter** (Windows) or **Return** (Mac) to go to the next line. Type the following:

```
event.currentTarget
.gotoAndPlay(flipBack);
```

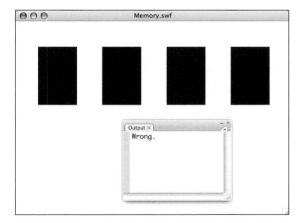

---

9 Choose **File > Save** to save **MemoryGame.as**, and then press **Ctrl+Enter** (Windows) or **Cmd+Return** (Mac) to test the movie. When the player window opens, click the two outside cards.

Sweet! The cards flip over, you get the "Wrong." message, and then both the cards flip back over.

10 Now click the same two cards.

These two cards flip over, but there's no error message, and they don't flip back over. Why? Since the event listeners were removed the first time the **checkCards()** event handler ran, the next time the cards are clicked, the handler doesn't run at all. You need to add the listeners back in if there isn't a match.

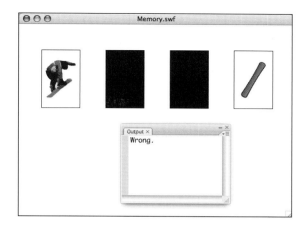

11 Close the player window and the **Output** panel. Position your cursor at the end of Line 70 in **MemoryGame.as**, and press **Enter** (Windows) or **Return** (Mac). Type the following:

```
_firstCard.addEventListener
(MouseEvent.CLICK, checkCards);
```

```
63                trace("Match!");
64                _firstCard = undefined;
65            }
66            else
67            {
68                trace("Wrong.");
69                _firstCard.gotoAndPlay("flipBack");
70                event.currentTarget.gotoAndPlay("flipBack");
71                _firstCard.addEventListener(MouseEvent.CLICK, checkCards);
72                _firstCard = undefined;
73            }
74        }
75    }
76 }
```
Line 71 of 76, Col 63

12 Select the code on Line 71 you just wrote, and press **Ctrl+C** (Windows) or **Cmd+C** (Mac) to copy it.

13 Position your cursor at the end of Line 72, press **Enter** (Windows) or **Return** (Mac), and press **Ctrl+V** (Windows) or **Cmd+V** (Mac) to paste the code.

```
65            }
66            else
67            {
68                trace("Wrong.");
69                _firstCard.gotoAndPlay("flipBack");
70                event.currentTarget.gotoAndPlay("flipBack");
71                _firstCard.addEventListener(MouseEvent.CLICK, checkCards);
72                _firstCard = undefined;
73                event.currentTarget.addEventListener(MouseEvent.CLICK, checkCards);
74            }
75        }
76    }
77 }
```
Line 73 of 77, Col 18

14 Change **_firstCard** on Line 73 to **event.currentTarget**.

15 Save **MemoryGame.as** by choosing
File > Save. Press **Ctrl+Enter** (Windows) or
Cmd+Return (Mac) to test the movie. Click
the outside two cards.

Since the cards are not a match, they flip
back over.

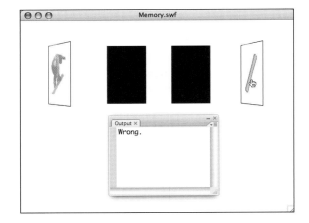

16 Click the cards again.

These cards are not a match this time either, but
they still flip back over. Great! All this trouble was
caused because the event listener was removed
on Line 55 in case of a match. Luckily, the fix is
easy. You just add it back in the conditional statement that runs if there is not a match.

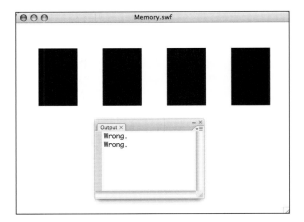

17 Close the player window and the **Output** panel. Close **MemoryGame.as**, **Card.as**, and **Memory.fla**.

9 | Determining a Win

In this exercise, you'll code how Flash determines when the game is won. To determine a win, you'll create two variables: one that holds the number of current matches and one that holds the number of possible matches. Every time a user makes a match, it's added to the current matches. If the variables are ever equal, the game will be won.

---

1 Choose **File > Open**, and open **Memory.fla**, **Card.as**, and **MemoryGame.as** from the **9-9** folder in the **chap_09** folder on your desktop.

---

2 Select **MemoryGame.as**. Insert your code at the end of Line 16 after the last variable, and press **Enter** (Windows) or **Return** (Mac) to go to the next line. Type the following:

```
private var
_totalMatches:Number;
private var
_currentMatches:Number;
```

Now that you've defined the two variables, you'll set their initial values in the `MemoryGame` constructor function.

```
import flash.display.MovieClip;
import Card;
import Boarder;
import BlueBoard;
import flash.events.MouseEvent;

public class MemoryGame extends MovieClip
{
    private var _card:Card;
    private var _boarder:Boarder;
    private var _blueBoard:BlueBoard;
    private var _cardX:Number;
    private var _cardY:Number;
    private var _firstCard:*;
    private var _totalMatches:Number;
    private var _currentMatches:Number;
```

---

3 Position your cursor at the end of Line 20 after the left curly brace of the constructor function, and press **Enter** (Windows) or **Return** (Mac) to go to the next line. Type the following:

```
_totalMatches = 2;
_currentMatches = 0;
```

```
    private var _cardX:Number;
    private var _cardY:Number;
    private var _firstCard:*;
    private var _totalMatches:Number;
    private var _currentMatches:Number;

    public function MemoryGame()
    {
        _totalMatches = 2;
        _currentMatches = 0;
        createCards();
    }
```

Since there are two sets of cards, two snowboarders and two boards, there are two sets of possible matches, so you set this variable to 2. **_currentMatches** is set to 0 since everyone starts the game with no matches.

4 Position your cursor at the end of Line 67 after **_firstCard = undefined;** in the **else if** statement, and press **Enter** (Windows) or **Return** (Mac) to go to the next line. Type the following:

```
65        else if(String(_firstCard._type) == String(event.currentTarget._type))
66        {
67            trace("Match!");
68            _firstCard = undefined;
69            _currentMatches ++;
70        }
71        else
72        {
73            trace("Wrong.");
```
Line 20 of 82, Col 38

```
_currentMatches ++;
```

++ is a mathematical operator that adds 1 to the value of **_currentMatches**. Every time a match is made, per the condition in the **else if** statement, this operation will run.

The next step is to check whether **_currentMatches** is equal to or greater than **_totalMatches**. You'll write this as a nested **if** statement in the **else if** statement.

---

5 Position your cursor at the end of Line 68 after the code you just typed, and press **Enter** (Windows) or **Return** (Mac) to go to the next line. Type the following:

```
if(_currentMatches >= _totalMatches)
```

---

6 Press **Enter** (Windows) or **Return** (Mac) to go to the next line. Type the following:

```
{
    trace("YOU WIN!!!")
}
```

```
61        else if(String(_firstCard._type) == String(event.currentTarget._type))
62        {
63            trace("Match!");
64            _firstCard = undefined;
65            _currentMatches ++;
66            if(_currentMatches >= _totalMatches)
67            {
68                trace("YOU WIN!!!")
69            }
70        }
71        else
72        {
73            trace("Wrong.");
```
Line 68 of 82, Col 24

---

7 Save **MemoryGame.as** by choosing **File > Save**, and then press **Ctrl+Enter** (Windows) or **Cmd+Return** (Mac) to test the movie. When the player window opens, click the two left cards.

There's one match. Think you can beat it?

---

8 Now click the two right cards.

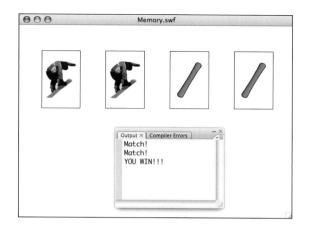

You win!!! Congratulations. Me too.

I'll admit the difficulty level of this game is some-what low, especially considering you've probably memorized all the cards already. In the next exer-cise, you'll add additional cards to make the game a little more exciting.

---

9 Close the player window and the **Output** panel. Close **MemoryGame.as**, **Card.as**, and **Memory.fla**.

In this exercise, you'll learn how to add more cards to your memory game.

---

1 Choose **File > Open**, and open **Memory.fla**, **Card.as**, and **MemoryGame.as** from the **9-10** folder in the **chap_09** folder on your desktop.

You'll need one more asset for this exercise.

---

2 Choose **File > Import > Open External Library**. In the **Open as Library** dialog box, select **Snow.fla** from the **9-10** folder, and click **Open**.

---

3 When the **Library** panel opens, click and drag the **Snow** symbol to the **Library** panel of **Memory.fla**. Close the **Snow.fla** library.

Now, just like with Boarder and blueBoard, you'll need to export Snow and the other card graphic, RedBoard, for use in ActionScript by updating the Linkage properties.

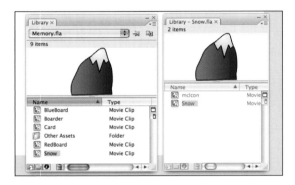

---

4 **Right-click** (Windows) or **Ctrl-click** (Mac) the **RedBoard** symbol in the **Library** panel, and choose **Linkage** in the contextual menu. When the **Linkage Properties** dialog box opens, select **Export for ActionScript**. Click **OK**, and click **OK** again to dismiss Flash's warning message.

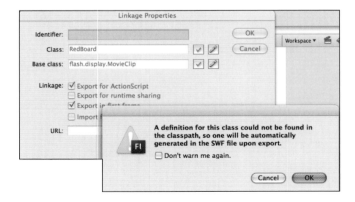

---

5 **Right-click** (Windows) or **Ctrl-click** (Mac) the **Snow** symbol in the **Library** panel, and choose **Linkage** in the contextual menu. When the **Linkage Properties** dialog box opens, select **Export for ActionScript**. Click **OK**, and click **OK** again to dismiss Flash's warning message.

6 Select **MemoryGame.as**. Insert your code at the end of Line 7 after the last **import** statement, and press **Enter** (Windows) or **Return** (Mac) to go to the next line. Type the following:

```
import RedBoard;
import Snow;
```

Now you'll need to create variables to hold the new instances of these classes.

```
package
{
    import flash.display.MovieClip;
    import Card;
    import Boarder;
    import BlueBoard;
    import flash.events.MouseEvent;
    import RedBoard;
    import Snow;

    public class MemoryGame extends MovieClip
    {
        private var _card:Card;
        private var _boarder:Boarder;
        private var _blueBoard:BlueBoard;
        private var _cardX:Number;
```

Line 9 of 88, Col 14

7 Position your cursor at the end of Line 20 after the last variable, and press **Enter** (Windows) or **Return** (Mac) to go to the next line. Type the following:

```
private var _redBoard:RedBoard;
private var _snow:Snow;
```

The next step is to generate card instances with these two graphic types.

```
    public class MemoryGame extends MovieClip
    {
        private var _card:Card;
        private var _boarder:Boarder;
        private var _blueBoard:BlueBoard;
        private var _cardX:Number;
        private var _cardY:Number;
        private var _firstCard:*;
        private var _totalMatches:Number;
        private var _currentMatches:Number;
        private var _redBoard:RedBoard;
        private var _snow:Snow;

        public function MemoryGame()
        {
            _totalMatches = 2;
```

Line 22 of 90, Col 3

8 Select Lines 36–58, both **for** statements in the **checkCards()** function. Press **Ctrl+C** (Windows) or **Cmd+C** (Mac) to copy them.

9 Position your cursor at the end of Line 58, and press **Enter** (Windows) or **Return** (Mac) twice. Press **Ctrl+V** (Windows) or **Cmd+V** (Mac) to paste the code.

10 Select the three instances of **i** on Line 60, and change them to **k**.

```
            for(var k:Number = 0; k < 2; k++)
            {
                _card = new Card();
                addChild(_card);
                _boarder = new Boarder();
                _card.setType(_boarder);
                _card.x = _cardX;
                _card.y = _cardY;
                _cardX += _card.width + 50;
                _card.addEventListener(MouseEvent.CLICK, checkCards);
            }

            for(var j:Number = 0; j < 2; j++)
            {
                _card = new Card();
```

Line 60 of 114, Col 34

11 Select the three instances of **j** on Line 72, and change them to **l**.

12 Select the word **_boarder** on Lines 64 and 65, and change it to **_redBoard**. Change **Boarder** on Line 64 to **RedBoard**.

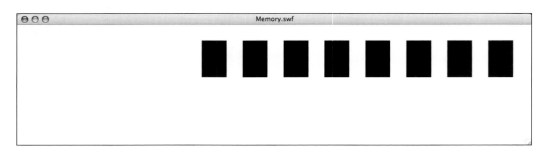

```
59
60              for(var k:Number = 0; k < 2; k++)
61              {
62              _card = new Card();
63              addChild(_card);
64              _redBoard = new RedBoard();
65              _card.setType(_redBoard);
66              _card.x = _cardX;
67              _card.y = _cardY;
68              _cardX += _card.width + 50;
69              _card.addEventListener(MouseEvent.CLICK, checkCards);
70              }
71
```

Line 60 of 114, Col 37

13 Select the word **_blueBoard** on Lines 76 and 77, and change it to **_snow**. Change **BlueBoard** on Line 77 to **Snow**.

14 Choose **File > Save All** to save your changes, and then press **Ctrl+Enter** (Windows) or **Cmd+Return** (Mac) to test the movie.

Notice that there are still four cards present. However, if you expand the size of your Flash player window, you'll see the other four cards, stacked to the right of the first four. That's fine, but what you really need here is a new row. All you have to do is reset the original X and original Y for the second two sets of cards.

15 Close the player window and the **Output** panel, if it's open.

16 Position your cursor at the end of Line 59 before the third **for** statement, and press **Enter** (Windows) or **Return** (Mac) twice. Press the **up arrow** key once, and type the following:

```
_cardX = 45;
_cardY += _card.height+50;
```

This code starts the second set of cards back at 45 pixels, but it moves them 50 pixels plus the length of the card height down from the last row.

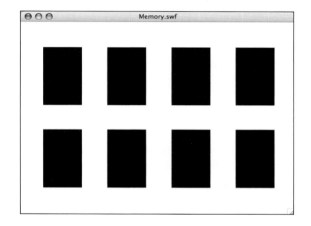

17 Save **MemoryGame.as** by choosing **File > Save**, and then press **Ctrl+Enter** (Windows) or **Cmd+Return** (Mac) to test the movie.

Excellent! Now you have two rows. Click any card from the first row and any card from the second to see that the second set of cards behaves exactly like the first, flipping and turning back when there is not a match.

18 Click the upper-right pair of cards, and click the upper-left pair of cards to create another match.

Notice the Output panel reads, "Wrong, Match!, Match! YOU WIN!!!" "Wrong" was from Step 9. All is well and good. "Match!" makes sense since your first and second matches was correct. But the third message, "YOU WIN!!!" doesn't seem right now that there are four sets of cards—you got only two out of four pairs, after all, and 50 percent is not a passing grade.

All you need to do to correct this is update the **_totalMatches** variable.

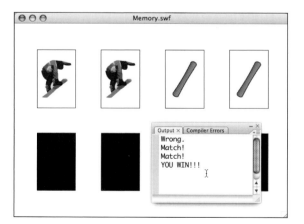

19 Close the player window and the **Output** panel. Return to **MemoryGame.as**.

20 Scroll up and select the number **2** on Line 26, and change it to **4**.

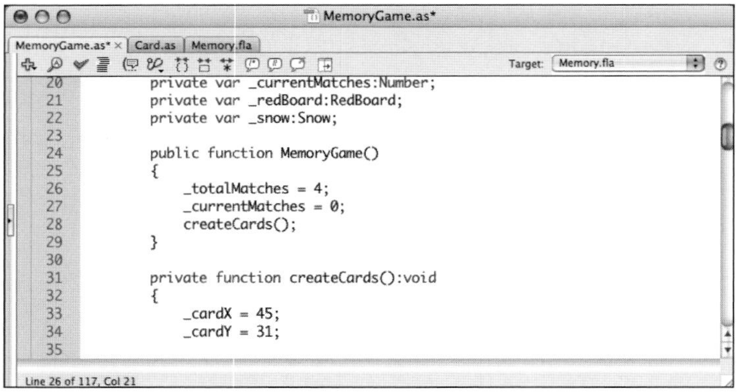

MemoryGame.as*
MemoryGame.as*
Card.as
Memory.fla
Target:
Memory.fla
20 private var _currentMatches:Number;
21 private var _redBoard:RedBoard;
22 private var _snow:Snow;
23
24 public function MemoryGame()
25 {
26 _totalMatches = 4;
27 _currentMatches = 0;
28 createCards();
29 }
30
31 private function createCards():void
32 {
33 _cardX = 45;
34 _cardY = 31;
35
Line 26 of 117, Col 21

21 Save **MemoryGame.as** by choosing **File > Save**. Press **Ctrl+Enter** (Windows) or **Cmd+Return** (Mac) to test the movie.

22 Click the upper-right pair of cards, the upper-left pair of cards, the lower-left pair, and the lower-right pair to make all four matches.

Now the Output panel reads, "Match!, Match!, Match!, Match!, YOU WIN!!!" The "You Win!!!" trace statement doesn't run until four correct matches have been made. To take this game to the next level, you can randomize the positions of the cards every time the game is loaded. Check out the video mentioned next for more information.

23 Close **MemoryGame.as**, **Card.as**, and **Memory.fla**.

VIDEO: | **randomizingcards.mov**

For more information on how to randomize the order in which the cards are placed on the **Stage**, check out **randomizingcards.mov** in the **videos** folder on the **ActionScript HOT CD-ROM**.

A round of applause! You finished the game and this chapter. You reviewed key concepts from the previous eight chapters and applied them in a different way. In the next chapter, you'll start coding color.

10

Using Advanced Graphics and Animation Tools

In this chapter, you'll create shapes, apply filters, and change the color of objects using code. Having the ability to create these graphic elements using ActionScript means you can create features that aren't even possible in design mode, such as generating random color changes and dynamically applying and animating filters. Using these tools can add loads to the design and interactivity of a Flash-driven application.

1 | Drawing with Code

In this exercise, you'll learn how to draw a simple shape on the **Stage** using ActionScript, without using any of the drawing tools in design mode.

---

1 Choose **File > New**, and click **Flash File (ActionScript 3.0)** in the **New Document** window.

---

2 Double-click the first layer, and rename it **actions**.

---

3 Select **Frame 1** on the **actions** layer, and press **F9** (Windows) or **Opt+F9** (Mac) to open the **Actions** panel.

The first step when you draw a shape with ActionScript is to create a variable to represent the shape.

---

4 On the first line, type the following:

```
var shape:Shape = new Shape();
```

The new **shape** variable will represent a new instance of the **Shape** class, which happens to be the data type **Shape**. That's a lot of shapes! Now it's time to actually draw the object.

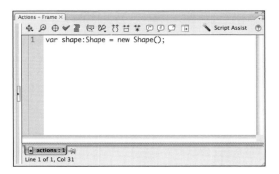

---

5 Press **Enter** (Windows) or **Return** (Mac) twice to insert two new lines, and type the following:

```
shape.graphics.lineStyle(
```

graphics and **lineStyle** are properties of the **Shape** class. In the parentheses, you can make modifications to the shape's stroke. Only two values are of concern now: thickness or stroke width and color.

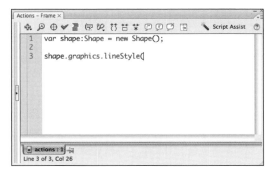

---

6 After the left parenthesis, type the following:

```
1, 0x00FF00);
```

The stroke width is measured in pixels: 1 means the shape stroke will be 1-pixel wide. The stroke color is represented by a hexadecimal value, just like when you were working with fonts in Chapter 8, *"Using Text and Arrays."* 00FF00 will make your stroke green.

Now you'll define the shape fill.

---

7 Press **Enter** (Windows) or **Return** (Mac), and type the following:

```
shape.graphics.beginFill(
```

`beginFill()` accepts only two values: the color, which is required, and the alpha, which is optional.

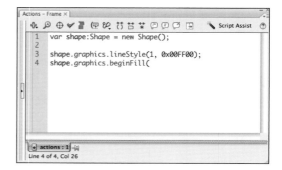

---

8 After the left parenthesis, type the following:

```
0x000000);
```

000000 is the hexadecimal value for black.

---

9 Press **Enter** (Windows) or **Return** (Mac), and type the following:

```
shape.graphics.drawCircle(
```

`drawCircle()` is a method that will draw the shape instance on the Stage. In fact, it will draw a circle. When you draw a circle, you must specify the *x* and *y* positions and the radius of the circle.

---

10 After the left parenthesis, type the following:

```
100,100,50);
```

These parameters give the circle an *x* and *y* position of 100 pixels and a radius of 50 pixels.

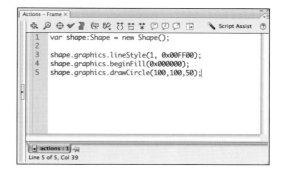

11 Press **Enter** (Windows) or **Return** (Mac), and type the following:

```
shape.graphics.endFill();
```

The Flash Player will not render the fill until the **endFill()** method is called. This step is optional since shape-drawing methods such as **drawCircle()** call **endFill()** automatically, but it is considered a best practice.

Finally, like any other object you create via ActionScript, you must add the new object to the display list using **addChild()**.

---

12 Press **Enter** (Windows) or **Return** (Mac), and type the following:

```
addChild(shape);
```

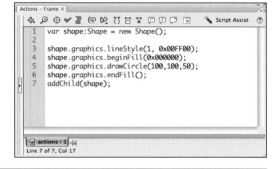

---

13 Press **Ctrl+Enter** (Windows) or **Cmd+Return** (Mac) to test the movie.

There you have it! A circle with a black fill and green stroke is placed 100 pixels down and 100 pixels from the left. Now, the stroke is a little hard to see. Instead of choosing the correct color and thickness from the Stroke Color box, choosing the Ink Bottle tool, and clicking to change the stroke, you can update this with a change to the 1 in the ActionScript code.

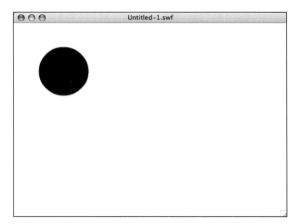

---

14 Close the player window. Select the **1** in the **lineStyle** statement on Line 3, and change it to **5**.

---

15 Press **Ctrl+Enter** (Windows) or **Cmd+Return** (Mac) to test the movie again.

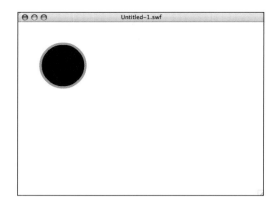

Voila! The stroke has been updated to a 5-pixel stroke. Now you may be thinking, that was an awful lot of work to draw a simple shape. Seven lines of code? Wouldn't it be easier to draw one using Flash's Ellipse tool? Well, you have a good point there. It is not always necessary or even recommended that you draw shapes with ActionScript. In fact, this goes for every exercise in this book. You shouldn't use ActionScript exclusively to create the content in your Flash documents. But there are situations when it might be beneficial.

Let's say you want to create an interface where a user could draw their own shapes. You'd have to use ActionScript to create it. Another example would be where you want to generate a random number of different-colored shapes. Only ActionScript can do that. But in order to build more complicated code like that, you first you need to know how to create a basic shape. And now you know!

Before moving on to these more complicated applications, let's review the code for drawing rectangles.

---

16 Close the player window. Select the `drawCircle` statement on Line 5, and press **Delete**. Replace this statement with the following:

```
shape.graphics.drawRect(100,100,200,100);
```

`drawRect()` accepts four parameters, in the following order: x position, y position, width, and height.

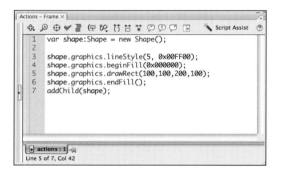

---

17 Press **Ctrl+Enter** (Windows) or **Cmd+Return** (Mac) to test the movie again.

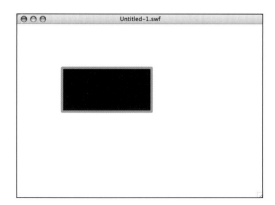

There's your rectangle. The fill and stroke are the same; just the shape style is different. You can draw many more shapes with ActionScript. To examine the methods and parameters required to draw each shape, look up the `shape.graphics` class in the Flash Help menu. You can access Flash Help anytime by pressing F1 on your keyboard or by choosing Help > Flash Help.

But there's one more thing I'd like to show you. Any visible object, such as a movie clip, can draw shapes. You don't have to use the **Shape** class.

ActionScript 3.0 for Adobe Flash CS3 Professional : H•O•T

18 Close the player window. Change the two instances of the word **Shape** on Line 1 to **MovieClip**.

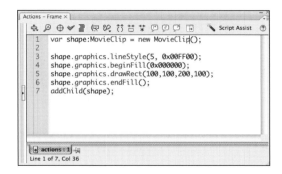

```
1   var shape:MovieClip = new MovieClip();
2
3   shape.graphics.lineStyle(5, 0x00FF00);
4   shape.graphics.beginFill(0x000000);
5   shape.graphics.drawRect(100,100,200,100);
6   shape.graphics.endFill();
7   addChild(shape);
```

19 Press **Ctrl+Enter** (Windows) or **Cmd+Return** (Mac) to test the movie.

You get the same shape when you create a new instance of the **MovieClip** class instead of the **Shape** class. All visible objects in Flash have a **graphics** property that lets you draw vector shapes.

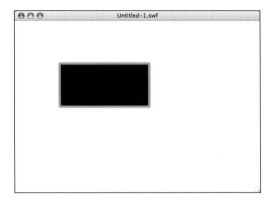

20 Close the preview window, and close your Flash file. You don't need to save your changes.

2 | Creating a Color Change

In this exercise, you'll learn how to modify the color of a movie clip using code.

1 Open **Color_Change.fla** from the **chap_10** exercise folder.

First you'll create a color change in design mode.

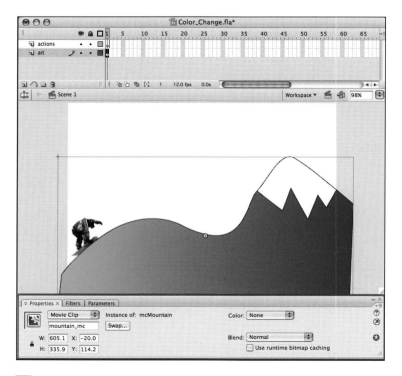

2 Choose **Window > Properties > Properties** to open the **Property inspector**, if it is not already open. Select the **Selection** tool, click the mountain on the **Stage**, and then look at the **Property inspector**.

This object is a movie clip instance named mountain_mc.

3 Click the **Color** pop-up menu, and choose **Tint**.

The color of the mountain is automatically tinted with a percentage of the default color selected in the Tint Color box. Your color may not be the same as mine.

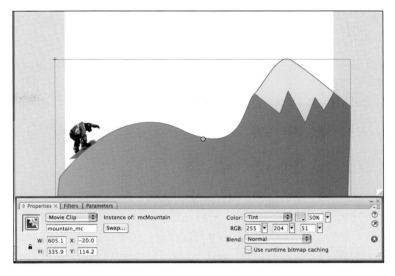

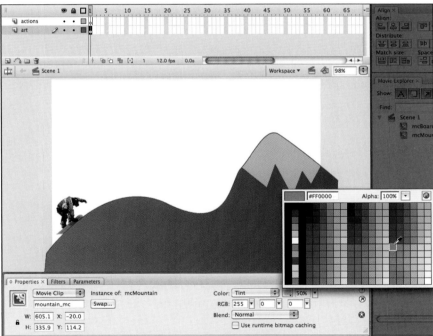

Click the color box, and position your cursor over the different swatches to see how the color of the mountain movie clip changes. Click away from the color picker to close the swatches.

This is the same effect you'll be creating in ActionScript. You may be thinking, why would I ever want to create a color transformation in code? Well, let's say you wanted to grab a random color for the tint of an object. The only way to do this would be with ActionScript. In this exercise, you'll create a simple color change, but in the next one you'll learn how to randomize it. So onward and upward!

4 Click the **Tint** pop-up menu again, and choose **None** to return the mountain to its original color.

---

5 Select **Frame 1** on the **actions** layer, and press **F9** (Windows) or **Opt+F9** (Mac) to open the **Actions** panel, if it is not already open.

Creating a color change with ActionScript consists of three steps: first you create a new instance of the `ColorTransform` class, then you apply your changes to the instance, and finally you link the `ColorTransform` instance to the object on the Stage you want to transform. This is similar to the process you use to style text in ActionScript.

---

6 Position your cursor on the first line, and type the following:

```
var colorT:ColorTransform = new ColorTransform();
```

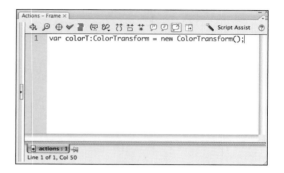

---

7 Press **Enter** (Windows) or **Return** (Mac) twice, and type the following:

```
colorT.blueOffset = -100;
```

Changes to colors with the `ColorTransform` object are made using offsets and multipliers. Offsets allow you to subtract or add intensity to either the red, green, or blue channels; multipliers allow you to increase or decrease the intensity of each channel by a percentage (expressed as a point value, such as .3). Offsets accept values from -255 to 255. Multipliers accept values between 0 and 1.

The `blueOffset` property is used to offset the value of the blue channel of the object being modified. Subtracting 100 from the current blue value decreases the amount of blue in the color. You'll increase the red value next by the same amount using the `redOffset` property.

---

8 Press **Enter** (Windows) or **Return** (Mac), and type the following:

```
colorT.redOffset = 100;
```

Now that the second step is complete and you've modified properties of the `ColorTransform` object, the third step is to apply the object to the mountain movie clip.

---

9 Press **Enter** (Windows) or **Return** (Mac) twice, and type the following:

`mountain_mc.transform.colorTransform = colorT;`

`colorTransform` is a property residing in the `transform` property of a movie clip. Here you are defining the `colorTransform` property of mountain_mc equal to the new `colorT` instance you created in the previous steps.

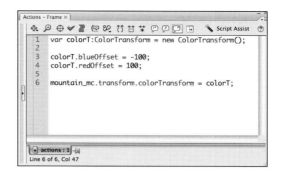

10 Press **Ctrl+Enter** (Windows) or **Cmd+Return** (Mac) to test the movie.

The mountain now appears slightly green and brown, since you reduced the amount of blue and increased the red. You can change the same `ColorTransform` object to any display object. To change the color of the boarder movie clip, you'd just replace `mountain_mc` on Line 6 of your code with `boarder_mc`.

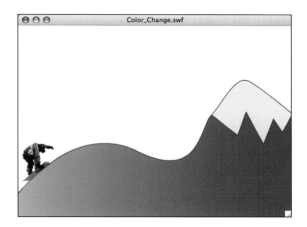

11 Close the player window, and return to the **Actions** panel. Replace `mountain_mc` on Line 6 with `boarder_mc`.

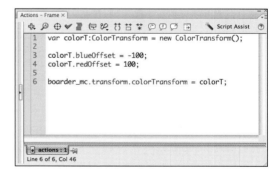

12 Press **Ctrl+Enter** (Windows) or **Cmd+Return** (Mac) to test the movie again.

Notice the color of the snowboarder is different from what the mountain was when you applied the color transform. It has more of an orange tint. That's because you are not setting the exact value for the RGB channels of the object, you are *offsetting* the values.

13 Close the player window, and return to the **Actions** panel. Select the word `ColorTransform` on the first line of your code, and choose **Help > Flash Help**.

The Help menu opens automatically to the `ColorTransform` definition. Scroll down to the Public Properties section for a list of the other properties you can modify with this class.

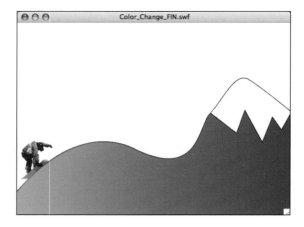

14 Close the **Help** window, and close **Color_Change.fla**. You don't need to save your changes.

In the next exercise, you'll learn how to randomize your color transformations.

3 | Generating a Random Color Change

In this exercise, you'll learn how to generate and apply a random color to objects on the **Stage**.

1 Choose **File > Open**, and open **Random_Color.fla** the **chap_10** folder on your desktop.

This file contains some of the same content as the previous file, Color_Change.fla. There are instances of the mcMountain and mcBoarder movie clips on the Stage, named mountain_mc and boarder_mc, respectively. There's also a new movie clip called mcRandom. The idea is that when you click the random movie clip button, a random color will be assigned to the snowboarder and the mountain.

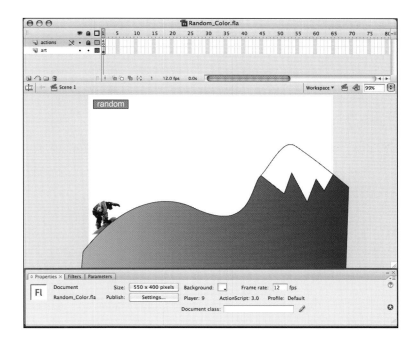

2 Select **Frame 1** on the **actions** layer, and press **F9** (Windows) or **Opt+F9** (Mac) to open the **Actions** panel, if it is not already open.

The top six lines of the code contain the code you wrote in the previous exercise. At the bottom of the panel, there is a new event listener for random_mc and an empty event handler.

```
1  var colorT:ColorTransform = new ColorTransform();
2
3  colorT.blueOffset = -100;
4  colorT.redOffset = 100;
5
6  boarder_mc.transform.colorTransform = colorT;
7
8
9
10
11 random_mc.addEventListener(MouseEvent.CLICK, onClick);
12
13 function onClick(event:MouseEvent):void
14 {
15
16 }
```

3 Select Lines 3–6 of the code, and press **Ctrl+X** (Windows) or **Cmd+X** (Mac) to cut them. Delete all but two of the lines between Line 1 and the event listener.

Don't worry—you'll paste this code back in the event handler.

___

4 Click Line 8 in the event handler, and press **Ctrl+V** (Windows) or **Cmd+V** (Mac) to paste the code.

If any of the lines you pasted lose their indention, position your cursor at the beginning of the lines, and press the Tab key.

Now you'll change the **offset** property values to random numbers.

```
1   var colorT:ColorTransform = new ColorTransform();
2
3
4   random_mc.addEventListener(MouseEvent.CLICK, onClick);
5
6   function onClick(event:MouseEvent):void
7   {
8       colorT.blueOffset = -100;
9       colorT.redOffset = 100;
10
11      boarder_mc.transform.colorTransform = colorT;
12  }
```

Line 11 of 12, Col 2

___

5 Select **-100** on Line 8, and replace it with the following:

`Math.round(Math.random() *`

You've seen this code before. You're generating a random number and using the nearest rounding method to round it to a whole number. Next, you'll multiply it by some value to create a number that fits within the possible values for the **offset** property. But there's a bit of a problem. It seems natural to use 255, which would result in a random number between 0 and 255. The problem is, we're looking for values between 255 and -255.

```
1   var colorT:ColorTransform = new ColorTransform();
2
3
4   random_mc.addEventListener(MouseEvent.CLICK, onClick);
5
6   function onClick(event:MouseEvent):void
7   {
8       colorT.blueOffset = Math.round(Math.random() * |
9       colorT.redOffset = 100;
10
11      boarder_mc.transform.colorTransform = colorT;
12  }
```

Line 8 of 12, Col 49

Here's a thought. This range is actually 510 numbers, 255 negative numbers and 255 positive numbers, plus zero. If you multiply the random number results by 510 and then subtract 255, you'll have a range between 255 and -255, including zero. Let's try this!

___

6 Now type the following:

`510) - 255;`

So if the random method generates a value of 510, then 255 will be subtracted, and you'll be left with 255, the highest number in the desired range. If the `random()` function generates a value of 0, then 255 will be subtracted, and you'll still be within the correct range.

```
Actions - Frame
                                              Script Assist
1  var colorT:ColorTransform = new ColorTransform();
2
3
4  random_mc.addEventListener(MouseEvent.CLICK, onClick);
5
6  function onClick(event:MouseEvent):void
7  {
8      colorT.blueOffset = Math.round(Math.random() * 510) - 255;
9      colorT.redOffset = 100;
10
11     boarder_mc.transform.colorTransform = colorT;
12 }
```
actions : 1
Line 10 of 12, Col 1

---

7 Select `Math.round(Math.random() * 510) - 255;` and press **Ctrl+C** (Windows) or **Cmd+C** (Mac) to copy the code.

---

8 Select `100;` in the next line of code, Line 9, and press **Ctrl+V** (Windows) or **Cmd+V** (Mac) to replace it with the `Math` expression you copied from Line 8.

While you're at it, you might as well apply a `greenOffset` as well.

```
Actions - Frame
                                              Script Assist
1  var colorT:ColorTransform = new ColorTransform();
2
3
4  random_mc.addEventListener(MouseEvent.CLICK, onClick);
5
6  function onClick(event:MouseEvent):void
7  {
8      colorT.blueOffset = Math.round(Math.random() * 510) - 255;
9      colorT.redOffset = Math.round(Math.random() * 510) - 255;
10
11     boarder_mc.transform.colorTransform = colorT;
12 }
```
actions : 1
Line 9 of 12, Col 59

---

9 Select all the code on Line 9, and press **Ctrl+C** (Windows) or **Cmd+C** (Mac) to copy the code. Go to the end of Line 9, and press **Enter** (Windows) or **Return** (Mac) to type a new line. Now press **Ctrl+V** **(Windows) or** Cmd+V **(Mac)** to paste the code.

---

10 Select the word `redOffset` on Line 10, and change it to `greenOffset`.

11 Press **Ctrl+Enter** (Windows) or **Cmd+Return** (Mac) to test the movie. When the player window opens, click the **random** button several times.

Nice! Every time you click the button, the snowboarder turns a different color.

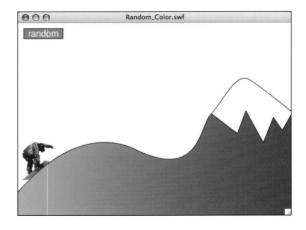

---

12 Close the player window, and return to the **Actions** panel.

If you wanted to apply a color change to the mountain, you could copy and paste Line 12 and change `boarder_mc` to `mountain_mc`. But the two objects would change the same color every time the button was clicked. To generate a unique color for the mountain, you'd need to generate new random numbers.

---

13 Select the code on Lines 8–12, and press **Ctrl+C** (Windows) or **Cmd+C** (Mac) to copy the code. Go to the end of Line 12, and press **Enter** (Windows) or **Return** (Mac) twice. Now press **Ctrl+V** (Windows) or **Cmd+V** (Mac) to paste the code.

---

14 Select the word **boarder_mc** on Line 18, and change it to **mountain_mc**.

```
1  var colorT:ColorTransform = new ColorTransform();
2
3
4  random_mc.addEventListener(MouseEvent.CLICK, onClick);
5
6  function onClick(event:MouseEvent):void
7  {
8      colorT.blueOffset = Math.round(Math.random() * 510) - 255;
9      colorT.redOffset = Math.round(Math.random() * 510) - 255;
10     colorT.greenOffset = Math.round(Math.random() * 510) - 255;
11
12     boarder_mc.transform.colorTransform = colorT;
13
14     colorT.blueOffset = Math.round(Math.random() * 510) - 255;
15     colorT.redOffset = Math.round(Math.random() * 510) - 255;
16     colorT.greenOffset = Math.round(Math.random() * 510) - 255;
17
18     mountain_mc.transform.colorTransform = colorT;
19  }
```

15 Press **Ctrl+Enter** (Windows) or **Cmd+Return** (Mac) to test the movie again. When the player window opens, click the **random** button several times.

Now the colors of the snowboarder and the mountain are randomly selected, independent of one another. The key to this exercise was making sure the random number range corresponded to the values required by the **offset** properties.

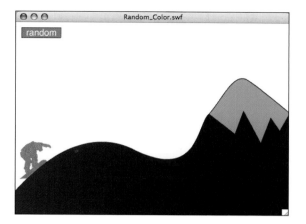

16 Close the player window, and close **Random_Color.fla**. You don't need to save your changes.

4 | Animating a Color Change

In this exercise, you'll learn how to animate a color change.

---

1 Choose **File > Open**, and open **Animate_Color.fla** from the **chap_10** folder on your desktop.

This file contains both boarder_mc and mountain_mc, similar to the exercise files used in the previous exercises.

---

2 Select **Frame 1** on the **actions** layer, and press **F9** (Windows) or **Opt+F9** (Mac) to open the **Actions** panel, if it is not already open.

This code contains a new instance of the `ColorTransform` object. Now you'll use the `ENTER_FRAME` event, which you first explored in Chapter 4, *"Responding to Events,"* to animate this color transformation.

---

3 Press **Enter** (Windows) or **Return** (Mac) twice to go to Line 3. Type the following:

```
this.addEventListener(Event.ENTER_FRAME,
animateColor);
```

---

4 Press **Enter** (Windows) or **Return** (Mac) twice, and type the following:

```
function animateColor(event:Event):void
{
}
```

Now that the event listener and the handler are set up, you'll set the initial values of the `ColorTransform` object.

5 Position your cursor at the end of Line 1, and press **Enter** (Windows) or **Return** (Mac). Type the following:

```
colorT.redOffset = -255;
```

6 Position your cursor in the curly braces of the event handler on Line 8, and type the following:

```
colorT.redOffset ++;
```

Because you are using **ENTER_FRAME**, this event handler will be triggered during every frame on the movie, which is currently set at 12 fps (frames per second).

When the movie starts, the **redOffset** value will be set at -255, as you wrote on Line 2. Then every

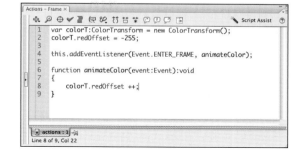

frame, the **redOffset** value will increment by 1. Remember that ++ is the mathematical operator meaning "add 1 to the current value." Before you test the movie, **colorT** needs to be linked to an object on the Stage.

7 Press **Enter** (Windows) or **Return** (Mac) to insert a new line, and type the following:

```
mountain_mc.transform.colorTransform = colorT;
```

8 Press **Ctrl+Enter** (Windows) or **Cmd+Return** (Mac) to test the movie, and watch the mountain closely.

Without any interference, the mountain cap gradually changes from a light blue to white, and the mountain changes to pink. Let's make this animate a little bit faster.

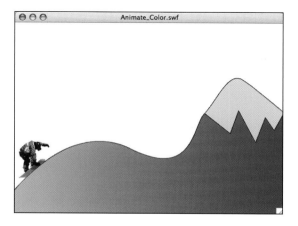

9 Close the player window, and return to the **Actions** panel.

---

10 Select the ++ operator on Line 8, and change it to **+= 10**.

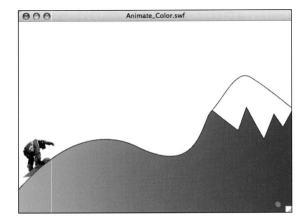

```
1  var colorT:ColorTransform = new ColorTransform();
2  colorT.redOffset = -255;
3
4  this.addEventListener(Event.ENTER_FRAME, animateColor);
5
6  function animateColor(event:Event):void
7  {
8      colorT.redOffset += 10;
9      mountain_mc.transform.colorTransform =  colorT;
10 }
```

---

11 Press **Ctrl+Enter** (Windows) or **Cmd+Return** (Mac) to test the movie again, and watch the mountain.

Now the color change is a little more obvious. That's how to animate a color change with ActionScript. You can animate it by using the `ENTER_FRAME` event listener (or using a timer) and changing the `ColorTransform` properties within the event handler.

---

12 Close the player window, and close **Animate_Color.fla**. You don't need to save your changes.

5 | Using Filters

In this exercise, you'll learn how to create filters using code. First of all, it's important to address why you would create filters in code at all. Filters are intense graphic elements that take up a lot of space in your Flash files. If you can make them appear dynamically, only when they're needed, so much the better. In other words, if the user does not need to see a filter until a certain time, you can introduce it at that time. If they never need to see it, you don't have to increase the file size unnecessarily as you would if you had to build it into the design. You wind up with a more effective and a more efficient Flash movie.

Another reason you might build a filter in Flash through code is if you wanted the filter to be applied based on the user's mouse position. For example, you could have a drag and drop object on the Stage that had a drop shadow. If you wanted the drop shadow to change positions based on the user's mouse movements, you would have to use ActionScript. Coding filters with ActionScript is just another way to optimize your Flash movie.

---

1 Choose **File > Open**, and open **Filters.fla** from the **chap_10** folder on your desktop.

---

2 Select **Frame 1** on the **actions** layer, and press **F9** (Windows) or **Opt+F9** (Mac) to open the **Actions** panel, if it is not already open.

Applying a filter to an object in ActionScript is actually simple. The snowboarder on the Stage is already labeled boarder_mc, so you'll use that to start.

---

3 Insert your cursor on Line 1, and type the following:

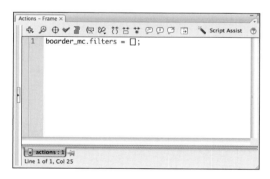

`boarder_mc.filters = [];`

The **filters** property of boarder_mc, which is the same for any display object, can hold an array of filters, as signified by the square brackets. So, you can apply more than one filter to a single object. You can even create custom filters, which you'll learn about in the next exercise.

4 Position your cursor in the square brackets, and type the following:

new DropShadowFilter()

And you're done! This will create a new instance of the **DropShadowFilter** class. The drop shadow will use the default values for this filter, just like if you selected the movie clip on the Stage and applied a drop shadow. It has a default depth, angle, and so on.

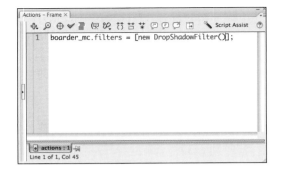

5 Press **Ctrl+Enter** (Windows) or **Cmd+Return** (Mac) to test the movie.

Voila! Notice the black area or shadow around the snowboarder. You've just applied this drop shadow with code. It's almost as easy as doing it in design mode, and as I explained earlier, there can be many benefits to applying filters with code instead. Next you'll apply a blur filter.

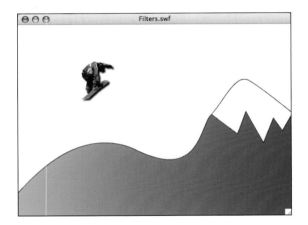

6 Close the player window, and return to the **Actions** panel. Select **DropShadow** (just these words) in the first line of code, and replace it with **Blur**.

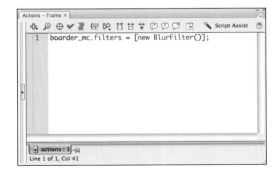

7 Press **Ctrl+Enter** (Windows) or **Cmd+Return** (Mac) to test the movie.

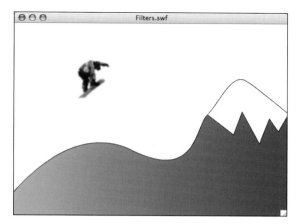

Now you have a blurry snowboarder. You could replace BlurFilter with BevelFilter, GlowFilter, GradientGlowFilter, and so on. All the filters available in design mode can be applied using this syntax.

8 Close the player window, and close **Filters.fla**. You don't need to save your changes.

EXERCISE

6 | Modifying Filter Properties

In this exercise, you'll learn how to modify filter properties with ActionScript.

---

1 Choose **File > Open**, and open **Filter_Properties.fla** from the **chap_10** folder on your desktop.

This file is the same as the other files you've been working with in this chapter. In this exercise, you'll have the snowboarder cast a shadow on the mountain.

---

2 Select **Frame 1** on the **actions** layer, and press **F9** (Windows) or **Opt+F9** (Mac) to open the **Actions** panel, if it's not already open.

---

3 Position your cursor on the first line, and type the following:

```
var boarderShadow:DropShadowFilter = new
DropShadowFilter();
```

This variable will represent the new instance of the drop shadow filter.

---

4 Press **Enter** (Windows) or **Return** (Mac), and type the following:

```
boarderShadow.
```

The Code Hint menu should pop up. You can modify a variety of properties for each filter. To get a full description of each property, choose Help > Flash Help.

---

5 Next type the following:

```
color = 0x0B77A9;
```

Like other color properties, this one accepts a hexadecimal value. 0B77A9 is a dark blue color that I sampled from the mountain on the Stage.

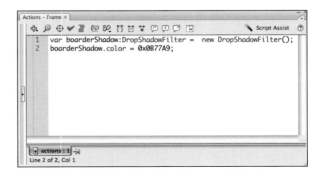

---

6 Press **Enter** (Windows) or **Return** (Mac), and type the following:

```
boarderShadow.blurX = 10;
boarderShadow.blurY = 10;
```

blurX and **blurY** are the horizontal and vertical blur amounts for the drop shadow.

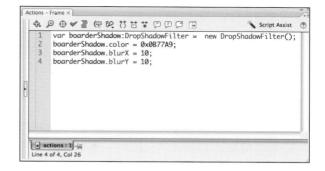

7 Press **Enter** (Windows) or **Return** (Mac), and type the following:

```
boarderShadow.angle = 66;
```

Note: Angles in Flash go from -180 to 180 degrees.

8 Press **Enter** (Windows) or **Return** (Mac), and type the following:

```
boarderShadow.distance = 200;
```

This is the last property you'll modify, but it's an important one, because it makes the shadow fall all the way down onto the mountain.

Now you just have to apply this drop shadow to the boarder object.

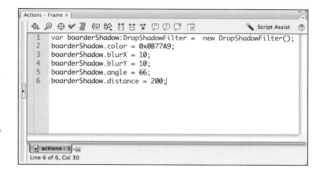

9 Press **Enter** (Windows) or **Return** (Mac) twice, and type the following:

```
boarder_mc.filters = [boarderShadow];
```

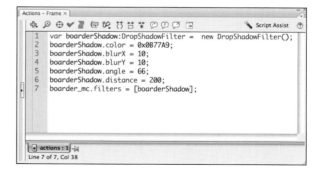

10 Press **Ctrl+Enter** (Windows) or
Cmd+Return (Mac) to test the movie.

There you go. The snowboarder casts a shadow
on the mountain. If you're wondering where I
got all these specific values for the filter from, I
actually applied the filter first in design mode,
modified the properties with the Filters panel,
wrote them down, and then used them in my
ActionScript.

If you are not seeing the drop shadow, it may
be because the mountain is on top of the
snowboarder in the object stacking order. If so,
close the player window and the Actions panel. Right-click (Windows) or Ctrl-click (Mac)
the mountain on the Stage, and choose Arrange > Send to Back in the contextual menu.

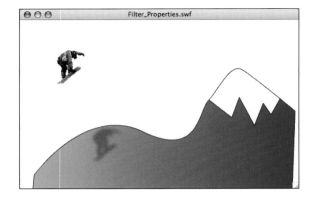

---

11 Close the player window, and close **Filter_Properties.fla**. You don't need to save your changes.

---

7 | Animating Filters

In this exercise, you'll learn how to animate a filter.

---

1 Choose **File > Open**, and open **Animating_Filters.fla** from the **chap_10** folder on your desktop.

Again, there's a snowboarder and the mountain on the Stage.

---

2 Select **Frame 1** on the **actions** layer, and press **F9** (Windows) or **Opt+F9** (Mac) to open the **Actions** panel, if it is not already open.

This file already contains quite a bit of script. The new **DropShadowFilter** instance has already been created, the properties are modified, and there's an **ENTER_FRAME** event listener and an event handler that moves the snowboarder up and over 5 pixels every frame.

```
Actions - Frame ×                                          Script Assist ?
1   var boarderShadow:DropShadowFilter = new DropShadowFilter();
2   boarderShadow.color = 0x0B77A9;
3   boarderShadow.blurX = 0;
4   boarderShadow.blurY = 0;
5   boarderShadow.angle = 90;
6   boarderShadow.distance = 100;
7
8
9   this.addEventListener(Event.ENTER_FRAME, moveShadow);
10
11  function moveShadow(event:Event):void
12  {
13      boarder_mc.y -= 5;
14      boarder_mc.x += 5;
15  }

actions : 1
Line 15 of 15, Col 2
```

---

3 Press **Ctrl+Enter** (Windows) or **Cmd+Return** (Mac) to test the movie.

Notice that the filter hasn't yet been applied to the snowboarder.

---

4 Close the player window, and return to the **Actions** panel. Position your cursor at the end of Line 14, press **Enter** (Windows) or **Return** (Mac), and then type the following:

`boarder_mc.filters = [boarderShadow];`

```
Actions - Frame ×                                          Script Assist ?
1   var boarderShadow:DropShadowFilter = new DropShadowFilter();
2   boarderShadow.color = 0x0B77A9;
3   boarderShadow.blurX = 0;
4   boarderShadow.blurY = 0;
5   boarderShadow.angle = 90;
6   boarderShadow.distance = 100;
7
8
9   this.addEventListener(Event.ENTER_FRAME, moveShadow);
10
11  function moveShadow(event:Event):void
12  {
13      boarder_mc.y -= 5;
14      boarder_mc.x += 5;
15      boarder_mc.filters = [boarderShadow];
16  }

actions : 1
Line 15 of 16, Col 39
```

5 Press **Ctrl+Enter** (Windows) or **Cmd+Return** (Mac) to test the movie.

Now the shadow is there, but it moves along with the snowboarder into the sky, which doesn't look very realistic. The shadow's distance needs to be increased as the boarder moves.

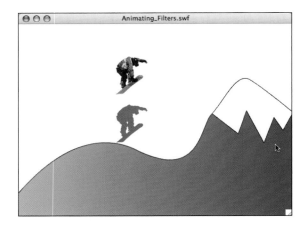

---

6 Close the player window, and return to the **Actions** panel. Position your cursor at the end of Line 14, and press **Enter** (Windows) or **Return** (Mac) to go to the next line. Type the following:

```
boarderShadow.distance += 5;
```

So as the snowboarder rises 5 pixels every frame, the shadow will fall 5 pixels.

---

7 Press **Enter** (Windows) or **Return** (Mac) to go to the next line. Type the following:

```
boarderShadow.blurX ++;
```

This causes the shadow to get blurrier as the shadow gets higher, adding to the realism of the effect.

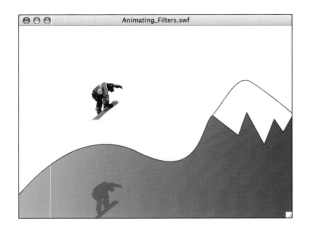

---

8 Select Line 16, the line of code your wrote in the previous step, and press **Ctrl+C** (Windows) or **Cmd+C** (Mac) to copy the code.

ActionScript 3.0 for Adobe Flash CS3 Professional : H·O·T

9 Position your cursor at the end of Line 16, and press **Enter** (Windows) or **Return** (Mac) to go to the next line. Press **Ctrl+V** (Windows) or **Cmd+V** (Mac) to paste the code, and then change `blurX` to `blurY`.

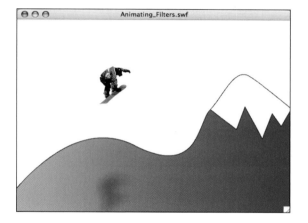

```
 3    boarderShadow.blurX = 0;
 4    boarderShadow.blurY = 0;
 5    boarderShadow.angle = 90;
 6    boarderShadow.distance = 100;
 7
 8
 9    this.addEventListener(Event.ENTER_FRAME, moveShadow);
10
11    function moveShadow(event:Event):void
12    {
13        boarder_mc.y -= 5;
14        boarder_mc.x += 5;
15        boarderShadow.distance += 5;
16        boarderShadow.blurX ++;
17        boarderShadow.blurY ++;
18        boarder_mc.filters = [boarderShadow];
19    }
```

10 Press **Ctrl+Enter** (Windows) or **Cmd+Return** (Mac) to test the movie. Watch the shadow closely.

Now the shadow gets even blurry as it moves across the mountain.

11 Close the player window, and close **Animating_Filters.fla**. You don't need to save your changes.

And that's how you animate filters. Just like when you animate color changes, you can use either the `ENTER_FRAME` or `TIMER` event.

In the next chapter, you'll learn about how to convert even more tasks that are usually performed in design mode, such as adding sounds and importing videos, into ActionScript code. See you there!

11

Working with Multimedia

You've already learned how to link to external Web sites and import external text files, but in this chapter, you'll learn how to import other types of objects into your Adobe Flash movies using ActionScript. You can import Apple QuickTime movies, a variety of sound formats, and even Flash video using just a few lines of code. You'll also learn how to control the playback of these items by adding stop and start buttons and volume controls.

1 | Loading External Images and SWFs

In this exercise, you'll learn how to load a variety of images and external SWF files into a Flash movie using ActionScript.

1 Copy the **chap_11** folder from the **Exercises Files** folder to your desktop. Choose **File > Open**, and open **Loading_Images.fla** from the **11-1** folder in the **chap_11** folder you copied to your desktop.

There's nothing on the Stage or in the Library panel of this file yet. You'll add a series of images by loading them from external files.

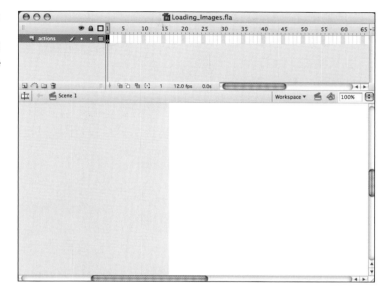

2 Select **Frame 1** on the **actions** layer, and press **F9** (Windows) or **Opt+F9** (Mac) to open the **Actions** panel.

First you'll create a **URLRequest** variable that will represent the location of the external image file.

3 On the first line, type the following:

```
var imageRequest:URLRequest = new
URLRequest("snowboard.jpg");
```

The next step in loading an external file is to create an image **Loader**, which is a Flash object similar to a **URLLoader**.

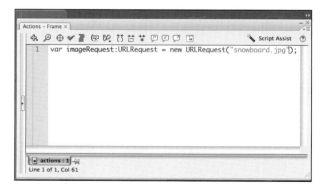

4 Press **Enter** (Windows) or **Return** (Mac), and type the following:

```
var imageLoader:Loader = new Loader();
```

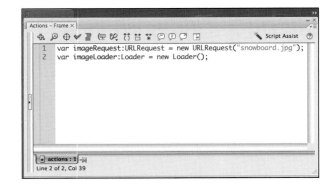

---

5 Press **Enter** (Windows) or **Return** (Mac), and type the following:

```
imageLoader.load(imageRequest);
```

load() is a method instructing the **Loader** to load the **imageRequest** file, snowboard.jpg. There's only one more step before you can see this image: you need to use the **addChild()** method to add this object to the display list.

---

6 Press **Enter** (Windows) or **Return** (Mac), and type the following:

```
addChild(imageLoader);
```

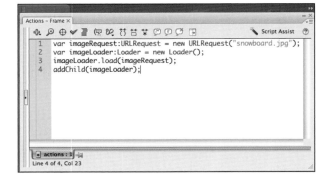

---

7 Press **Ctrl+Enter** (Windows) or **Cmd+Return** (Mac) to test the movie.

A snowboard image will appear on the far left side of the Stage. It's that easy to load an external image! Now you'll try loading some different types of images.

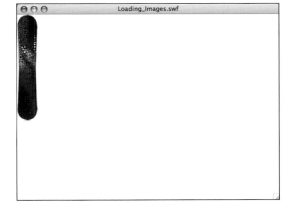

NOTE:

What Kind of Image Files Can I Use in My Flash Project?

Using the **Loader** class, you can load JPEG, PNG, and GIF files. GIF stands for Graphics Interchange Format. GIFs are best suited for graphics and logos, rather than photographs or more complicated images, because of the limited color palette, and they are widely supported. GIFs use 256 colors in the 24-bit RGB (**R**ed, **G**reen, **B**lue) color space.

PNG stands for Portable Network Graphics. PNGs are similar to GIF files and used mainly for less color intensive graphics that are intended for use on the Web. Unlike GIFs, PNGs do not support animation, but they do support more transparency and can produce smaller file sizes than GIFs.

JPEG stands for Joint Photographic Experts Group, which was the name of the group that created the standards behind the file format. JPEG uses a special lossy compression method, which results in smaller file sizes for photographic images than PNG or GIF, which use lossless compression methods. JPEG is the most popular choice for photographs that are destined for the Web.

Note: **Lossless** compression methods reduce file size without sacrificing quality, whereas **lossy** compression methods discard some information under the theory that it is not visible to the human eye. If lossy images are edited and saved more than once, they can suffer some loss of quality, because information is continually discarded. That's why digital photographs are usually exported to the JPEG format as the final step after editing.

The format you choose is really up to you. If you are concerned about the size of your final movie, you might decide to export your image in a variety of file formats and then compare the resulting file sizes. As you can see from the illustration here, the compression methods really do affect the final file.

8 Close the preview window, and return to the **Actions** panel. Replace the **.jpg** extension in Line 1 with **.gif**.

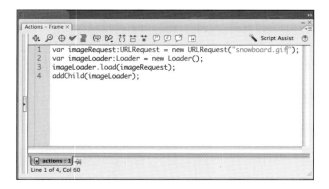

9 Press **Ctrl+Enter** (Windows) or **Cmd+Return** (Mac) to test the movie.

You may notice that the snowboard in this test movie looks a bit better than the previous image, a .jpg, but the file is also almost twice as large.

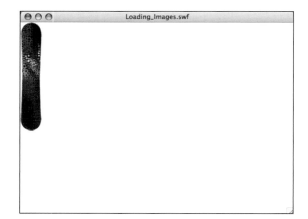

10 Close the preview window, and return to the **Actions** panel. Replace the **.gif** extension in Line 1 with **.png**.

11 Press **Ctrl+Enter** (Windows) or **Cmd+Return** (Mac) to test the movie.

The .png file should look very similar to the .jpg and .gif files, but again, the file size is somewhat larger. If you are using a lot of external assets in your movie, it can really add up.

Now on to external movies! You can actually use this same syntax to load a SWF file.

12 Close the preview window, and return to the **Actions** panel. Replace `snowboard.png` in Line 1 with `movie.swf`.

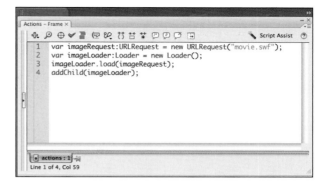

13 Press **Ctrl+Enter** (Windows) or **Cmd+Return** (Mac) to test the movie.

You can't tell by looking at it, since the image is static, but this is actually an external SWF file you're seeing. An occasion where you might want to load a SWF into another SWF file is when you intend to use the movie throughout your site. SWF files are another type of reusable asset that can be used in different projects or replicated throughout a single project. Another benefit of loading an external SWF is that it is cached in the user's browser only once. So if you decide to use it in multiple locations throughout a Web site, the user doesn't have to keep downloading the file, and the whole experience is more seamless.

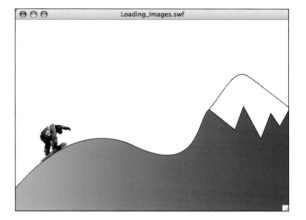

14 Close the preview window, and close **Loading_Images.fla**. You don't need to save your changes.

In the next exercise, you'll learn how to communicate with a loaded SWF file.

2 | Communicating with Loaded Movies

In this exercise, you'll learn how to modify objects in an external SWF file that has been loaded into another Flash movie using ActionScript.

---

1 Open **Communicating.fla** and **movie.fla** from the **11-2** folder in the **chap_11** exercise folder you copied to your desktop.

First let's look at the ActionScript in Communicating.fla.

---

2 Choose **Communicating.fla**. Select **Frame 1** on the **actions** layer, and press **F9** (Windows) or **Opt+F9** (Mac) to open the **Actions** panel, if it is not already open.

This file contains all the code you wrote in the previous movie: the **URLRequest** and **Loader** variables, the **load()** method that loads the **URLRequest**, and the **addChild()** method that adds the new object (movie.swf) to the movie's display list.

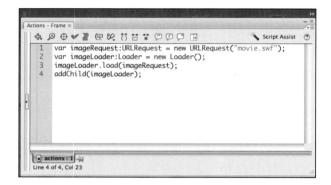

```
1   var imageRequest:URLRequest = new URLRequest("movie.swf");
2   var imageLoader:Loader = new Loader();
3   imageLoader.load(imageRequest);
4   addChild(imageLoader);
```

---

3 Press **Ctrl+Enter** (Windows) or **Cmd+Return** (Mac) to test the movie.

Communicating.swf loads the movie.swf content automatically. The objective of this exercise is to communicate with the snowboarder you see on the Stage, meaning the movie clip residing in the external movie.swf file, and make him jump in the air. Actually, once you've broken that barrier between the SWF file and the nested SWF file, you can make the snowboarder do anything you want.

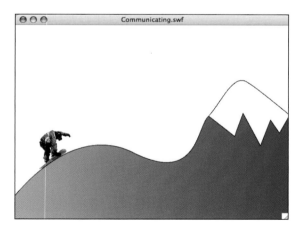

---

4 Close the preview window, and return to the **Actions** panel. Position your cursor at the end of Line 4, and press **Enter** (Windows) or **Return** (Mac) twice to insert two new lines.

The first step is to create the code that will respond when the movie.swf file is finished loading. To do this, you'll add a **COMPLETE** event listener.

---

5 On Line 6, type the following:

`imageLoader.contentLoaderInfo`
`.addEventListener(Event.COMPLETE,`
`onComplete);`

`contentLoaderInfo` is a property of the **Loader** class that contains all the information about the target file, the file that is being loaded. In this case, it's movie.swf. This code will trigger the `onComplete` event when movie.swf is finished loading.

```
1  var imageRequest:URLRequest = new URLRequest("movie.swf");
2  var imageLoader:Loader = new Loader();
3  imageLoader.load(imageRequest);
4  addChild(imageLoader);
5
6  imageLoader.contentLoaderInfo.addEventListener(Event.COMPLETE, onComplete);
```

Line 6 of 6, Col 76

6 Press **Enter** (Windows) or **Return** (Mac) twice to insert two new lines, and type the following:

`function onComplete(event:Event)`
`:void`
`{`
`}`

Make sure to leave an empty line between the left and right curly braces. This is where you will place the code that will let you communicate with the loaded SWF file. But before you add this code, you need to make a few changes to the SWF file's project file, movie.fla.

```
1   var imageRequest:URLRequest = new URLRequest("movie.swf");
2   var imageLoader:Loader = new Loader();
3   imageLoader.load(imageRequest);
4   addChild(imageLoader);
5
6   imageLoader.contentLoaderInfo.addEventListener(Event.COMPLETE, onComplete);
7
8   function onComplete(event:Event):void
9   {
10
11  }
```

Line 10 of 11, Col 2

---

7 Close the **Actions** panel. Select the **movie.fla** document tab to maximize the file.

---

8 Choose **Window > Library** to open the **Library** panel, if it is not already open. Select **mcBoarder**, **right-click** (Windows) or **Ctrl-click** (Mac) the movie clip's icon, and choose **Linkage** in the contextual menu.

9 Select **Export for ActionScript**, and click **OK** to close the **Linkage Properties** dialog box.

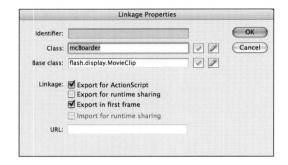

Remember that if you want to communicate with an object via an external ActionScript file, you need to export the class definition for that object at run time. In previous chapters, you did this when you were working with external ActionScript files; in this case, the ActionScript resides in an external FLA file.

---

10 Click **OK** to close the Flash warning dialog box.

This dialog box is just letting you know that Flash will create a class definition for mcBoarder on export.

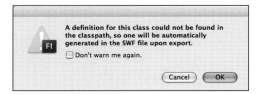

---

11 Choose **File > Save** to save **movie.fla**, and return to **Communicating.fla**. Select **Frame 1** on the **actions** layer, and press **F9** (Windows) or **Opt+F9** (Mac) to open the **Actions** panel.

---

12 Position your cursor on Line 10 between the curly braces of the event handler, and type the following:

```
event.target.content.boarder
_mc.y -= 100;
```

This is a long string of code. Let's review: **event.target** is the object being targeted by the event listener, which is called **contentLoaderInfo**. The keyword **contentLoaderInfo** refers to the movie.swf file in general.

```
 1   var imageRequest:URLRequest = new URLRequest("movie.swf");
 2   var imageLoader:Loader = new Loader();
 3   imageLoader.load(imageRequest);
 4   addChild(imageLoader);
 5
 6   imageLoader.contentLoaderInfo.addEventListener(Event.COMPLETE, onComplete);
 7
 8   function onComplete(event:Event):void
 9   {
10       event.target.content.boarder_mc.y -= 100;
11   }
```

content is a property referring to the actual objects in the movie.

boarder_mc is the instance name of the mcBoarder movie clip residing in the movie. You can communicate with this object because you exported it for ActionScript in Step 9.

The rest of the code, **y -= 100;**, causes the boarder to jump up 100 pixels once the movie.swf is finished loading.

---

13 Press **Ctrl+Enter** (Windows) or **Cmd+Return** (Mac) to test the movie.

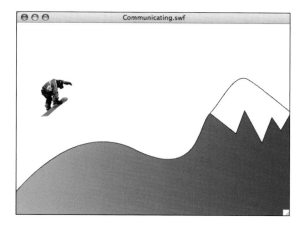

The movie.swf file loads, and the snowboarder jumps in the air! Cool!

If you want to communicate with other loaded content in your movies, remember to add the event listener not to the **Loader** itself but to the **contentLoaderInfo** property. When you build the event handler, use the **event.target.content** chain, followed by the instance name of the object you want to communicate with. And don't forget to export the object in the external movie for use in ActionScript!!

---

14 Close the preview window, and close **Communicating.fla** and **movie.fla**. You don't need to save your changes.

In the next exercise, you'll learn how to load another type of media, sound.

---

3 | Loading Sounds

In the next few exercises, you'll learn how to work with sound in your Flash files. First you'll learn how to load an external sound file.

---

1 Choose **File > Open**, and open **Sound.fla** in the **11-3** folder in the **chap_11** folder on your desktop.

---

2 Select **Frame 1** on the **actions** layer, and press **F9** (Windows) or **Opt+F9** (Mac) to open the **Actions** panel, if it is not already open.

The code to import a sound file starts like any other file import script. First you create a **URLRequest** that points to the sound file.

---

3 Position your cursor on the first line, and type the following:

```
var soundReq:URLRequest = new
URLRequest("free_fade.mp3");
```

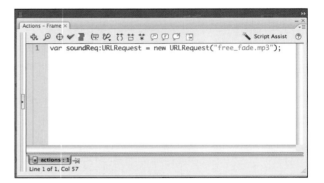

---

4 Press **Enter** (Windows) or **Return** (Mac) to go to the next line. Type the following:

```
var sound:Sound = new Sound();
```

This variable is a new instance of the **Sound** class that will hold the free_fade.mp3 sound you'll import in the next step.

Acceptable Sound Formats

You can use three types of sound files in Flash CS3, and you can use six more if you expect your users to have QuickTime 4 (or newer) installed on their machines. You can import 8-bit or 16-bit sounds. Although 16-bit is recommended, if you have limited memory and hard drive space, you can stick to 8-bit sounds. The following chart describes the sound file formats that you can use in Flash:

Sound Formats			
Format	Windows	Mac	Description
WAV	X		Microsoft standard for storing audio files on PCs. Uncompressed WAV files are fairly large and not as popular as the smaller MP3 format.
AIFF		X	A uncompressed file format developed by Apple that is usually used with professional audio and video applications.
MP3	X	X	A compressed audio file format that results in smaller file sizes than WAV and AIFF and is compatible with both Windows and Mac computers.
If you have QuickTime 4 (or newer), you can use the following:			
AIFF	X	X	See the earlier description.
Sound Designer II (.SDII)		X	A sound file format originally designed for Mac-based audio- and video-editing programs. This is commonly used for transferring files between applications.
MOV (QuickTime Audio Only)	X	X	Media container file that can contain its own set of audio file formats, including MIDI, MPEG-2, and MPEG-4.
Sun AU (.AU)	X	X	Audio file format developed by Sun Microsystems.
System 7 (.SND)		X	Legacy audio file format used by Mac OS 7.
WAV	X	X	Windows audio format. This format can be played in QuickTime on the Mac.

5 Press **Enter** (Windows) or **Return** (Mac) to go to the next line. Type the following:

```
sound.load(soundReq);
```

This line of code will load the **URLRequest** for free_fade.mp3. You now need to make sure the sound plays once the file is fully loaded.

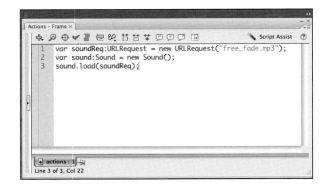

6 Press **Enter** (Windows) or **Return** (Mac) twice, and type the following:

```
sound.addEventListener(Event.COMPLETE, onComplete);
```

7 Press **Enter** (Windows) or **Return** (Mac) twice, and type the following:

```
function onComplete(event:Event):void
{
    sound.play();
}
```

Once the sound file is fully loaded, this event handler will be triggered, and the sound will play.

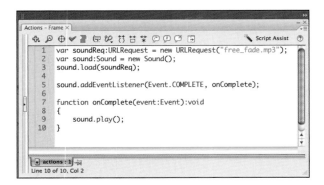

8 Press **Ctrl+Enter** (Windows) or **Cmd+Return** (Mac) to test the movie.

The SWF file doesn't contain any artwork, but the sound should start playing immediately. You've successfully made the sound load! In the next exercise, you'll learn how to control the playback of a sound.

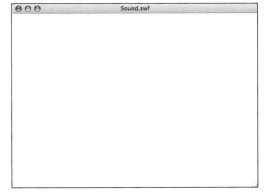

9 Close the player window, and close **Sound.fla**. You don't need to save your changes.

4 | Starting and Stopping Sound

In this exercise, you'll learn how to attach ActionScript to buttons in order to start and stop a sound.

1 Choose **File > Open**, and open **Starting_Stopping.fla** in the **11-4** folder on the **chap_11** folder on your desktop.

This file contains two separate button instances named play_btn and stop_btn, which are located on the art layer of the Timeline.

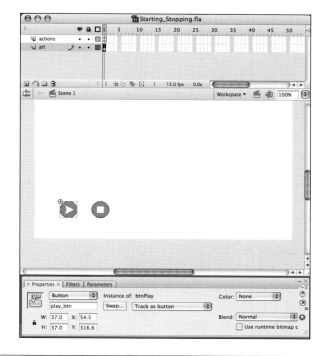

2 Select **Frame 1** on the **actions** layer, and press **F9** (Windows) or **Opt+F9** (Mac) to open the **Actions** panel, if it is not already open.

This is the code you wrote in the previous movie: a **URLRequest** that links to the sound file's location, a new **sound** variable, and a **load()** method that loads the **URLRequest** into the **sound** object. The event listener checks when the sound is finished loading and triggers the event handler, which causes the sound to play.

However, your ability to control sound playback using the **Sound** class is minimal. The **Sound** class is designed just to hold the sound file. To control the playback, you need to use another class, **SoundChannel**.

```
1   var soundReq:URLRequest = new URLRequest("free_fade.mp3");
2   var sound:Sound = new Sound();
3   sound.load(soundReq);
4
5   sound.addEventListener(Event.COMPLETE, onComplete);
6
7   function onComplete(event:Event):void
8   {
9       sound.play();
10  }
11
12  /*function playSound(event:MouseEvent):void
13  {
14
15  }
16
17  function stopSound(event:MouseEvent):void
18  {
19
20  }*/
```

3 Position your cursor at the end of Line 2, and press **Enter** (Windows) or **Return** (Mac) to go to Line 3. Type the following:

```
var soundControl:SoundChannel = new
SoundChannel();
```

This code creates a new instance of the **SoundChannel** class named **soundControl**. Now you can start adding interactivity to the movie through the buttons on the Stage.

```
var soundReq:URLRequest = new URLRequest("free_fade.mp3");
var sound:Sound = new Sound();
var soundControl:SoundChannel = new SoundChannel();
sound.load(soundReq);

sound.addEventListener(Event.COMPLETE, onComplete);

function onComplete(event:Event):void
{
    sound.play();
}
```

---

4 Position your cursor at the end of Line 6 after the event listener, press **Enter** (Windows) or **Return** (Mac), and type the following:

```
play_btn.addEventListener(MouseEvent.CLICK, playSound);
```

This code will trigger the empty event handler, **playSound()**, which is commented out on Line 14.

---

5 Select the code your just typed on Line 7, and press **Ctrl+C** (Windows) or **Cmd+C** (Mac) to copy it. Position your cursor at the end of Line 7, press **Enter** (Windows) or **Return** (Mac) to go to the next line, and then press **Ctrl+V** (Windows) or **Cmd+V** (Mac) to paste the code. Change **play_btn** to **stop_btn** and **playSound** to **stopSound**.

Now you can take the comments away from the event handler.

```
var soundReq:URLRequest = new URLRequest("free_fade.mp3");
var sound:Sound = new Sound();
var soundControl:SoundChannel = new SoundChannel();
sound.load(soundReq);

sound.addEventListener(Event.COMPLETE, onComplete);
play_btn.addEventListener(MouseEvent.CLICK, playSound);
stop_btn.addEventListener(MouseEvent.CLICK, stopSound);

function onComplete(event:Event):void
{
    sound.play();
}
```

---

6 Select Lines 15–23, and click the **Remove Comment** button at the top of the **Actions** panel.

The code should change from gray to black and blue. Now you need to write the actions that will run in the event handlers.

```
var soundReq:URLRequest = new URLRequest("free_fade.mp3");
var sound:Sound = new Sound();
var soundControl:SoundChannel = new SoundChannel();
sound.load(soundReq);

sound.addEventListener(Event.COMPLETE, onComplete);
play_btn.addEventListener(MouseEvent.CLICK, playSound);
stop_btn.addEventListener(MouseEvent.CLICK, stopSound);

function onComplete(event:Event):void
{
    sound.play();
}

/*function playSound(event:MouseEvent):void
{

}

function stopSound(event:MouseEvent):void
{

}*/
```

7 Select the code on Line 12 (**sound.play();**), and press **Ctrl+X** (Windows) or **Cmd+X** (Mac) to cut the code. Position your cursor on Line 17, and press **Ctrl+V** (Windows) or **Cmd+V** (Mac) to paste the code. Position your cursor at the beginning of this line, and type **soundControl = .**

This code causes **soundControl** to play the movie, shifting the function from the **Sound** object to the **SoundChannel** object. Remember you use the **SoundChannel** class because **Sound** can't be used to control playback. For a description of the different sound-related classes in Flash and their behaviors, check out the sidebar "Sound Classes."

```
Actions - Frame
                                                        Script Assist

 1   var soundReq:URLRequest = new URLRequest("free_fade.mp3");
 2   var sound:Sound = new Sound();
 3   var soundControl:SoundChannel = new SoundChannel();
 4   sound.load(soundReq);
 5
 6   sound.addEventListener(Event.COMPLETE, onComplete);
 7   play_btn.addEventListener(MouseEvent.CLICK, playSound);
 8   stop_btn.addEventListener(MouseEvent.CLICK, stopSound);
 9
10   function onComplete(event:Event):void
11   {
12
13   }
14
15   function playSound(event:MouseEvent):void
16   {
17       soundControl = sound.play();
18   }
19
20   function stopSound(event:MouseEvent):void
21   {
22
23   }
```

actions : 1
Line 17 of 23, Col 30

NOTE:

Sound Classes

The following chart lists a few of the sound-related classes and their uses in Flash. These classes are all part of the **flash.media** package.

Sound Classes	
Class	**Description**
Sound	This loads sounds and starts a sound playing.
SoundChannel	Once a sound plays in Flash, a corresponding **SoundChannel** object is created for that sound. **SoundChannel** is used to control the playback (for example, the starting and stopping) of a single sound.
SoundMixer	This controls the playback of all sounds that are currently playing in a Flash movie.
Microphone	This captures audio input and controls the properties of the sound stream.
SoundTransform	This controls the volume of a sound. A **SoundTransform** object can be applied to **Sound**, **SoundChannel**, and **Microphone** objects, and more.

8 Select the code on Line 7–8 (the event listeners), and press **Ctrl+X** (Windows) or **Cmd+X** (Mac) to cut the code. Position your cursor on Line 11, and press **Ctrl+V** (Windows) or **Cmd+V** (Mac) to paste the code.

It's considered a best practice to include the event listeners in the **onComplete** function. This way, they'll be added after the sound is finished loading. If they were added sooner, the user could click the Play or Stop button before the sound finishes loading and might receive an error message.

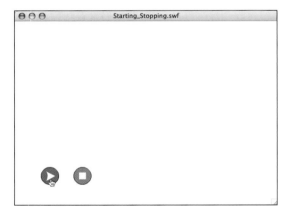

```
Actions - Frame ×
                                                        Script Assist
   1   var soundReq:URLRequest = new URLRequest("free_fade.mp3");
   2   var sound:Sound = new Sound();
   3   var soundControl:SoundChannel = new SoundChannel();
   4   sound.load(soundReq);
   5
   6   sound.addEventListener(Event.COMPLETE, onComplete);
   7
   8
   9   function onComplete(event:Event):void
  10   {
  11       play_btn.addEventListener(MouseEvent.CLICK, playSound);
  12       stop_btn.addEventListener(MouseEvent.CLICK, stopSound);
  13   }
  14
  15   function playSound(event:MouseEvent):void
  16   {
  17       soundControl = sound.play();
  18   }
  19
  20   function stopSound(event:MouseEvent):void
  21   {
  22
  23   }
```

actions : 1
Line 12 of 23, Col 57

9 Press **Ctrl+Enter** (Windows) or **Cmd+Return** (Mac) to test the movie. When the preview window opens, press the **Play** button.

The sound should start playing when you click the Play button but not before.

10 Close the player window, and return to the **Actions** panel. Position your cursor on Line 22, and type the following:

```
soundControl.stop();
```

```
Actions - Frame
                                                          Script Assist
 1   var soundReq:URLRequest = new URLRequest("free_fade.mp3");
 2   var sound:Sound = new Sound();
 3   var soundControl:SoundChannel = new SoundChannel();
 4   sound.load(soundReq);
 5
 6   sound.addEventListener(Event.COMPLETE, onComplete);
 7
 8
 9   function onComplete(event:Event):void
10   {
11       play_btn.addEventListener(MouseEvent.CLICK, playSound);
12       stop_btn.addEventListener(MouseEvent.CLICK, stopSound);
13   }
14
15   function playSound(event:MouseEvent):void
16   {
17       soundControl = sound.play();
18   }
19
20   function stopSound(event:MouseEvent):void
21   {
22       soundControl.stop();
23   }

actions : 1
Line 22 of 23, Col 22
```

11 Press **Ctrl+Enter** (Windows) or **Cmd+Return** (Mac) to test the movie again. When the preview window opens, click the **Play** button to start the sound, and then click the **Stop** button to stop it.

The sound should start playing and then stop again once you click the Stop button.

VIDEO: **pausingsounds.mov**

In this exercise, if you clicked the **Play** button again, the sound would start playing over from the *beginning* of the audio track. Instead of a **Play** button, it is usually better to add **Play/Pause** buttons to pause and resume the sound so that the sound starts to play from wherever the user stopped the track. To learn how to add a **Pause** button to a movie, check out **pausingsounds.mov** in the **videos** folder on the **ActionScript HOT CD-ROM**.

12 Close the player window, and close **Starting_Stopping.fla**. You don't need to save your changes.

Managing the Volume of Sound

In this exercise, you'll learn how to control the volume of a sound in Flash.

---

1 Choose **File > Open**, and open **Volume_Control.fla** in the **11-6** folder from the **chap_11** folder on your desktop.

In this file, the playback controls have been modified slightly. A Play/Pause button has replaced the Play button.

There are also two new volumes controls: one called up_btn and one called down_btn. Let's take a look at the code that is powering these buttons.

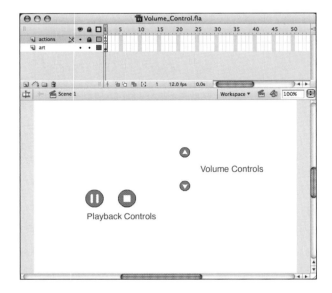

2 Select **Frame 1** on the **actions** layer, and press **F9** (Windows) or **Opt+F9** (Mac) to open the **Actions** panel, if it is not already open.

This file has a few new additions to the code. Lines 9 and 10 contain event listeners for the two volume control buttons. The event handlers are called **increaseVolume** and **decreaseVolume** and are located on Lines 47–55 of the code.

At this point, you have quite a bit of code here. It can be difficult to navigate between related sections, such as the event listeners and the event handlers I just mentioned. Luckily, Flash has a great tool that allows you to collapse sections of the code.

```
1   var soundReq:URLRequest = new URLRequest("free_fade.mp3");
2   var sound:Sound = new Sound();
3   var soundControl:SoundChannel = new SoundChannel();
4   var resumeTime:Number = 0;
5
6   sound.load(soundReq);
7
8   sound.addEventListener(Event.COMPLETE, onComplete);
9   up_btn.addEventListener(MouseEvent.CLICK, increaseVolume);
10  down_btn.addEventListener(MouseEvent.CLICK, decreaseVolume);
11
12
13  function onComplete(event:Event):void
14  {
15      play_btn.addEventListener(MouseEvent.CLICK, playSound);
16      stop_btn.addEventListener(MouseEvent.CLICK, stopSound);
17  }
18
19  function playSound(event:MouseEvent):void
20  {
21      soundControl = sound.play(resumeTime);
22      pause_btn.visible = true;
23      pause_btn.addEventListener(MouseEvent.CLICK, pauseSound);
24      play_btn.visible = false;
25      play_btn.removeEventListener(MouseEvent.CLICK, playSound);
26  }
27
28  function pauseSound(event:MouseEvent):void
29  {
30      resumeTime = soundControl.position;
31      soundControl.stop();
32      play_btn.visible = true;
```

3 Select the line of code on Line 45, and drag up to Line 13 to select all the code in between. Click the triangle that appears to the left of the point at which your selection ends, Line 13. (**Tip:** The triangle appears in the gray bar to the left of the **Actions** panel, just to the right of the line numbers.)

And *voila*! Those 32 lines of code are collapsed into a neat group. If you need to expand them again, simply click the triangle again.

Now let's return to the code. You know that when you are dealing with the playback of a sound, you need to use the **SoundChannel** class. When you are dealing with the volume of a sound, you use another class called **SoundTransform**.

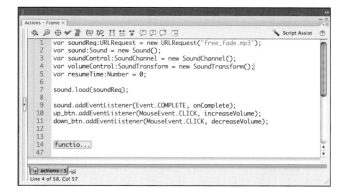

4 Position your cursor at the end of Line 3, press **Enter** (Windows) or **Return** (Mac) to insert a new line, and type the following:

```
var volumeControl:SoundTransform = new
SoundTransform();
```

This creates a new instance of the **SoundTransform** class.

5 Position your cursor on Line 50 in the `increaseVolume()` event handler, and type the following:

```
volumeControl.volume += .1;
```

volume is a sound property that has a possible value of 0–1. Typing .1 will increase the current volume by 10 percent every time the up button is clicked.

6 Press **Enter** (Windows) or **Return** (Mac) to insert a new line, and type the following:

`soundControl.soundTransform = volumeControl;`

This code associates the `volumeControl` object with the sound. Note that you link it to the **SoundChannel** object, not the **Sound** itself.

```
 8
 9    sound.addEventListener(Event.COMPLETE, onComplete);
10    up_btn.addEventListener(MouseEvent.CLICK, increaseVolume);
11    down_btn.addEventListener(MouseEvent.CLICK, decreaseVolume);
12
13
14    functio...
47
48    function increaseVolume(event:MouseEvent):void
49    {
50        volumeControl.volume += .1;
51        soundControl.soundTransform = volumeControl;
52    }
53
54    function decreaseVolume(event:MouseEvent):void
55    {
56
57    }
58
59    pause_btn.visible = false;
```

Line 51 of 59, Col 46

7 Select Lines 50–51, the two lines of code you just wrote, and press **Ctrl+C** (Windows) or **Cmd+C** (Mac) to copy them. Position your cursor on Line 56 in the **decreaseVolume()** event handler, and press **Ctrl+V** (Windows) or **Cmd+V** (Mac) to paste the code.

8 Change the plus sign on Line 56 to a minus sign.

The volume will be decreased by 10 percent when the down button is clicked.

```
14    functio...
47
48    function increaseVolume(event:MouseEvent):void
49    {
50        volumeControl.volume += .1;
51        soundControl.soundTransform = volumeControl;
52    }
53
54    function decreaseVolume(event:MouseEvent):void
55    {
56        volumeControl.volume -= .1;
57        soundControl.soundTransform = volumeControl;
58    }
59
60    pause_btn.visible = false;
```

Line 56 of 60, Col 29

9 Press **Ctrl+Enter** (Windows) or **Cmd+Return** (Mac) to test the movie. When the preview window opens, click the **Play** button, and then click the volume buttons to check the volume controls.

Excellent! The sound gets louder and softer as you click the buttons.

To quickly recap, to apply volume controls to a movie, you simply create a new **SoundTransform** object, increase or decrease by adding or subtracting from the volume property of that object, and then associate the **SoundTransform** instance with the **SoundChannel** object by setting the **SoundChannel** object's **soundTransform** property to the new **SoundTransform** instance name.

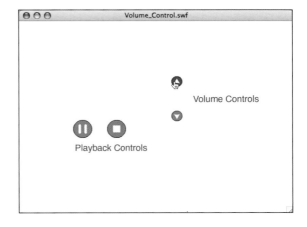

10 Close the player window, and close **Volume_Control.fla**. You don't need to save your changes.

6 | Loading Video

In this exercise, you'll learn how to load Flash video into a SWF file.

---

1 Choose **File > Open**, and open **Loading_Video.fla** from the **11-8** folder in the **chap_11** folder on your desktop.

VIDEO: | **understandingvideo.mov**

For a better understanding of the Flash video architecture before you begin this exercise, check out **understandingvideo.mov** in the **videos** folder on the **ActionScript HOT CD-ROM**.

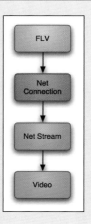

---

2 Select **Frame 1** on the **actions** layer, and press **F9** (Windows) or **Opt+F9** (Mac) to open the **Actions** panel, if it is not already open.

The first step in loading a video is to create a new variable that will represent your **NetConnection** class object. A **NetConnection** object provides the means to stream a video from a local drive or a server. Basically, it directs Flash to the proper location.

---

3 Position your cursor on the first line, and type the following:

```
var videoConnection:NetConnection =  new
NetConnection();
```

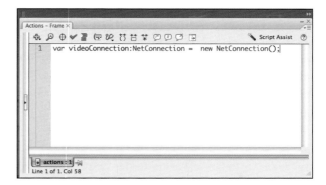

---

4 Press **Enter** (Windows) or **Return** (Mac), and type the following:

```
videoConnection.connect(
```

In these parentheses, you'll pass in the connection name. Flash is looking for a string.

---

5 Next type the following:

```
null);
```

Usually you'd type the server address, but since you're going to be accessing the video from the exercise files folder on your desktop, you'll use the keyword **null**. If you'd like to learn more about connecting to a server, select the word *NetConnection* on Line 1, and press F1 or choose Help > Flash Help to read more about the **connect()** method of this class.

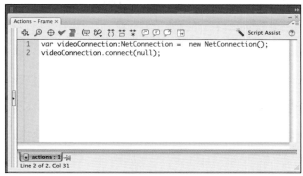

Now you need to create a **NetStream** object. **NetStream** controls the playback of the video files.

---

6 Press **Enter** (Windows) or **Return** (Mac), and type the following:

```
var videoStream:NetStream = new
NetStream(videoConnection);
```

When you create a new instance of the **NetStream** class, unlike most other variables, you need to pass in the **NetConnection** name right away.

---

7 Press **Enter** (Windows) or **Return** (Mac), and type the following:

```
videoStream.play("short_jump.flv");
```

So the **NetStream** object connects to your hard drive using the **NetConnection** path and streams the video passed through in the parentheses. However, you won't be able to see the video until you connect the stream to a video object on the Stage.

8 Press **Enter** (Windows) or **Return** (Mac), and type the following:

```
var video:Video = new Video();
```

Now you just need to attach the stream to the video instance and add it to the movie's display list.

9 Press **Enter** (Windows) or **Return** (Mac), and type the following:

```
video.attachNetStream(videoStream);
addChild(video);
```

Now it's time to test the movie!

10 Press **Ctrl+Enter** (Windows) or **Cmd+Return** (Mac) to test the movie.

The video opens in the player window and seems to play OK. However, an error message pops up in the Output panel, called "Error #2044: Unhandled AsyncErrorEvent...." This means there is some event happening in the movie that is not being addressed in your ActionScript. No worries. You'll address this issue in the next exercise.

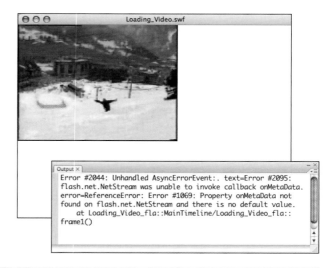

11 Close the player window and the **Output** panel, and close **Loading_Video.fla**. You don't need to save your changes.

7 | Controlling Video Playback

In this exercise, you'll learn how to control the playback of loaded FLV files and how to address error messages that might pop up during playback.

---

1 Choose **File > Open**, and open **Video_Playback.fla** from the **11-9** folder in the **chap_11** folder on your desktop.

This file contains a Play button and a Stop button on the Stage, similar to the file you worked with in Exercise 4. The instance names are play_btn and stop_btn.

---

2 Select **Frame 1** on the **actions** layer, and press **F9** (Windows) or **Opt+F9** (Mac) to open the **Actions** panel, if it is not already open.

This script in this file is the same as the code you wrote in the previous exercise.

```
1  var videoConnection:NetConnection = new NetConnection();
2  videoConnection.connect(null);
3  var videoStream:NetStream = new NetStream(videoConnection);
4  videoStream.play("short_jump.flv");
5  var video:Video = new Video();
6  video.attachNetStream(videoStream);
7  addChild(video);
```

3 Press **Ctrl+Enter** (Windows) or
Cmd+Return (Mac) to test the movie.

The video plays, but an error message pops
up in the Output panel. It tells you there is an
unhandled event. If you scroll down, you'll
see the sentence "Property onMetaData not
found on flash.net.NetStream and there is no
default value." This is the key to this problem. What is **onMetaData**? Let's find out.

4 Close the player window and
the **Output** panel, and return to the
Actions panel. Position your cursor
at the end of Line 7, press **Enter**
(Windows) or **Return** (Mac), and then
type **onMetaData**. Select this word, and
then choose **Help > Flash Help** to
open the **Help** menu.

Read the code description. **onMetaData**
is an event that occurs when Flash
receives descriptive information, or
metadata, that is embedded in the
Flash file. This could be the title,
author, comments, captions, or any
number of types of data. Also notice
that the Help documentation says
you cannot use the **addEventListener**
method to listen for or process this

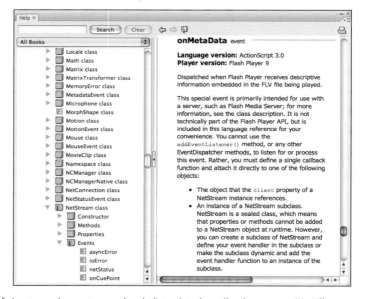

event. Instead, you'll need to use one of the two alternate methods listed to handle the event. You'll
apply the listener to the object that the **client** property of a **NetStream** instance references. That might
not make a lot of sense right now, but it should become clear in the next few steps.

5 Close the **Help** window, and delete the word **onMetaData** on **Line 8** of the **Actions** panel.

Here's the plan: You'll create a generic object that will hold the **onMetaData** information. Then you'll associate the generic object with the **NetStream** and add the event listener to the **NetStream** object.

6 Position your cursor at the end of Line 4, and press **Enter** (Windows) or **Return** (Mac) to go to the next line. Type the following:

```
var metaListener:Object = new Object();
```

An instance of the **Object** class accepts all the methods and properties of any object descended from it, like, for example, a Flash video. **Object** is a dynamic class. Classes such as **MovieClip** that do not accept new methods and properties are called **static classes**.

---

7 Press **Enter** (Windows) or **Return** (Mac) to go to the next line. Type the following:

```
metaListener.onMetaData = onMetaData;
```

This code associates the new **onMetaData()** method, or soon to be *event handler,* with the generic object **metaListener**.

```
1  var videoConnection:NetConnection = new NetConnection();
2  videoConnection.connect(null);
3  var videoStream:NetStream = new NetStream(videoConnection);
4  videoStream.play("short_jump.flv");
5  var metaListener:Object = new Object();
6  metaListener.onMetaData = onMetaData;
7  var video:Video = new Video();
8  video.attachNetStream(videoStream);
9  addChild(video);
```

Line 6 of 9, Col 38

---

8 Press **Enter** (Windows) or **Return** (Mac) to go to the next line. Type the following:

```
videoStream.client = metaListener;
```

videoStream.client was formerly one of the only two objects you could apply the event listener to in this file. By associating it with the generic object, you can also listen for **onMetaData**.

---

9 Position your cursor at the end of Line 10, and press **Enter** (Windows) or **Return** (Mac) twice to insert two new lines. Type the following:

```
function onMetaData(data:Object):void
{
}
```

Now if you test the movie, the event is being addressed, and the error message won't pop up anymore. It doesn't matter that the event handler is empty; it's still handling the event.

```
1  var videoConnection:NetConnection = new NetConnection();
2  videoConnection.connect(null);
3  var videoStream:NetStream = new NetStream(videoConnection);
4  videoStream.play("short_jump.flv");
5  var metaListener:Object = new Object();
6  metaListener.onMetaData = onMetaData;
7  videoStream.client = metaListener;
8  var video:Video = new Video();
9  video.attachNetStream(videoStream);
10 addChild(video);
11
12 function onMetaData(data:Object):void
13 {
14
15 }
```

Line 14 of 15, Col 2

10 Press **Ctrl+Enter** (Windows) or **Cmd+Return** (Mac) to test the movie.

The video will start to play automatically, and no error message will pop up. Now you can add event listeners to the buttons on the Stage so you can control the video playback.

11 Close the player window, and return to the **Actions** panel. Position your cursor on **Line 14** between the curly braces of the new function, and type the following:

```
play_btn.addEventListener
(MouseEvent.CLICK, playMovie);
stop_btn.addEventListener
(MouseEvent.CLICK, stopMovie);
```

The reason you put the event listeners in the function is because that way the buttons will be ready to use once the data is fully loaded.

```
 1  var videoConnection:NetConnection = new NetConnection();
 2  videoConnection.connect(null);
 3  var videoStream:NetStream = new NetStream(videoConnection);
 4  videoStream.play("short_jump.flv");
 5  var metaListener:Object = new Object();
 6  metaListener.onMetaData = onMetaData;
 7  videoStream.client = metaListener;
 8  var video:Video = new Video();
 9  video.attachNetStream(videoStream);
10  addChild(video);
11
12  function onMetaData(data:Object):void
13  {
14      play_btn.addEventListener(MouseEvent.CLICK, playMovie);
15      stop_btn.addEventListener(MouseEvent.CLICK, stopMovie);
16  }
```

Line 15 of 16, Col 57

12 Position your cursor on **Line 16** after the right curly brace, press **Enter** (Windows) or **Return** (Mac) twice, and type the following:

```
function playMovie(event:MouseEvent):void
{
  videoStream.play("short_jump.flv");
}
```

You communicate with the **NetStream** object, called **videoStream** in this case, not directly to the FLV, but you do need to pass in the video name in the parentheses.

13 Select Line 18–21, and press **Ctrl+C** (Windows) or **Cmd+C** (Mac) to copy them. Position your cursor after Line 21, press **Enter** (Windows) or **Return** (Mac) twice, and press **Ctrl+V** (Windows) or **Cmd+V** (Mac) to paste the code. Change **playMovie** to **stopMovie** and **play("short_jump.flv")** to **pause()**.

14 Press **Ctrl+Enter** (Windows) or **Cmd+Return** (Mac) to test the movie. When the player window opens, click the **Stop** button to stop the movie, and then click the **Play** button to start the movie again.

Cool! By recycling and tweaking this code just a bit, you can create a custom Flash player for any Flash video!

15 Close the preview window, and close **Video_Playback.fla**. You don't need to save your changes.

I hope you enjoyed this chapter. Incorporating multimedia into your Flash movies is an important part of interesting and engaging designs in Flash. Using ActionScript, you can customize your projects even further.

12

Adding Advanced Interactivity

In this chapter, you'll take everything you've learned throughout this entire book and apply it to create a drag-and-drop puzzle game. Just like the other games you created in this book, this game will show you how everything you have learned up to this point fits together in one application.

1 | Creating a Drag-and-Drop Class

In this exercise, you'll review the finished game and then learn how to create a drag-and-drop object class that will be the basis for the puzzle game.

1 Copy the **chap_12** folder from the **Exercises Files** folder onto your desktop. Open the **12-1** folder, and double-click **Drag_Class.swf** to open it in your default browser.

This file contains all the aspects of the finished game. The pieces on the left side of the screen are randomly placed every time the movie runs. Each piece can be dragged and dropped anywhere in the rectangle on the right side. The goal of the game is to drag and drop the pieces into the correct order in the box on the right side of the window. When you select a puzzle piece, a drop shadow appears around the object. If you drop the piece in the right location, it snaps into place and then becomes disabled. If you drop the piece in a wrong location, the piece snaps back to the top of the pile on the left. Ready to start? The first "piece" will be creating that drag-and-drop interactivity.

2 Close the player window, and open Flash. Choose **File > Open**, and open **Drag_Class.fla, DragGame.as**, and **DragDrop.as** from the **12-2** folder in the **chap_12** folder you copied to your desktop.

Before you begin coding, let's review the contents and organization of these files.

3 Choose **Drag_Class.fla**. Drag the **edit bar** down so you can see all the layers.

Notice that the bottom layer is called stroke. This layer contains the rectangle on the Stage. Above this layer is a guide layer called original.

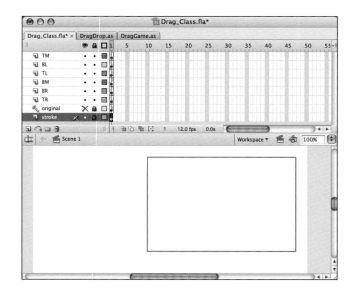

4 Click the **Show Layer** icon (the red X) next to the **original** layer to reveal the layer's contents.

This is what the puzzle will look like when it is complete.

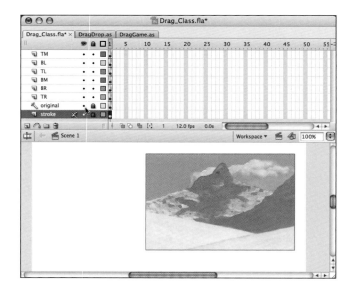

ActionScript 3.0 for Adobe Flash CS3 Professional : H•O•T

5 Click **Hide Layer** to hide the **original** layer. Double-click the **lock** icon at the top of the **Timeline**, above the layers, to unlock all the layers. Click anywhere in the rectangle, and look at the selected object's properties in the **Property inspector**.

Notice that a corresponding layer in the Timeline is highlighted when you select the object. The object is one of six target pieces, which define the areas where the puzzle pieces should be placed. Also notice that the Alpha setting for these objects is set to 0. These objects will represent the target areas.

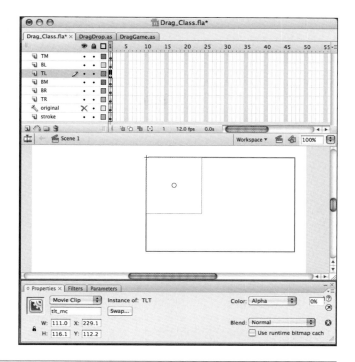

6 Click the **lock** icon above the layers again to lock them all. Choose **Window > Library** to open the **Library** panel, if it is not already open. Double-click the **Puzzle Pieces** folder icon to reveal the folder contents.

All the puzzle pieces have been converted to movie clip symbols and named according to their positions on the Stage. TL refers to top left, TM stands for top middle, BR stands for bottom right, and so on. There are six pieces.

7 Double-click the **Target Pieces** folder icon to reveal the folder contents.

There are six symbols in this folder as well. The symbols use the same naming convention as the pieces in the Puzzle Pieces folder, plus a *T* for Target.

8 Now choose the **DragGame.as** file to examine the ActionScript code.

This file will represent the document class. I've already set up a skeleton for most of the code. This will just make it easier and faster for you to write the rest.

Before you examine DragDrop.as, you'll add DragGame.as as the document class for Drag_Class.fla.

```
package
{
    import flash.display.MovieClip;

    public class DragGame extends MovieClip
    {
        public function DragGame()
        {

        }
    }
}
```

9 Choose **Drag_Class.fla** again. Click anywhere off the main **Stage** area, and then type **DragGame** in the **Document Class** field in the **Property inspector**. Click again in the gray area off the **Stage** to commit the change.

10 Choose **DragDrop.as**.

This file is also a skeleton for a class file, just like DragGame.as. This file will hold the drag-and-drop behavior for the puzzle pieces.

```
package
{
    import flash.display.MovieClip;

    public class DragDrop extends MovieClip
    {
        public function DragDrop()
        {

        }
    }
}
```

11 Position your cursor at the end of Line 3, and press **Enter** (Windows) or **Return** (Mac) to insert a new line. Type the following:

```
import flash.events.MouseEvent;
```

You'll use mouse events to detect whether the user's mouse is up or down so that they can either drag or drop the piece.

12 Position your cursor on Line 10, and type the following:

```
this.addEventListener(MouseEvent.
MOUSE_DOWN, dragMovie);
this.addEventListener(MouseEvent.
MOUSE_UP, dropMovie);
```

```
1  package
2  {
3      import flash.display.MovieClip;
4      import flash.events.MouseEvent;
5
6      public class DragDrop extends MovieClip
7      {
8          public function DragDrop()
9          {
10             this.addEventListener(MouseEvent.MOUSE_DOWN, dragMovie);
11             this.addEventListener(MouseEvent.MOUSE_UP, dropMovie);
12         }
13     }
14  }
```

13 Position your cursor after the right curly brace of the constructor function on Line 12, press **Enter** (Windows) or **Return** (Mac) twice to insert two new lines, and type the following:

```
private function dragMovie
(event:MouseEvent):void
{
   this.startDrag();
}
```

When the mouse is pressed, the puzzle piece will become draggable.

```
5
6      public class DragDrop extends MovieClip
7      {
8          public function DragDrop()
9          {
10             this.addEventListener(MouseEvent.MOUSE_DOWN, dragMovie);
11             this.addEventListener(MouseEvent.MOUSE_UP, dropMovie);
12         }
13
14         private function dragMovie(event:MouseEvent):void
15         {
16             this.startDrag();
17         }
18     }
19  }
```

14 Select the lines of code you wrote in Step 13, Lines 14–17, and press **Ctrl+C** (Windows) or **Cmd+C** (Mac) to copy them. Click after the right curly brace on Line 17, press **Enter** (Windows) or **Return** (Mac) to insert a new line, and then press **Ctrl+V** (Windows) or **Cmd+V** (Mac) to paste the code. Change `dragMovie` to `dropMovie` and `startDrag` to `stopDrag`.

15 Save **DragDrop.as** by choosing **File > Save**.

16 Select **Drag_Class.fla**.

In this file, you'll associate the `DragDrop` class with the puzzle pieces in the Library panel. To do this, you'll change the Linkage properties of the symbols in the Library panel.

17 In the **Library** panel, **right-click** (Windows) or **Ctrl-click** (Mac) the **BL** symbol in the **Puzzle Pieces** folder. Choose **Linkage** in the contextual menu.

18 Select **Export for ActionScript**, and change the **Base class** name to **DragDrop**. Click **OK** to close the **Linkage Properties** dialog box, and click **OK** again to close Flash's warning message.

This will convert the puzzle piece to a **DragDrop** class object but preserve the symbol's unique class name of BL.

19 Repeat Steps 17 and 18 for the five remaining symbols in the **Puzzle Pieces** folder in the **Library** panel. Make sure to change the base class for all the symbols to **DragDrop**.

Now that all the puzzle pieces are converted, you need to drag instances to the Stage—using ActionScript, of course.

20 Select **DragGame.as**. Position your cursor at the end of Line 3, and press **Enter** (Windows) or **Return** (Mac) to insert a new line. Type the following:

```
import DragDrop;
import BL;
```

You need to import both the **DragDrop** class and the individual puzzle piece class definitions in order to reference them in this ActionScript file.

```
package
{
    import flash.display.MovieClip;
    import DragDrop;
    import BL;

    public class DragGame extends MovieClip
    {
        public function DragGame()
        {

        }
    }
}
```

21 Position your cursor at the end of Line 8 after the right curly brace, press **Enter** (Windows) or **Return** (Mac) twice, and then press the **up arrow** key once. Type the following:

```
private var bl:BL;
```

22 Position your cursor at the end of Line 14 after the right curly brace, and press **Enter** (Windows) or **Return** (Mac) twice. Type the following:

```
private function createPieces():void
{
  b1 = new BL();
  addChild(b1);
}
```

This code makes the **b1** variable you created on Line 9 equal to a new instance of the **BL** class and adds the instance to the display list.

```
package
{
    import flash.display.MovieClip;
    import DragDrop;
    import BL;

    public class DragGame extends MovieClip
    {
        private var b1:BL;

        public function DragGame()
        {

        }

        private function createPieces():void
        {
            b1 = new BL();
            addChild(b1);
        }
    }
}
```
Line 21 of 22, Col 3

---

23 Position your cursor on Line 13 in the **dragGame()** function, and type the following:

```
createPieces();
```

This runs the **createPieces()** function as soon as the **DragGame** document class is called when the movie loads.

Now you just need to repeat these steps for the five remaining puzzle pieces.

---

24 Position your cursor at the end of Line 5, and press **Enter** (Windows) or **Return** (Mac) to insert a new line. Type the following:

```
import BR;
import BM;
import TL;
import TR;
import TM;
```

This imports the class definitions for the rest of the pieces.

```
package
{
    import flash.display.MovieClip;
    import DragDrop;
    import BL;
    import BR;
    import BM;
    import TL;
    import TR;
    import TM;

    public class DragGame extends MovieClip
    {
        private var b1:BL;

        public function DragGame()
        {
            createPieces();
        }
```
Line 10 of 27, Col 12

25 Position your cursor at the end of Line 14, and press **Enter** (Windows) or **Return** (Mac) to insert a new line. Type the following:

```
private var br:BR;
private var bm:BM;
private var tl:TL;
private var tr:TR;
private var tm:TM;
```

This creates new variables for each of the pieces.

```
package
{
    import flash.display.MovieClip;
    import DragDrop;
    import BL;
    import BR;
    import BM;
    import TL;
    import TR;
    import TM;

    public class DragGame extends MovieClip
    {
        private var bl:BL;
        private var br:BR;
        private var bm:BM;
        private var tl:TL;
        private var tr:TR;
        private var tm:TM;
```

Line 19 of 32, Col 21

26 Position your cursor at the end of Line 29, and press **Enter** (Windows) or **Return** (Mac) to insert a new line. Type the following:

```
br = new BR();
addChild(br);
bm = new BM;
addChild(bm);
tl = new TL();
addChild(tl);
tr = new TR();
addChild(tr);
tm = new TM();
addChild(tm);
```

```
        private function createPieces():void
        {
            bl = new BL();
            addChild(bl);
            br = new BR();
            addChild(br);
            bm = new BM;
            addChild(bm);
            tl = new TL();
            addChild(tl);
            tr = new TR();
            addChild(tr);
            tm = new TM();
            addChild(tm);
        }
```

Line 36 of 42, Col 18

This creates a new instance of each piece and adds the pieces to the Stage. Let's add one more thing to indicate these pieces are interactive objects.

27 Select **DragDrop.as**. Position your cursor at the end of Line 9 after the left curly brace, and press **Enter** (Windows) or **Return** (Mac) to insert a new line. Type the following:

```
this.buttonMode = true;
```

As you may recall, this line of code will ensure the user's cursor turns into a hand icon when the user moves the cursor over the pieces, indicating they are clickable objects.

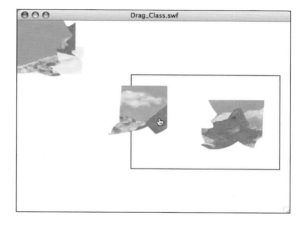

28 Choose **File > Save All** to save your changes to all three files. Then press **Ctrl+Enter** (Windows) or **Cmd+Return** (Mac) to test the movie.

All six puzzle pieces are piled in the top-left corner of the Stage. Move your cursor over them, and your cursor should change to the hand icon. Click and drag the pieces to different locations, and release your mouse to test the drag-and-drop functionality. That's not bad at all! It's a great start. In the next exercise, you'll learn how to test whether the pieces are in the correct target movie clip area when they are dropped.

29 Close the player window. Choose **File > Close All** to close the open files.

2 | Detecting Collisions

In this exercise, you'll use ActionScript code to detect whether a puzzle piece is touching a target piece when the pieces are dragged into the rectangle.

---

1 Open **Drag_Class.fla**, **DragDrop.as**, and **DragGame.as** from the **12-3** folder in the **chap_12** exercise folder you copied to your desktop. Choose **Drag_Class.fla**.

First let's look at the instance names of the target pieces on the Stage.

---

2 Choose **Window > Properties > Properties** to open the **Property inspector**, if it is not already open. Select the **Selection** tool, and click in the top-left corner of the rectangle on the **Stage** to select one of the target pieces and examine its properties in the **Property inspector**.

This instance name of this piece is tlt_mc, or Top Left Target Movie Clip. The rest of the target pieces use the same naming convention. These are the objects for which you'll be looking to detect hits. First you'll create a variable to hold the location of the object that is being dragged and dropped by the user.

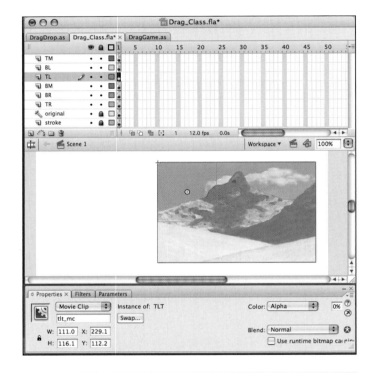

3 Choose **DragDrop.as**. Position your cursor after the left curly brace at the end of Line 7, and press **Enter** (Windows) or **Return** (Mac) twice to insert two new lines. Press the **up arrow** key once, and then type the following:

```
public var _targetPiece:*;
```

This variable is defined as public so you can call it outside this ActionScript file. Remember from Chapter 9, *"Creating a Memory Game,"* that by using an asterisk, a wildcard, for the data type, this variable will accept multiple data types. This makes the `DragDrop` class that much more reusable.

---

4 Save **DragDrop.as** by choosing **File > Save**. Choose **DragGame.as**.

The next step is to associate the puzzle pieces with the matching target pieces. You'll add this code in the `createPieces()` function.

---

5 Position your cursor at the end of Line 29 after the first `addChild()` method in the `createPieces()` function, and press **Enter** (Windows) or **Return** (Mac) to insert a new line. Type the following:

```
bl._targetPiece = blt_mc;
bl.addEventListener(MouseEvent.
MOUSE_UP, checkTarget);
```

The target piece property for the bl puzzle piece is now set to the blt target piece, and you've also added an event listener that will trigger the `checkTarget()` event (which you will write a little later in this exercise) when the user releases their mouse. Now you just need to repeat this step for the five remaining puzzle pieces!

6 Select these two lines of code, copy them by pressing **Ctrl+C** (Windows) or **Cmd+C** (Mac), and then paste them below each **addChild()** method in this function. That's five times! Remember to replace the puzzle piece instance name and target piece instance name. When you are finished, your code should look like the illustration shown here.

And now that you've added all these mouse events, you need to import the definition so that Flash knows what to do with them.

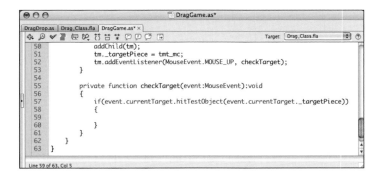

```
26          private function createPieces():void
27          {
28              bl = new BL();
29              addChild(bl);
30              bl._targetPiece = blt_mc;
31              bl.addEventListener(MouseEvent.MOUSE_UP, checkTarget);
32              br = new BR();
33              addChild(br);
34              br._targetPiece = brt_mc;
35              br.addEventListener(MouseEvent.MOUSE_UP, checkTarget);
36              bm = new BM();
37              addChild(bm);
38              bm._targetPiece = bmt_mc;
39              bm.addEventListener(MouseEvent.MOUSE_UP, checkTarget);
40              tl = new TL();
41              addChild(tl);
42              tl._targetPiece = tlt_mc;
43              tl.addEventListener(MouseEvent.MOUSE_UP, checkTarget);
44              tr = new TR();
45              addChild(tr);
46              tr._targetPiece = trt_mc;
47              tr.addEventListener(MouseEvent.MOUSE_UP, checkTarget);
48              tm = new TM();
49              addChild(tm);
50              tm._targetPiece = tmt_mc;
51              tm.addEventListener(MouseEvent.MOUSE_UP, checkTarget);
52          }
```

7 Position your cursor at the end on Line 3 after the first **import** statement, and press **Enter** (Windows) or **Return** (Mac) to insert a new line. Type the following:

```
import flash.events.MouseEvent;
```

Moving on! Now you need to write the **checkTarget()** event handler. This is a crucial part of the code that will detect whether the puzzle piece the user is dropping in the rectangle matches the target piece in that area.

```
50              addChild(tm);
51              tm._targetPiece = tmt_mc;
52              tm.addEventListener(MouseEvent.MOUSE_UP, checkTarget);
53          }
54
55          private function checkTarget(event:MouseEvent):void
56          {
57              if(event.currentTarget.hitTestObject(event.currentTarget._targetPiece))
58              {
59
60              }
61          }
62      }
63  }
```

8 Position your cursor after the right curly brace on Line 53, and press **Enter** (Windows) or **Return** (Mac) twice to insert two new lines. Type the following:

```
private function checkTarget(event:MouseEvent):void
{
  if(event.currentTarget.hitTestObject(event.currentTarget._targetPiece))
  {
  }
}
```

This function tests whether two objects are touching. The critical bit is `hitTestObject()`, a method you haven't worked with before in this book. `hitTestObject()` does almost exactly what it sounds like; it determines whether a object is touching or hitting another object passed in through the parentheses. `event.currentTarget` is the puzzle piece the user will have just released. `event.currentTartget._targetPiece` is this puzzle piece's related target piece, which you defined in Steps 6 and 7.

9 Position your cursor after the `if` statement you just wrote on Line 57, and press **Enter** (Windows) or **Return** (Mac) to insert a new line. Type the following:

```
{
    trace("whoooooot!");
}
```

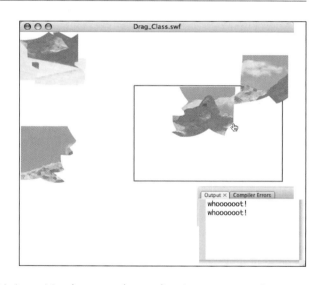

The trace statement will notify you when you have a match. "Whoooooot!" just happens to be one of my favorites victory cries, although you could pick something else.

10 Save your changes by choosing **File > Save**, and then press **Ctrl+Enter** (Windows) or **Cmd+Return** (Mac) to test the movie. When the player window opens, click and drag one of the puzzle pieces to the rectangle.

Once you've successfully placed a piece, the Output panel will open with the congratulatory message "whoooooot!" If you missed the target, try, try again! Note that the placement doesn't have to be precise. As long as any part of the puzzle piece is touching the target, you'll get the message. Also notice that if you drag the pieces elsewhere on the Stage, you do not get the message. You get it only when you make a match.

Congratulations. You've successfully detected a collision between two objects on the Stage. This is exciting because the application can run on its own and perform actions depending on whether they've found a match. In the next exercise, you'll do just this, writing what happens when the pieces collide—and also when they don't.

11 Close the player window, and return to Flash. Choose **File > Save All** to save all your changes, and then close the files.

3 | Responding to Collisions

In this exercise, you'll add code to the project files that will determine what happens when a user successfully drops a puzzle piece in the correct location. On the flip side, you also need to write code to handle the occasions when they don't.

1 Choose **File > Open**, and open **Drag_Class.fla**, **DragDrop.as**, and **DragGame.as** in the **12-4** folder in the **chap_12** folder on your desktop.

2 Choose **DragDrop.as**. Position your cursor on Line 8 after the first **private var** statement, and press **Enter** (Windows) or **Return** (Mac) to insert a new line. Type the following:

```
public var _origX:Number;
public var _origY:Number;
```

The code creates variables that will eventually hold the original X and Y positions of the **DragDrop** class objects. You're making these public properties so they can be accessed outside this file.

3 Position your cursor on Line 13 after the left curly brace, press **Enter** (Windows) or **Return** (Mac) to insert a new line, and type the following:

```
_origX = this.x;
_origY = this.x;
```

This code will set the variables you just created to the original X and Y values of the **DragDrop** object when they are first created.

4 Choose **DragGame.as**. Scroll to the bottom of the code. Position your cursor at the end of Line 59 after the trace statement, and press **Enter** (Windows) or **Return** (Mac) to go to the next line. Type the following:

```
event.currentTarget.x =
event.currentTarget._targetPiece.x;
event.currentTarget.y =
event.currentTarget._targetPiece.y;
```

This code resides in the **if** conditional statement that is checking for a match. So if there is a match, the X and Y positions of **currentTarget**, the puzzle piece the user has dropped, will be set to match the positions of the target piece. This is the "snap into place" effect you saw illustrated in the finished file in Exercise 1.

Now if there is not a match, you'll set the X and Y values of the puzzle pieces back to their original X and Y values. This will cause nonmatching pieces to snap back to the pile on the left side of the Stage.

5 Position your cursor on Line 62 after the right curly brace, and press **Enter** (Windows) or **Return** (Mac) to go to the next line. Type the following:

```
else
{
    event.currentTarget.x = event.currentTarget._origX;
    event.currentTarget.y = event.currentTarget._origY;
}
```

The **else** function will be triggered if the condition specified in the **if** statement (if the puzzle piece targeted by the user is in the hit area of the related target piece) is false. And, as I mentioned previously, this will send the puzzle pieces to their original X and Y positions.

6 Choose **File > Save All** to save your changes to these three files. Press **Ctrl+Enter** (Windows) or **Cmd+Return** (Mac) to test the movie. When the player window opens, drag a puzzle piece to the correct location.

The Output panel opens with the "whoooo001!" message, and the puzzle piece now snaps into place.

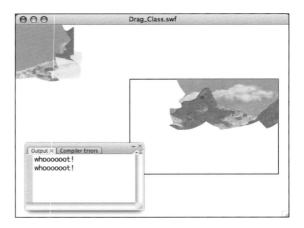

7 Now drag another puzzle piece to the wrong spot.

Notice that the puzzle piece snaps back immediately to its original position in the top-left corner of the Stage. So far, so good! But there's one more problem. If you were to click one of the puzzle pieces that has already been correctly placed, you'd find you could click and drag it back around the Stage. After they are placed correctly, these pieces should really be locked.

8 Close the player window and the **Output** panel. Return to **DragGame.as**.

```
54
55          private function checkTarget(event:MouseEvent):void
56          {
57              if(event.currentTarget.hitTestObject(event.currentTarget._targetPiece))
58              {
59                  trace("whooooot!");
60                  event.currentTarget.removeEventListener(MouseEvent.MOUSE_UP, checkTarget);
61                  event.currentTarget.x = event.currentTarget._targetPiece.x;
62                  event.currentTarget.y = event.currentTarget._targetPiece.y;
63              }
64              else
65              {
66                  event.currentTarget.x = event.currentTarget._origX;
67                  event.currentTarget.y = event.currentTarget._origY;
68              }
69          }
70      }
71  }
```

Line 60 of 71, Col 79

9 Position your cursor at the end of Line 59 in the **if** statement, and press **Enter** (Windows) or **Return** (Mac) to go to the next line. Type the following:

```
event.currentTarget.removeEventListener(MouseEvent.MOUSE_UP, checkTarget);
```

This line of code turns off the event listener so that the piece will no longer respond to MOUSE_UP events. You also have to turn off the interactivity in DragDrop.as to make the pieces fully locked.

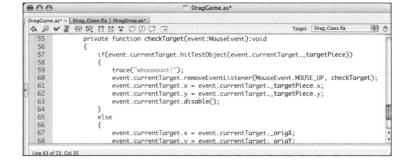

10 Choose **DragDrop.as**. Position your cursor on Line 29 after the right curly brace of the **dropMovie()** event handler, and press **Enter** (Windows) or **Return** (Mac) twice to go to the next line. Type the following:

```
public function disable():void
{
  this.removeEventListener(MouseEvent.MOUSE_DOWN, dragMovie);
  this.removeEventListener(MouseEvent.MOUSE_UP, dropMovie);
  this.buttonMode = false;
}
```

Now you just need to call this function after the pieces have been correctly placed, which would be in DragGame.as.

11 Choose **DragGame.as**. Position your cursor at the end of Line 62, and press **Enter** (Windows) or **Return** (Mac) to go to the next line. Type the following:

```
event.currentTarget.disable();
```

All this code does is run the **disable()** function from DragDrop.as. Remember, you made this a public function for just this purpose so it could be called from another file.

12 Save your changes to all the open files by choosing **File > Save All**. Press **Ctrl+Enter** (Windows) or **Cmd+Return** (Mac) to test the movie. When the player window opens, drag a puzzle piece to the correct location.

The puzzle piece snaps into place, and the Output panel opens with your message. Now try to click and drag the piece back out of the puzzle. You can't do it! Perfect. In the next exercise, you'll add the code that will detect when the game is won.

13 Close the player window, and choose **File > Close All** to close the open files in Flash.

Detecting a Win

In this exercise, you'll set up the puzzle game to detect a win. The game is won when all the puzzle pieces are put in place properly.

1 Choose **File > Open**, and open **Drag_Class.fla**, **DragDrop.as**, and **DragGame.as** in the **12-5** folder on the **chap_12** folder on your desktop.

To detect a win, you'll use a method similar to the one you used in Chapter 9, *"Creating a Memory Game."* You create two variables to hold the total possible matches and the number of current matches the user has made and then create a conditional statement that runs if the possible matches are greater or equal to the total matches. First you'll create the variables.

2 Select **DragGame.as**. Scroll down to Lines 15–20. This is the section where you create all your variables. Position your cursor after Line 20, and press **Enter** (Windows) or **Return** (Mac) to go to the next line. Type the following:

```
private var _totalPieces:Number;
private var _currentPieces:Number;
```

Now you'll need to set initial values for `totalPieces` and `currentPieces`.

```
12
13        public class DragGame extends MovieClip
14        {
15            private var bl:BL;
16            private var br:BR;
17            private var bm:BM;
18            private var tl:TL;
19            private var tr:TR;
20            private var tm:TM;
21            private var _totalPieces:Number;
22            private var _currentPieces:Number;
23
```
Line 22 of 74, Col 3

3 Position your cursor at the end of Line 25 after the left curly brace of the **DragGame()** function, and press **Enter** (Windows) or **Return** (Mac) to go to the next line. Type the following:

```
_totalPieces = 6;
_currentPieces = 0;
```

You're inserting these statements in the constructor function that runs as soon as the document class is loaded at run time so that the initial values are set immediately. Remember, there are six puzzle pieces and six total matches possible. When the game starts, the initial `_currentPieces` value will always be 0.

```
20            private var tm:TM;
21            private var _totalPieces:Number;
22            private var _currentPieces:Number;
23
24
25            public function DragGame()
26            {
27                _totalPieces = 6;
28                _currentPieces = 0;
29                createPieces();
30            }
31
```
Line 28 of 76, Col 23

Now you just need to add to the `_currentPieces` variable every time a piece is dropped in the right place. A match is detected in the `if` statement at the bottom of the code, so it would be most appropriate to add the `_currentPieces` addition there. Next step!

4 Scroll to the bottom of the code. Position your cursor at the end of Line 66 after the statement that runs the `disable()` function, press **Enter** (Windows) or **Return** (Mac), and type the following:

`_currentPieces ++;`

This code will add 1 to the value of **_currentPieces** every time there is a match. Now you just need to compare **_currentPieces** to **_totalPieces** so that Flash can detect when there is a win.

```
       Target: Memory.fla
61        if(event.currentTarget.hitTestObject(event.currentTarget._targetPiece))
62        {
63            event.currentTarget.x = event.currentTarget._targetPiece.x;
64            event.currentTarget.y = event.currentTarget._targetPiece.y;
65            event.currentTarget.removeEventListener(MouseEvent.MOUSE_UP, checkTarget);
66            event.currentTarget.disable();
67            _currentPieces ++;
68            if(_currentPieces >= _totalPieces)
69            {
70                trace("You Win!");
71            }
72        }
Line 70 of 80, Col 22
```

5 Press **Enter** (Windows) or **Return** (Mac) to go to the next line, and type the following:

```
if(_currentPieces >= _totalPieces)
{
   trace("You Win!");
}
```

As I mentioned when you were creating the memory game, you can use two equals signs here, but I prefer to use greater than or equal to, just in case. For example, I might decide to add another piece, and it's one less part of the code I have to mess with.

6 Save your changes to all three files by choosing **File > Save All**. Press **Ctrl+Enter** (Windows) or **Cmd+Return** (Mac) to test the movie. When the preview window opens, click and drag the puzzle pieces to their correct locations in the rectangle.

If you make a mistake, the piece will snap back to the top of the pile, and you can just try again.

I removed the "whoooooot!" trace statement from these files, so you'll have to wait until all the pieces are correctly placed. At that point, the Output panel will open with the message "You Win!"

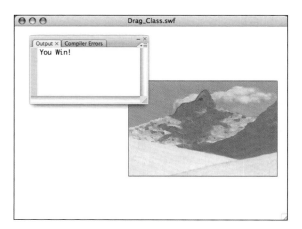

VIDEO: **addingdropshadows.mov**

To learn how to add drop shadows to the puzzle pieces when they are selected, check out **addingdropshadows.mov** in the **videos** folder on the **ActionScript HOT CD-ROM.**

7 Close the player window, and choose **File > Close All** to close the three open files.

Congratulations! You've successfully detected a win. In the next exercise, you'll learn how to randomize the order in which the puzzle pieces are created and placed on the Stage.

5 | Randomly Placing Objects

In this exercise, you'll write the code that will randomly place the puzzle pieces every time you play the game.

1 Choose **File > Open**, and open **Drag_Class.fla**, **DragGame.as**, and **DragDrop.as** in the **12-7** folder from the **chap_12** folder on your desktop.

These files are similar to where you left off in Exercise 4, except I have written the code that adds a drop shadow to the pieces when they are selected.

2 Choose **DragGame.as**. Scroll down to the bottom of your code. Position your cursor at the end of Line 78 after the right curly brace, press **Enter** (Windows) or **Return** (Mac) twice, and type the following:

```
private function randomPosition
(piece:*):void
```

This function will randomize the placement of the puzzle pieces. The **piece** variable will be passed into this function as soon as each instance is created.

3 Press **Enter** (Windows) or **Return** (Mac), and type the following:

```
{
   piece.x = Math.round(Math.random()
*
}
```

We're going to stop here for a minute, even though this statement isn't complete. You need a multiplier here to increase the randomly generated number so that it moves the pieces the correct amount on the Stage. Let's return to Drag_Class.fla to see how you would want to position the pieces in design mode.

4 Choose **Drag_Class.fla**. Click the **Insert Layer** button below the **Timeline** to insert a new layer. Click the layer name once to select the layer, and then select the **Rectangle** tool in the **Tools** panel. Make sure the **Object Drawing** option at the bottom of the **Tools** panel is deselected. Click and drag a rectangle on the **Stage**, about the same size and shape as the rectangle in the illustration shown here.

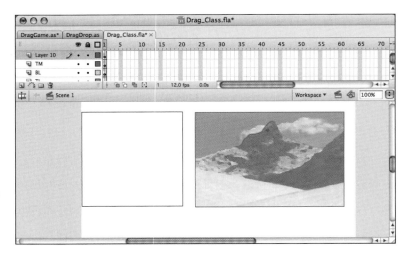

This rectangle is located in about the spot where you want to position the random assortment of pieces. Using the Property inspector, you can find out the exact dimensions and position of the rectangle.

---

5 Select the **Selection** tool in the **Tools** panel. Choose **Window > Properties > Properties** to open the **Property inspector**, if it is not already open. Now select the rectangle you just drew on the **Stage**, and examine its properties in the **Property inspector**.

Note the width of your rectangle. Mine is about 200 pixels wide. Yours may be different. I do want it flush with the other rectangle, so I will add a few pixels to that value.

---

6 Select the layer you added in Step 4, and press the **Delete Layer** button at the bottom of the **Timeline** to delete the layer and its contents, including the rectangle you just drew.

---

7 Choose **DragGame.as**. Position your cursor after the asterisk on Line 82, where you left off on Step 3. Press the **spacebar** to add a space, and type the following:

(225

If you left this as is, because their registration points are set to the top left, some of the puzzle pieces would overlap the hit areas of the rectangle. Subtracting the width of the puzzle piece ensures they will stay on the left side of the Stage.

---

8 Type a space, and then type the following:

```
- piece.width));
```

9 Press **Enter** (Windows) or **Return** (Mac) to go to the next line. Type the following:

```
piece.y = Math.round(Math.random() * (400 - piece.height));
```

You didn't bother to note the height of the rectangle you drew on the Stage because you want to use the height of the entire Stage as the placement area for the pieces; 400 happens to be the height of the Stage. Now that the `randomPosition()` function is finished, you just need to call it when the pieces are created.

10 Scroll up in your code, and position your cursor at the end of Line 36 after the first **b1** event listener. Press **Enter** (Windows) or **Return** (Mac) to go to the next line, and type the following:

```
randomPosition(b1);
```

Now you just need to add this code for the rest of the puzzle pieces.

11 Select the line of code you just wrote on Line 37, and press **Ctrl+C** (Windows) or **Cmd+C** (Mac). Position your cursor after the next event listener in this block of code on Line 41, press **Enter** (Windows) or **Return** (Mac) to go to the next line, and then press **Ctrl+V** (Windows) or **Cmd+V** (Mac) to paste it. Change **bl** to **br**. Repeat this step for the four remaining pieces. When you are finished this block of code, it should look like the illustration shown here.

12 Save your changes to these three files by choosing **File > Save All**. Test the movie by pressing **Ctrl+Enter** (Windows) or **Cmd+Return** (Mac).

Cool! All the pieces are in random positions, within a defined area on the left side of the Stage.

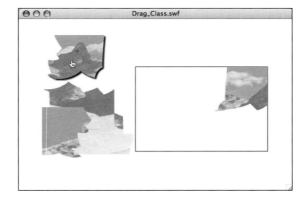

13 Press **Ctrl+Enter** (Windows) or **Cmd+Return** (Mac) to reload the movie. All the pieces will be placed in different positions. Drag one or two pieces to the correct locations in the puzzle to preview the drop shadow effect. Then drag a piece to an incorrect location.

Notice that the piece you placed in the wrong position snaps back to the upper-left corner of the screen. Before you finish with this exercise, let's fix this.

14 Close the player window and the **Output** panel, and return to **DragGame.as**. Position your cursor at the end of Line 89 after the last statement in the **randomPosition()** function, press **Enter** (Windows) or **Return** (Mac) to go to the next line, and type the following:

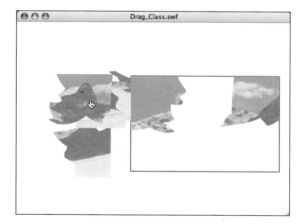

```
piece._origX = piece.x;
piece._origY = piece.y;
```

This resets the _origX and _origY variables to the random position values that are generated after the first two lines of this function runs. That way, when the **else** statement runs, when there is *not* a match, the pieces will return to the positions set by the **randomPosition()** function.

---

15 Choose **File > Save** to save your changes. Press **Ctrl+Enter** (Windows) or **Cmd+Return** (Mac) to test the movie again. All the pieces will be placed in random positions. Drag one or two pieces to the incorrect locations in the puzzle.

Great! The pieces snap back to the positions assigned by the **randomPosition()** function. You have successfully created a drag-and-drop game!

---

16 When you are finished, close the player window, and choose **File > Close All** to close the three open files.

Congratulations to you! You've made it through the whole book. You've learned about variables, functions, classes, conditional statements, arrays, and even how to create some games. I hope you've had as much fun following along with this book as I have writing it. ActionScript adds an amazing amount of power and interest to your Flash files. I also hope it gives you a good foundation so that you can move on and create more advanced applications on your own. To continue your learning and read more about ActionScript 3.0, check out the resources listed in Appendix B, *"ActionScript 3.0 and Flash CS3 Professional Resources."*

Troubleshooting FAQ and Technical Support

If you run into problems while following the exercises in this book, you might find the answers to your questions in the "Troubleshooting FAQ" section. If you don't find the information you're looking for, use the contact information provided in the "Technical Support Information" section.

Troubleshooting FAQ

Q On a Mac, why can't I see any FLA files when I choose **File > Open**?

A If an FLA file was created in Windows, you might experience a problem seeing the file when you try to open it on a Mac. You can correct this problem by changing the **Show** option to **All Files**.

Q On a Mac, an FLA file won't open when I double-click it. Why?

A If the FLA file was created in Windows, you might not be able to double-click it to open the file. If this is the case, open Adobe Flash CS3, and choose **File > Open** to open the FLA file. If you don't see the FLA file listed when you choose **File > Open**, see the previous question. After you save the FLA file (originally created on in Windows) on your Mac, you will be able to double-click the FLA to open it.

Q All of my panels have disappeared. What should I do?

A Press the **Tab** key to show them and even hide them again. If you don't like their arrangement, you can restore them to their default onscreen positions by choosing **Window > Workspace > Default**. This command is especially helpful when someone else has undocked and changed the combination of your panels.

Q Why does Flash create extra files when I press **F12** (Windows) or **Cmd+F12** (Mac)?

A Pressing **F12** (Windows) or **Cmd+F12** (Mac) is a shortcut for the **Publish Preview** command, which publishes an SWF file and an HTML file. Flash CS3 creates these files in the same directory as the FLA file. If you want to preview your movie without publishing any other files, choose **Control > Test Movie** or **File > Publish Preview > Flash** to create only the SWF file.

Q Why do all the objects on my **Stage** appear faded?

A This occurs when you double-click a symbol instance or **right-click** (Windows) or **Ctrl-click** (Mac) a symbol instance and choose **Edit in Place**. This is a quick way to make changes to a symbol without having to access the **Library** panel; however, it can be confusing if that's not what you intended to do. In the **edit bar**, click **Scene 1** to exit this editing mode and return to the main **Timeline**. In the illustration shown here, **Scene 1** was renamed main. So, in this example, you would click the word **main** in the **edit bar** to return to the main **Timeline**.

Q Why won't my movie clips play when I click the **Play** button?

A You preview your movie clips on the main **Timeline** within the Flash CS3 authoring environment. You can preview movie clips in their own **Timeline**, in the **Library** panel, or in the Flash Player (by choosing **Control > Test Movie**).

Q I made an input text field, but when I test it by choosing **Control > Test Movie** and trying to type in it, nothing happens. Why?

A When you created the text box, you most likely set the text color to the same color as the background of the movie. Try changing the text color and testing the movie again. Also, make sure you have **Input Text** set for the text type.

Q I want to learn more about the many actions in the **Actions** panel. How do I do this?

A In the **Actions** panel, type any action or keyword you need more information about. Then choose **Help > Flash Help** to open the content-sensitive **Help** menu. A complete description of the action or keyword will appear in the window.

Technical Support Information

The following is a list of technical support resources you can use if you need help.

lynda.com

If you run into any problems as you work through this book, check the companion Web site for updates:

www.lynda.com/info/books/as3

If you don't find what you're looking for on the companion Web site, send an email to **books-errata@lynda.com**.

We encourage and welcome your feedback, comments, and error reports.

Peachpit Press

If your book has a defective CD-ROM, please contact the customer service department at Peachpit Press:

customer_service@peachpit.com

Adobe Technical Support

If you're having problems with Flash CS3 Professional unrelated to this book, please visit the following Web site to access the Adobe Flash Support Center:

www.adobe.com/support/flash/

To contact Adobe Technical Support, use the email form at the following Web site:

www.adobe.com/support/email/cscontact/

Adobe Technical Support can help you with typical problems, such as an expired trial version.

You can also try to contact Adobe directly by phone:

United States and Canada 1-800-470-7211 (toll-free)

Outside the United States and Canada +1-415-553-7186

B

ActionScript 3.0 and Flash CS3 Professional Resources

Adobe Flash CS3 Professional users have a great many resources for finding information about Flash and ActionScript. You have ample choices among a variety of newsgroups, conferences, and third-party Web sites that can really help you get the most out of the new skills you've developed by reading this book. In this appendix, you'll find a list of the best resources for further developing your skills with ActionScript and Flash.

lynda.com Training Resources

lynda.com is a leader in software books and video training for Web and graphics professionals. To help further develop your skills in Flash, check out the following training resources from lynda.com.

lynda.com Books

The **Hands-On Training** series was originally developed by **Lynda Weinman**, author of the revolutionary book *Designing Web Graphics*, first released in 1996. Lynda believes people learn best from doing and has developed the Hands-On Training series to teach users software programs and technologies through a progressive learning process.

Check out the following books from lynda.com:

Adobe Dreamweaver CS3 Hands-On Training
by Garrick Chow
lynda.com/books and Peachpit Press
ISBN: 0321509854

Adobe Flash CS3 Professional Hands-On Training
by Todd Perkins
lynda.com/books and Peachpit Press
ISBN: 0321509838

Designing Web Graphics 4
by Lynda Weinman
New Riders
ISBN: 0735710791

lynda.com Video-Based Training

lynda.com offers video training as stand-alone CD-ROM and DVD-ROM products and through a subscription to the lynda.com **Online Training Library**.

For a free, 24-hour trial pass to the lynda.com Online Training Library, register your copy of *ActionScript 3.0 for Flash CS3 Professional HOT* at the following link:

www.lynda.com/register/HOT/as3

Note: This offer is available for new subscribers only and does not apply to current or past subscribers of the lynda.com Online Training Library.

To help you build your skills with Flash, check out the following video training titles from lynda.com:

ActionScript 3.0 in Flash CS3 Professional Beyond the Basics
with Todd Perkins

Flash CS3 Professional Essential Training
with Rich Schupe

Illustrator CS3 and Flash CS3 Professional Integration
with Mordy Golding

Flashforward Conference and Film Festival

The **Flashforward** conference and film festival is an international educational conference dedicated to Adobe Flash. Flashforward was first hosted by Lynda Weinman, founder of lynda.com, and Stewart McBride, founder of United Digital Artists. Flashforward is now owned exclusively by lynda.com and strives to provide the best conferences for designers and developers to present their technical and artistic work in an educational setting.

For more information about the Flashforward conference and film festival, visit **www.flashforwardconference.com**.

Online Resources

The following are online resources for Flash information:

www.actionscript.org
This site is a massive forum dedicated to helping answer all of your ActionScript questions, and it's one of the best ActionScript resources out there.

www.adobe.com/devnet/flash/
This is a great resource for learning ActionScript 3.0 and just about anything imaginable related to Flash.

http://livedocs.adobe.com/flex/2/langref/migration.html
This site is a must if you are migrating from ActionScript 2.0 to ActionScript 3.0. Here, you will find a massive index of ActionScript 2.0 code and learn how to implement the same code in ActionScript 3.0.

Adobe Flash Developer Center
www.adobe.com/devnet/flash
Adobe has created a section of its Web site called the Adobe Flash Developer Center. This is a one-stop shop for everything Flash. For example, you can read tutorials and articles on Flash CS3,

download sample applications, access links to other Flash resources, and even read the white papers written on topics related to Flash CS3. This is the perfect link to use if you want to learn more about components or even video in Flash CS3.

www.adobe.com/cfusion/webforums/forum/
Adobe has set up several Web-based online forums for Adobe Flash. This is a great place to ask questions and get help from thousands of Flash users. These online forums are used by beginning to advanced Flash users, so you should have no problem finding the type of help you need, regardless of your experience with the program. The following list describes several of Adobe's online forums:

Flash General Discussion: Online forum for general issues related to using Adobe Flash.

Flash Site Design: Online forum for design feedback on your Flash animations. This forum is dedicated to discussing Flash design and animation principles and practices. Other issues not specific to the Flash tools yet important to Flash designers are also discussed here.

Flash ActionScript: Online forum for discussing creating interactive Flash projects using ActionScript.

Flash Remoting: Online forum that discusses issues involved with Flash Remoting, which supplies the infrastructure that allows users to connect to remote services exposed by application server developers and Web services. Examples of these are message boards, shopping carts, and even up-to-the-minute stock quote graphs.

Flash Exchange Extensions: Online forum for issues relating to Flash extensions, including how to use them and how to troubleshoot any problems with them. (See also the "Adobe Exchange for Flash" section next.)

Adobe Exchange for Flash

www.adobe.com/exchange/flash/
Adobe has set up another section of its Web site, called the Adobe Flash Exchange. Here you'll find hundreds of free extensions written by third-party users and developers that can help you build new features into your Web site. These features are not part of the Flash CS3 product, but you can download them when you need them. Many of these extensions have features that would otherwise require an advanced level of ActionScript skills. For example, some of these behaviors let you password-protect areas of your site and create pop-up menus, scroll bars, complex text effects, and so on.

The Adobe site is not just for developers but for any Flash user who wants to take Flash to the next level. If you are a developer, this is a great place to learn how to write your own behaviors to share with the rest of the Flash community.

You can also visit **www.adobe.com/cfusion/ webforums/forum/** and click the **Flash Exchange Extensions** link to access the online forum for Flash extensions.

Adobe TechNote Index

www.adobe.com/support/flash/technotes.html
This section of the Adobe Web site lists all the issues that have been reported and answered by the Flash staff members.

Third-Party Web Sites

The following are helpful third-party Web sites:

www.flashkit.com/

www.ultrashock.com/

http://virtual-fx.net/

www.actionscripts.org/

www.flzone.net/

http://flashmove.com/

http://flazoom.com/

www.were-here.com/

www.popedeflash.com/

Index

Symbols

&& (AND) operator, in compound conditional statements, 147–148

!= (not equal to), conditional operator, 144

( ) (parenthesis)
  conditional statements and, 9
  defining functions and, 7–8, 47
  statement syntax and, 67

* (asterisk)
  as multiplication operator, 167, 211
  multiplying scale with, 116

*/ (asterisk with slash), for multiline comments, 38–39

. (period)
  for ending statements, 6
  naming conventions and, 18

/ (forward slash)
  as division operator, 167
  naming conventions and, 18

// (double slashes), indicating comments, 37

; (semicolon), for ending statements, 6

[ ] (brackets), for arrays, 197, 277–278

{} (curly braces), in defining functions, 47–48, 69

' (single quotations), for use with strings, 86

" (quotation marks), string data types and, 6, 31

+ (plus) sign, in string concatenation, 205

++ (increment operator)
  adding value in memory game, 250
  animating color changes, 275–276
  as numeric operator, 152

< (less than), conditional operator, 140, 145

= (equals), 140

== (equals), conditional operator, 140, 147

> (greater than), conditional operator, 139, 145

A

abstract classes
  Timer class as, 98
  URLRequest class as, 86

Actions panel
  accessing, 31
  Actions toolbox, 24–25
  adding actions to keyframes, 43
  adding text to text fields, 179
  areas of, 24
  communicating with loaded movies, 292–295
  "Current selection cannot have actions applied to it" message, 28
  learning about actions in, 344
  loading external images and SWFs, 287–291
  loading video, 308–310
  tool tips, 44
  trace statements and, 33
  turning on Script Assist, 10

Actions toolbox
  Actions panel interface, 24–25
  finding methods, 43–44

ActionScript Virtual Machine (AVM), 3

ActionScript, getting started, 2–12
  Adobe players, 11
  Apollo and, 11–12
  CGI and, 12
  classes, 9
  comparing versions, 4–5
  conditional statements, 9
  core elements, 6
  events, event handlers, and event listeners, 8–9
  functions and methods, 7–8
  instances and instance names, 7
  introduction to ActionScript 3.0, 3
  JavaScript and Flash CS3 and, 12

disable( ), collision detection, 333

display lists
    adding objects to, 123, 155–156
    adding shape object to, 261
    adding text field to, 179
    overview of, 124

division operator (/), 167

document class
    defining, 120–125
    linking to, 129
    reasons for using, 120
    what's new, 4
    writing for memory game, 222–223

dot syntax, modifying properties, 7

double slashes (//), indicating comments, 37

down_btn, managing volume of sound, 304

DragDrop class, 317–325
    collision detection, 327
    collision response, 330
    creating, 321–322

drawCircle( ) method, 43, 260

drawing, code for, 259–263

drawRect( ) method, 262

drop shadows
    adding to puzzle pieces when selected, 336
    animating, 283–285
    creating with code, 278
    modifying filter properties, 280–281

dynamic text fields, 187

E

ECMAScript languages, 3

elements, ActionScript
    classes, 9
    conditional statements, 9
    events, event handlers, and event listeners, 8–9
    functions and methods, 7–8
    instances and instance names, 7
    overview of, 6
    properties, 7
    variables, 6–7

Ellipse tool, 262

else if keyword
    checking alternate conditions, 144–145
    checking matching cards in memory game, 238

else keyword
    checking alternate conditions, 144–146
    evaluating if condition is not true, 140–142
    use with if keyword, 137
    writing conditional statements, 9

endFill( ) method, 261

Enter (Windows), autocompleting code hints, 27

ENTER_FRAME event
    color animation, 274–276
    creating animation with, 90–95
    filter animation, 283–285

equals (=), 140

equals (==), conditional operator, 140, 147

event handlers
    animation timer and, 99
    animation with, 91, 274–276
    checking matching cards in memory game, 236
    creating link to Web site, 85
    generating random colors, 270
    for keyboard events, 80
    for memory game, 219–220, 226
    for mouse events, 74
    overview of, 8–9
    writing, 68–72

event listeners
    for animation events, 89–90
    catching events with, 66–67
    checking matching cards in memory game, 235–236, 247–248
    creating link to Web site, 84
    for keyboard events, 79
    for mouse events, 73
    overview of, 8–9
    radio tower illustrating, 65
    timers and, 99

events
    controlling animation with timer event, 96–101
    creating animation with ENTER_FRAME event, 88–95
    linking to Web sites, 84–87
    listeners for catching, 66–67
    overview of, 8, 64
    responding to keyboard events, 79–83

responding to mouse events, 73–78
syntax for, 9
types of, 65
writing event handler, 68–72
Export for ActionScript
communicating with loaded movies, 294
creating `DragDrop` class, 322
in Linkage dialog, 114, 118, 221
symbols, 224, 252
`extends`, 107–109
eXtensible markup language (XML)
loading XML data into Flash applications, 193
overview of and resources for, 12
Eyedropper tool, sampling color with, 185

F

F1 (Help menu). *See* Help menu (F1)
F12 (Windows), Publish Preview, 10, 344
F8, Convert to Symbol dialog, 17, 118
F9 (Windows), Actions panel, 24
files
creating new, 30
naming, 104–105
Publish settings, 127
saving, 104–105, 113
Fill Color box
selecting color values, 16
Tint option, 20
fills
`beginFill( )` method, 260
`endFill( )` method, 261
filters
animating, 283–285
creating with code, 277–279
modifying properties, 280–282
Finder (Mac), finding folders with, 126
FLA files
ActionScript embedded in, 3
troubleshooting on Mac, 344
Flash CS3
common functions, 7
features of code editor, 26
JavaScript and, 12

technologies for extending, 11–12
Flash Developer Center, 348–349
Flash Exchange Extensions online forum, 349
Flash Exchange Web site, 349
Flash Player, 11
Flash Remoting online forum, 349
Flashfoward conference and film festival, 348
Flex Builder, 3
`floor( )` method, Math class, 173, 210
flow-control elements, 133
FLP (Flash project) files, 49
folders, ActionScript classes folder, 126–128, 130
fonts, `TextFormat` objects, 183
`for` keyword
checking array values, 199
creating multiple instances of `Card` class, 231
dragging multiple class instances from Library panel, 155–156
writing loops with, 151–153
formats
image, 289–290
sound, 297
text, 182
forward slash (/)
as division operator, 167
naming conventions and, 18
Free Transform tool (Q)
rotating objects with, 23, 50
selecting, 18
`function` keyword
creating functions, 8
defining custom function, 47
functions, 40–63
code reuse with, 7–8
creating custom, 46–48
creating modular, 50–54, 56–58
defined, 41
event handlers triggering, 71
modular coding and, 49–50
movement and rotation values, 58
operators, 55–56
overview of, 40–41
returning values with, 59–63
setting up to receive data, 52–53
working with built-in methods, 42–45

G

getURL( ), ActionScript 2.0, 85

GIF (Graphics Interchange Format) files, 289–290

gotoAndPlay( ), 7

gotoAndStop( ), 45

graphics
  adding symbols to memory game, 252–253
  adding to memory game, 224–229
  GIF and PNG formats, 289–290
  Shape class properties, 259
  vector image properties, 263

Graphics Interchange Format (GIF) files, 289–290

gray color indicator, for comments, 36, 38

greater than (>), conditional operator, 139, 145

green color indicator, for text, 36

guide layers, turning off visibility, 42

H

Hand icon
  cursor appearing as, 70
  indicating interactive element, 85

Height property, movie clips, 22

Help menu (F1)
  in Actions panel, 29
  ColorTransform options, 268
  method explanation, 44
  TextField properties, 181

hexadecimal values
  for black color, 260
  text color options, 184–185

Hide Layer icon, creating drag-and-drop class, 319

hitTestObject( ), 329

I

if keyword
  checking alternate conditions, 143
  checking array values, 200
  checking matching cards in memory game, 237–238

  evaluating if condition is true, 139, 141
  writing conditional statements, 9, 134, 136

if...else statement, detecting collisions, 331

if/then scenarios, 133. *See also* conditional statements

imageLoader, creating, 287–288

images
  adding to memory game, 224–229
  loading from external files, 287–291

import statements
  creating DragDrop class, 322
  detecting collisions, 328
  importing classes, 107
  importing classes and base class, 123

increaseVolume( ) event handler, 304–305

increment operator (++)
  adding value in memory game, 250
  animating color changes, 275–276
  as numeric operator, 152

indexes
  arrays and, 197
  finding method packages or classes, 44
  loops and, 151, 233

inheritance, 107–109

input text
  fields, 187
  in game example, 202–203
  troubleshooting, 344

Insert Layer button, 24

Instance Name field, Property inspector, 7

instances
  changing names, 23
  dragging multiple instances from Library panel, 155–156
  dragging to Stage, 19
  generating with loops, 154–156
  placing instances created by loops, 157–162
  referring to by name, not symbol, 7

interactivity
  creating DragDrop class, 317–325
  detecting a win, 334–336
  detecting collisions, 326–329
  randomly placing objects, 337–341
  responding to collisions, 330–333
  turning off in memory game, 240

interval property, for keyword, 199

J

JavaScript, 12

JPEG (Joint Photographic Experts Group) files, 289

K

KEY_DOWN event, 80–81, 89

KEY_UP event, 89

keyboard events, 79–83

`keyCode` property, 82–83

keyframes, actions added to, 43

L

layers
  adding functions to, 42
  creating `DragDrop` class, 318
  Insert Layer button, 24
  labels layer, 216
  locking, 24
  renaming, 30
  separating actions and artwork, 79
  symbol layer, 216

`length` property, arrays, 199

less than (<), conditional operator, 140, 145

Library panel
  creating instances by dragging symbol from, 7, 19
  dragging multiple class instances from Library panel, 155–156
  keyboard shortcuts for accessing, 113

`lineStyle` property, `Shape` class, 259

Linkage properties
  accessing Linkage dialog, 114
  adding symbols to memory game, 252
  associating movie clip symbol with Card class, 219
  Export for ActionScript, 118
  objects, 110

literal expressions, 190

`load( )` method
  communicating with loaded movies, 292–295
  loading external images, 287–288

`Loader` class
  communicating with loaded movies, 292–293
  creating new instance of, 9
  image types loaded by, 289

locking/unlocking layers, 24, 319

logical operators, 56

logos, using GIFs for, 289–290

loops
  checking array values, 199
  creating code loops, 151–153
  creating multiple instances of `Card` class, 230–231
  generating class instances with, 154–156
  overview of, 150
  placing instances created by loops, 157–162

lossless compression, 289

lossy compression, 289

lynda.com
  technical support, 344
  training resources, 347

M

Mac computers
  ActionScript Virtual Machine (AVM) and, 3
  Choose a Folder, 128
  Cmd+C (copy), 74
  Cmd+F12 (Publish Preview), 343
  Cmd+L (Library), 113
  Cmd+Return (movie preview), 27
  Cmd+S (save), 113
  Cmd+Shift+F12 (Publish settings dialog), 127
  Cmd+V (paste), 38, 53
  Cmd+X (cut), 92
  Cmd+Z (undo), 23
  Ctrl+click, for context menus, 114
  Finder, finding folders with, 126
  Opt+F12 (Mac), 10
  Opt+F9 (Mac), Actions panel, 24
  Return, for autocompleting code hints, 27
  troubleshooting FLA files, 344

`Math` class
  `ceil( )` method, 174
  `floor( )` method, 173
  `floor( )` method, 210

T

target, of event listeners, 72, 135

technical support information, 344

testing movies
  keyboard shortcut for, 27
  loading external images and SWFs, 291
  modular functions, 53–54
  trace statements and, 34–35

text
  capturing data from text field, 187–190
  creating text field, 179–181
  finishing text game, 210–213
  green color indicator for, 36
  loading external, 191–195
  overview of, 178
  in string data types, 6
  styling text fields, 181–186
  using with arrays to create game, 202–209
  wrapping, 194

text fields
  capturing data from, 187–190
  creating, 179–181
  loading from external files, 191–195
  styling, 181–186

text property, 180

textColor property, 182

TextField class, 181, 186

TextFormat class
  changing text styles, 195
  creating, 182–183
  fonts, 183
  hexadecimal values, 184–185
  text size, 184–186

textHeight property, 182

third-party Web sites, 349

this keyword, 111

Timeline
  adding class objects to, 110–119
  adding timers to, 98
  creating new layer, 24
  document class and, 120
  inserting blank keyframe, 43
  scrubbing playhead, 97
  sprites not containing, 111, 124

TIMER event, 99, 101

timers
  animating color changes, 276
  controlling animation with, 96–101
  repeat count, 100

Tint option, Color pop-up menu, 20, 265–266

tool tips
  method explanation, 44
  statement syntax and, 67

Tools panel
  Free Transform tool (Q), 18, 50
  Rectangle tool, 16, 117
  Selection tool (V), 16–17

trace keyword, 33

trace statements
  checking arrays, 198
  checking event listeners and event handlers, 69
  checking random number generator, 169
  disabling vs. deleting, 71
  finding keyCode property of pressed key, 83
  loops and, 152–153
  returning values with functions and, 62
  setting up, 33–35

transform property, movie clips, 267

transparency, alpha values for controlling, 75–77

troubleshooting FAQs, 343–344

true/false values
  in boolean data types, 6
  variables containing, 135–136

TXT files, 187

type, event, 67

U

Uniform Resource Locator (URL), 84

up_btn, 304

URL (Uniform Resource Locator), 84

URLLoader class, 192–193, 195

URLRequest class
  as abstract class, 86
  loading data to text field from external file, 192–195
  loading sounds, 296–298
  starting/stopping, 299–303
  URLLoader and, 192–193
  URLRequest object, 85

V

V. *See* Selection tool (V)

values, functions returning, 59–63

var keyword, 6, 31

variables
  as container holding information, 29
  creating, 30–32
  creating for function properties, 57
  creating for shapes, 259
  creating new class instances, 253
  determining a win in memory game, 249
  location in code, 135
  multiple. *See* arrays
  overview of, 6–7
  as placeholders, 123
  true/false values, 135–136

vector images, 263

versions, ActionScript, 4–5

visibility, turned off/on guide layer, 42

void, event handlers not returning data, 47, 69

volume controls, 304–307

W

WAV format, 297

Web sites, events linking to, 84–87

Welcome Screen, 15

width settings, text, 180

X

win, detecting a, 334–336

Windows computers
  Browse for Folder, 128
  Ctrl+C (copy), 74
  Ctrl+Enter (movie preview), 27
  Ctrl+L (Library), 113
  Ctrl+S (save), 113
  Ctrl+Shift+F12 (Publish settings), 127
  Ctrl+V (paste), 38, 53
  Ctrl+X (cut), 92
  Ctrl+Z (undo), 23
  Enter (autocompleting code hints), 27
  F12 (Publish Preview), 10, 344
  F9 (Actions panel), 24
  Right-click, for context menus, 114

Windows Explorer, finding folders with, 126

Word Wrap option, context menus, 206

wordWrap property, text, 194

X

X and **Y** properties
  for animation events, 94–95
  Card class, 231–232
  changing, 124–125
  event handlers and, 71
  of instances, 159–161
  modifying X position, 22
  rotating objects and, 50, 54

XML (eXtensible markup language)
  loading XML data into Flash applications, 193
  overview of and resources for, 12